THE WRITINGS OF RABASH

LETTERS

Volume One

LAITMAN
KABBALAH
PUBLISHERS

Rav Baruch Shalom Halevi Ashlag

The Writings of RABASH – Letters
Volume One

Copyright © 2016 by Michael Laitman
All rights reserved
Published by Laitman Kabbalah Publishers

Contact Information
E-mail: info@kabbalah.info
Web site: www.kabbalah.info
Toll free in USA and Canada: 1-866-LAITMAN

1057 Steeles Avenue West, Suite 532, Toronto,
ON, M2R 3X1, Canada
Tel. 1-416-274-7287

2009 85th Street #51, Brooklyn, New York, 11214, USA
Tel. 1-800-540-3234

Printed in Canada

No part of this book may be used or reproduced
in any manner without written permission of the publisher,
except in the case of brief quotations embodied
in critical articles or reviews.

ISBN: 978-1-77228-015-9
Library of Congress Control Number: 2016932119

Translation: Rinah Shalom, Chaim Ratz
Editors: Mary Pennock, Mary Miesem, Mordakhay Kholdarov
Transcription: Brenda Jones, Linda Narbonne, Jazmin Delgado,
David Prosser, Mary Miesem, Katia Wilson, Karen Larkins
Layout: Chaim Ratz
Cover: Baruch Khovov
Administrative Editor: Simona Gamarnik
Executive Editor: Chaim Ratz
Printing and Post Production: Uri Laitman

FIRST EDITION: SEPTEMBER 2016
First printing

Table of Contents

Letter No. 1 5
Letter No. 2 7
Letter No. 3 9
Letter No. 4 13
Letter No. 5 16
Letter No. 6 17
Letter No. 7 20
Letter No. 8 22
Letter No. 9 33
Letter No. 10 41
Letter No. 11 44
Letter No. 12 47
Letter No. 12b 50
Letter No. 13 52
Letter No. 14 55
Letter No. 15 58
Letter No. 16 60
Letter No. 17 64
Letter No. 18 70
Letter No. 19 75
Letter No. 20 79
Letter No. 21 83
Letter No. 22 91
Letter No. 23 95
Letter No. 24 98
Letter No. 25 101
Letter No. 26 104
Letter No. 27 106
Letter No. 28 111
Letter No. 29 120
Letter No. 30 134
Letter No. 31 136
Letter No. 32 145
Letter No. 33 148
Letter No. 34 152
Letter No. 35 157
Letter No. 36 160
Letter No. 37 167
Letter No. 38 169

Letter No. 38b ... 173
Letter No. 39 ... 178
Letter No. 40 ... 180
Letter No. 41 ... 187
Letter No. 42 ... 189
Letter No. 43 ... 191
Letter No. 44 ... 197
Letter No. 45 ... 199
Letter No. 46 ... 202
Letter No. 47 ... 205
Letter No. 48 ... 207
Letter No. 49 ... 209
Letter No. 50 ... 211
Letter No. 51 ... 213
Letter No. 52 ... 216
Letter No. 53 ... 220
Letter No. 54 ... 223
Letter No. 55 ... 226
Letter No. 56 ... 229
Letter No. 57 ... 235
Letter No. 58 ... 237
Letter No. 59 ... 240
Letter No. 60 ... 245
Letter No. 61 ... 248
Letter No. 62 ... 251
Letter No. 63 ... 256
Letter No. 64 ... 258
Letter No. 65 ... 265
Letter No. 66 ... 272
Letter No. 67 ... 276
Letter No. 68 ... 279
Letter No. 69 ... 283
Letter No. 70 ... 287
Letter No. 71 ... 290
Letter No. 72 ... 292
Letter No. 73 ... 295
Letter No. 74 ... 300
Letter No. 75 ... 302
Letter No. 76 ... 305
Letter No. 77 ... 308
Letter No. 78 ... 310

Letter No. 1

"And you shall speak unto all the wisehearted, whom I have filled with the spirit of wisdom," etc.

To My Honorable Father, may he live long and happily.

Concerning what we spoke about regarding the Study of Kabbalah in purity, etc., and what I don't know I will write, and you will answer all my questions.

I see that I have not much to write, but only general things. I cannot learn even one word in purity, since the way is to sort out the doubts from the many certainties, and not the certainties from the many doubts, but then one must learn properly.

This depends on whether a person is already qualified for it, namely that all his receptions are in purity, meaning receiving in order to bestow. When one who is not at that degree learns, his studies of kabbalah cannot be in purity, as it is written, "And you shall speak unto all the wisehearted, whom I have filled with the spirit of wisdom," namely whose heart is already purified with the spirit of the Creator.

Otherwise, it is utterly impossible, as our sages said, "A man sins only if a spirit of folly has entered him." It follows that one cannot be called a sinner unless he has the spirit of wisdom. And although one does not feel that he is forever a sinner, it is because one does not see one's own flaws. But the truth is that as long as one is not rewarded with the spirit of wisdom he is called a sinner. It is necessarily so, and precisely this depends on the Creator to fulfill...

(The rest of the letter is missing)

Letter No. 2

Tuesday, Portion *Toldot* [Generations], November 23, 1954, Tel Aviv

To my courageous friends ... may the Creator be with you.

Concerning what we spoke about while standing by the car, see in the book, *Beit Shaar Hakavanot* [*Gatehouse of Intentions*], item 70, and you will find an answer.

And concerning your joining the society, to which I conceded, I must admit that I did not examine it sufficiently. The reason is that while I was in Tiberias, I was thinking about the conflicting opinions existing in Tiberias, so I said that there is no need to consider them, and only the truth will show the way. But upon arrival at Tel Aviv I immediately sensed that there are views among our former friends, as well, meaning prior to the departure of the Light. Now their *Kelim* [vessels] are, and a hint suffices, and they will seek iniquities and transgressions to justify their deeds, namely that truth is only in Jerusalem, the place of ruin. So now I have come to revert from this, meaning not to join the above-mentioned society.

As for your question about the meaning of the verse, "Anyone with whom the spirit of people is pleased," I have found that I have written in the name of my father, who was asking saying that there was a difference of opinions even among the greatest and most famous. He reasoned saying that if they had said that "Anyone with whom people are pleased," then they could have asked that question. But since they said precisely "Anyone with whom the *spirit* of people is pleased," meaning that there are creations, meaning bodies, and the bodies have no relation to the spirit of the Creator. On the contrary, the view of landlords is opposite to the view of Torah. But the *spirit* of people is holy.

This is the spirit to which our sages referred, since "whosoever keeps one commandment," namely the commandment of faith, called "one letter," "sentences himself and the whole world to the scale of merit."

This brings up the question, "But do we neither see nor feel any merit in the public while there are righteous in the generation?" Baal HaSulam said about that that the righteous draws the abundance for the entire collective, but those who do not have vessels to clothe the Light cannot enjoy this abundance. However, the souls of each and every person receives a Surrounding Light from the abundance, hence "the spirit of people is pleased with him" since the spirit of the Creator illuminates into the spirit of people.

However, we are not speaking of, or concerned with, all those who have not yet clothed their spirits.

May you merit going from strength to strength.

Your friend who sends you regards and wishes you well,

Baruch Shalom Ashlag

Letter No. 3

Vayechi Yaakov [And Jacob Lived], January 2, 1955, Tel-Aviv

To my dear and faithful friends,

I read the letter signed by ... and I thoroughly enjoyed your taking upon yourself the work in love of friends. Concerning your first question, I cannot answer it in writing because they are matters for oral discussion and it is not advisable to write them down.

Concerning the second question, I am writing you an article about what I heard from my father, Baal HaSulam: "You preserve man and beast, O Lord." Our sages explained that "these are cunning people who pretend to be as beasts," and you are writing me that it is good to actually be a beast! Instead, you must walk in the ways of Torah and wisdom, and draw from the brightness of the upper pleasantness the sweetness of the palatable pleasure of the upper light. However, it must be as "The shepherds of Abraham's cattle," and not as "The shepherds of Lot's cattle."

You should understand these matters with what I said yesterday at the third meal before our friends concerning the verse, "I will go down to Egypt with you and also bring you up" ... as well as the verse, "And he said, 'For *EKYEH* [I will be] with you, and this shall be a sign unto you that *Anochi* [I] have sent you. When I shall bring the people out of Egypt, you shall worship God on this

Har [mountain].'" What is the connection between *EKYEH* [I will be], *Anochi* [I am] and the *Har* [mountain]?

In the book, *Letters of Rabbi Akiva*, item 5, it is written, *EKYEH Asher EKYEH* [I will be what I will be], said the Creator. I have created the world with the quality of goodness, with the quality of goodness I lead it, and with the quality of goodness I will make it new." Another thing, *EKYEH Asher EKYEH*, said the Creator. With the quality of faith I have created the world, with the quality of faith I guide it, and with the quality of faith I will make it new." We should understand the meaning of the verse "I will be what I will be [*EKYEH Asher EKYEH*]" with respect to the quality of goodness and the quality of faith. Our sages interpreted the verse, *EKYEH Asher EKYEH*, to mean, "I will be in this trouble, for I will be with them in their enslavement to the other kingdoms."

To understand the above, we need to know that when a person begins to observe Torah and *Mitzvot* on the line of *Lishma*, he feels that he is in trouble, called "Egypt," meaning that the king of Egypt constantly asks, "Who is the Lord that I should obey His voice?" This is when the labors of the mind arrive, when his thoughts begin with *Zivugim de Hakaa* that batter his mind. At times one thinks that all these foreign thoughts are only spies who come "to see the nakedness of the land," meaning to look through the chimneys and not more, and there is no connection between these thoughts and the work of the Creator. Other times one thinks, "We are honest, the sons of one father," namely that all our thoughts are only to cling to the one Creator, and we are strengthened and prevail over all the thoughts of "Who is the Lord that I should obey His voice?" and "What is this work for you?" which is called the "exile in Egypt."

The matter of *EKYEH* is the state of "from you onward," which is the state of above reason. This time is called, "I will go down to Egypt with you," for "I am the Lord your God," which is the burden of faith, regarded for him as having descended by the exile in Egypt. When we want to calm the body and make for it promises of reward, in the form of the will to receive, we tell it: "and I will also bring you up," meaning that afterwards you will also remain in the state of *Anochi* ["I am," or "selfish"], which is the state of faith.

And this is *Asher EKYEH* [what I will be], meaning afterwards, too, he will remain in the state of *EKYEH*, meaning that even "When you have brought the people out of Egypt, you shall serve God on this mountain." *Har* [mountain] comes from the word *Hirhurim* [reflections], namely that afterwards, too, he will be built on the foundation of the mountain, which is "as mountains hanging by a thread," as in "He hangs up the earth on nothing."

But afterwards, when we achieve *Dvekut* [adhesion] with the Creator, the "nothing" becomes "without what," where there is no place for the "what" to awaken. Instead, the *EKYEH Asher* becomes, "I have created it by the quality of goodness." And when we feel that He is all the goodness, we understand, "I created the world by the quality of faith."

This is the meaning of "My heart overflows with a good thing." Baal HaSulam explained that feeling is only in the heart, that it is not revealed from the heart to the mouth. The mouth refers to knowledge, meaning that the mouth reveals one's mind and thoughts, whereas the heart is only the reception in the heart, only a potential. Then, when one takes upon himself this potential, he is rewarded with a good thing, a feeling that there is nothing better in the world than faith. At that point he can say, "My works are for the king," namely to bestow and not to receive. From this one is rewarded with the state of "My tongue is the pen of a quick writer," which is the state of Moses.

This is the meaning of, "I will go down to Egypt with you," namely that during the exile one sees that nothing is worse or lower than the state of "*Anochi*" ["I Am" or "selfish"]. But when rewarded, they see that it is also the state of "I will also bring you up," that all the ascents are the state of *Anochi*. This is *EKYEH*

Asher EKYEH, meaning that first it was as trouble but now he regards it as good. This is "And it is time of trouble for Jacob, but he will be saved from it," for all the salvations are regarded as *Anochi*.

I conclude my letter with a wish that we may merit receiving the burden of the kingdom heaven in the state of *Anochi*.

Letter No. 4

February 10, 1955

To my friend ... Hello and all the best,

You surprise me ... for it has been a while since I have received any news from you regarding your health and strength.

It must be that you are lacking confidence and strength, and in my view it is because of the external thoughts and views that you absorb through the attached channels found when coming to an environment that disagrees with our spirit and way. And where alien thoughts were in "the *Nukva* [female] of the great deep" for you, meaning that the thoughts had no power or control for you have already cancelled them and cast them under your feet, for you can already trample them and walk over them, meaning there are still alien thoughts in your bodies, but they are no longer in control.

This is the meaning of the Shabbat [Sabbath]— although the *Klipot* [shells/peels] are present in the world and the correction has not been completed, when "darkness shines as light," but the place of the alien thoughts is in the *Nukva* of the great deep. That is, they have no grip over man at all. However, when departing from the authority of one to the authority of many, meaning when taking out the thoughts and works into the authority of many, for the many to look at them, and if we also insert the thoughts of the people of the authority of many into your authority of one, this is already called "desecration of Shabbat." This means that we give room for the awakening of those *Klipot* whose power has already ceased—who were already in the *Nukva* of the great deep—to come up into your thoughts.

At that time, you do not think that these alien thoughts are wittiness and erudition of people from the outside, that it is on offshoot of your mischief, and that now you are attached to the truth, meaning possess the true scrutiny, and now the conclusions you are drawing are through true and one hundred percent clean contemplation of the alien thoughts. And also, that until now, everything you did was only due to your insufficient scrutiny that one who wishes to walk on the path of truth should do.

And henceforth you need to walk on the path that is customary to people who are carried out by the currents of the world, and the results are quite predictable. And although I do not tend to speak, much less write, about these matters, I will change my way, although I know that it will be utterly useless, but only for the purpose of, "I saved my soul."

We had a party on the trees' New Year's Eve—on the month of *Shevat*, when the world is sentenced for the whip or for mercy. The month of *Shevat* is the fifth of the winter months. Through the curses and swears that we hear about the Torah and *Mitzvot* [commandments] when we arrive at the fifth discernment, which is the *Sefira*, *Hod*, we should correct and be sentenced favorably so that the pain will turn into splendor. At that time the whip becomes mercy, extending all five *Behinot* from *Hesed* to *Hod*, as it is written, "For I said, 'Let a world of mercy be built.'" For the light of *Hassadim* is called "above reason," and only there is the blessing.

For this reason, on the 15 of *Shevat* we bless on the fruits, as Baal HaSulam said, that the whole difference between *Kedusha* [holiness] and *Klipa* is in the fruits: the work yields fruits, but "another god is infertile and does not bear fruit." Also, being rewarded with fruits is only through the quality of *Hesed*, and then one is rewarded with a fruit-bearing tree. "For man is the tree of the field," namely that only through the way that we received from Baal HaSulam are we rewarded with fruits called being "fruitful and multiplying." Through the fruits we are always in a state of youthfulness, meaning as a youthful boy, as in, "Delight, young man, in your childhood."

This is the meaning of "Those whose hope is in the Lord will gain new strength," for only this is called "help from above." That is, when one comes into a state where there are arguments for both directions, one cannot sort out the truth. At that time one needs only help form above. This is called "Those whose hope is in the Lord," for he needs heaven's mercy.

May the Creator grant us with His salvation in corporeality and spirituality,

Your friend,

Baruch Shalom HaLevi Ashlag

Letter No. 5

February 24, 1955

To my friend,

I read your letter from after Shabbat of this week, and it gives me pleasure that you need to disclose the states that pass over time from letter to letter. Certainly, the Creator will open our eyes with His law.

My view on that is that you should do more in love of friends. It is impossible to achieve lasting love, unless through *Dvekut* [adhesion], meaning that the two of you will unite in a tight bond. This can be only if you try to "undress" the clothing in which the inner soul is placed. This clothing is called "self-love," for only this clothing separates two points. But if we walk on the straight path, the two points—which are discerned as two lines that refute one another—become a middle line that contains both lines together.

And when you feel that you are at war, each of you will know and feel that he needs the help of his friend, and without him, his own strength will wane, as well. Then, when you understand that you must save your life, each of you will forget he has a body he must preserve, and you will both be tied by the thought of how to defeat the enemy. Therefore, hurry, and the truth will show its way and you are certain to succeed.

And do continue corresponding.

Baruch Shalom HaLevi Ashlag

Letter No. 6

April 15, 1955, London

To the students,

I received the letter of ... and it is good that he interprets its details as much as he can. As for the rest of the matters that he informed me, I hope to sort everything out soon.

The Mishnah says, "Everyone is incumbent in seeing," meaning that each and every one must be seen at the Temple, as it is said, "All your males shall be seen." One who is regarded as a male, meaning a giver, must feel that the Creator sees him and watches over him.

Our sages said, "One who is blind in one of his eyes is exempted from seeing, as it is said, 'Will see, will see.' As one comes to see, one comes to be seen. As one comes to see with both eyes, one comes to be seen with both eyes" (*Hagigah* 4).

"Eyes" mean *Anochi* [I] and "You shall not have." *Anochi* is regarded as love, which is considered *Hassadim* [mercies], namely faith. "You shall not have" is regarded as a woman, considered left. Only then is one rewarded with greeting the face of the *Shechina* [Divinity].

"They shall not see My face empty handed, but rather each man with a gift according to his ability," meaning to the extent that he had an awakening from below, to the extent of the blessing of the Creator, and as much as the Creator illuminated for him during his work so he could persevere during his work. By this one can be rewarded with greeting the face of the *Shechina*.

In the Gemarah (p 4), it is written about what is written in the Mishnah, "Except for the deaf, the fool, and the little one. In the Tanya: "Who is a fool? He who loses what he is given." He is exempted from seeing, meaning that he cannot be granted any clothing of *Kedusha* [holiness].

By this I have interpreted the words of our sages, "Rabbi Yohanan said, 'Who is a wise disciple who is returned a loss by impression? He who is meticulous with his garment, to turn it inside out'" (Shabbat, 114). We need to understand the greatness about this.

In our way, it is simple: "His garment" is the clothing over the soul, meaning that he is meticulous with turning the will to receive to be in order to bestow. It is a rule that everyone is rewarded with an awakening from above at one time. But why does this awakening depart from him? It is because one sins only if a spirit of folly has permeated him.

This means that there is a wise one and there is a fool. The wise one is called the "Creator." A "wise disciple" means that one has learned the quality of the Creator—to be a giver. A "fool" is the opposite of the Creator—one who wishes to be a receiver for oneself. By the awakening of the vessels of reception, the awakening promptly leaves him.

But when he is meticulous about turning his garment inside out, meaning in order to bestow, his loss is promptly returned to him by impression, meaning that he is rewarded with eyes of *Kedusha*, with *Anochi* and "You shall not have."

However, we should know that there is a *Mitzva* [commandment] and there is Torah, as it is written, "a candle is a *Mitzva* and the light is Torah."

The holy *Zohar* explains the reason why he offered an offering of grain on Passover. The *Omer* was of grain because the moon was imperfect, meaning that there was circumcision without removal (and only on the first night it was as an awakening from above).

Circumcision is the removal of the foreskin, which is the casting off of the will to receive.

By this one is rewarded with a *Mitzva*, faith, called the "hand *Tefillin*, of the weaker hand." This discernment is called the "kingdom of heaven," regarded as a beast in *Gematria*, the name BON. Also, by the correction through the *Omer* count during the seven weeks, one is rewarded with receiving the Torah, which is heaven, *Zeir Anpin*, which is "man" [Adam] in *Gematria*. For this reason, on the eighth day of the assembly, two loafs were offered from the grain, which is food for man.

By this we will understand the Mishnah, "On Passover one is sentenced for the produce of the grain, and on the eight days of the assembly for the fruit of the tree. Rabbi Yehuda said in the name of Rabbi Akiva, 'Why did the Torah say, 'Bring harvest before me on Passover so that your produce in the field will be blessed.' And why did the Torah say, 'Bring two loafs of bread before me on the eight day of the assembly? It is because the assembly is the time of the fruit of the tree.' The Creator said, 'Bring two loafs of bread before Me so that the fruit of the tree will be blessed'" (Rosh Hashanah, 16).

We need to understand the connection between food for beasts and the produce of the fields, and the connection between food for man, which is grain, with the fruit of the tree. In our way, it is simple: *Omer* means food for beast, which is faith, *Mitzva*, fear of heaven, for *Malchut* is called "beast." The two loafs of bread are man's food, as RASHI interpreted, "According to Rabbi Yehuda, the tree that the first man ate was wheat, for man is called 'the tree of the field,' and the Torah is called a 'tree,' as it is written, 'She is a tree of life.' And when rewarded with Torah, it is called "being sentenced for the tree on the eighth day of the assembly."

I was not lengthy in this letter; I have no news and let us hope that all will be well.

Your friend

Letter No. 7

April 24, 1955

Hello and all the best to my friends who are standing guard against the clouds and shadows currently facing the nation of the Lord. After the great concealment that has descended upon our world at this time, the spark of the light of the Lord that they have acquired from Baal HaSulam still glitters in their hearts; they know how to keep the points in their hearts, and they are awaiting the eternal salvation...

I would like to add a few words regarding the casual conversation that took place on the 23rd of April. A great question was asked, "What is the reason for all the secular things in our world, namely the labor and pain, if the Creator wanted to benefit His creations with things of holiness, for the creatures to feel delight and pleasure in *Dvekut* [adhesion] with the Creator? This secularity, what is it for?"

In your opinion, holiness would be enough for the creatures, so why all the system of *Klipot* [shells]? What gain and what contentment and benefit does this bring to the Creator if we believe that He Himself has created this whole enterprise?

You also said that only above reason can we accept these matters. I, too, think that with all the spiritual matters we assume above reason, we are later granted with clothing of the knowledge of the Creator in complete clothing, as it is written, "and I will pour out for you unbounded blessing." But in the study, we can also understand the rhyme and reason according to the way of the Torah.

See in *The Zohar* (*Tazria* p 36 [item 105]), in the article, "There Is Advantage to Wisdom over Folly," and in the *Sulam*, where it explains that although there are many things in the world, but if there is nothing that can be held, there is no perception and sensation of all the wonderful things that exist in our world.

This means that we haven't the *Kelim* [vessels] to attain even the simplest things in which to feel the palatable taste, sweetness, and pleasantness. Only once we have the proper *Kelim*, called "desires to receive the good fillings," and when we cannot say that we would be able to receive and obtain these things without the craving for them.

To make an allegory, it is known that there is pleasure in passion, meaning that there is pleasure in passion for something, and there is pleasure in obtaining the matter. The measure of the pleasure in the passion depends on the measure of pain from not obtaining it. That is, if one feels that if he does not obtain the matter he will feel disappointment in his life, the pleasure dresses in the duration of the passion and longing.

Let us take something simpler as an example: When one drinks water in order to calm his thirst, the water grips to the size of the *Kli* [vessel], meaning to the degree of the suffering of his thirst. But if we ask a person, while drinking the water, if he is happy with the suffering of the thirst, by which he now receives great pleasure from the water, he will certainly say "Yes." And yet, if we advise a person, "If you want to enjoy the water eat salty foods and refrain from drinking half a day until your thirst is enough to make you enjoy drinking later," he will certainly say, "neither they nor their reward." Also, if we did not have the *Kelim*...

And concerning Rabbi Akiva, "All my life I have been tormenting, when will this matter come to me so I may keep it..." [The rest of the letter is missing.]

Letter No. 8

May 26, 1955, Tel-Aviv,
on the 48th day of the Omer Count, a day before *Shavuot*

Hello and all the best to my friends,

In response to your letter, I must tell you that for now, I have nothing to add in writing. Rather, as it is written, "Speak to the children of Israel and they will journey." Concerning journeys, you know that it refers to going from state A to state B, that this is the meaning of changing places, as Baal HaSulam said in an interpretation to the verse, "Day to day expresses speech." He wrote there that it is impossible to have another day without having a state of night in between, meaning that there is a break in the middle. Otherwise, it is called "a long day" and not "day after day." But the order of the work is precisely day after day. "And night to night reveals knowledge" means that there is a day in between, thus far his words.

This is the order of the journeys. Therefore, do not be afraid of any states, but only, as we said above, "journey," go forward. Each time, a new current must be streamed, as ... wrote me in his last letter, the verse, "They are new every morning; great is Your faith."

Incidentally, I am disclosing my thoughts and will to you although it is not usually my way. And yet, I wish to disclose before you what I thought about the people of Tiberias, to know how they regard us, amiably or rudely. In this letter, I will write to you how I picture and what I see of the people of Tiberias. And even though I did not describe the essence of Tiberias, still, I will write my thoughts to you.

Currently, I am becoming a little more relieved from my personal and general problems, and I am taking some time off to raise my head and behold the spectacle that is unfolding there. It is as though I see three kinds of people there, three images and forms clothed in three different types of bodies.

1) A large share, the vast majority, I do not think considers us unfavorably or favorably, or that they respect or disrespect us. In all honesty, I think we are beneath attention in their eyes. In other words, they neither think nor even feel us. It is as though we don't exist with them together in the world, on earth.

Even if they happen to hear that there is such a thing as students of the Rav Ashlag, it is of no interest to them. They are preoccupied with their own provision all day long—in their passions, or pursuit of respect, or in their spirituality. They have no need to consider such trifling matters as us—this tiny group of people—especially since they heard that there is a dispute within this tiny group.

"Scraps do not satisfy the lion." That is, the tiny group is too small and insignificant in their eyes to provide them with satiation and mental satisfaction if they let us into their minds to decide if we are good or bad. This is how inferior we are in their eyes—completely beneath scrutiny, unworthy of a moment's notice. And even though I think that this lion has all kinds of schemes in regard to us, there is actually nothing of the kind.

2) The second kind is those who respect us and in whom we already take up space in the world. They regard us as worthy people, respectable, and of certain stature. They do us the big favor of allocating time for us in their minds and in their thoughts during their free time. They take interest in us and note our stance and our activities to see if we are truly virtuous and

with integrity, to criticize us with an air of criticism if they find anything in us.

When they think about it, they see that at the end of the day, this is a group of people who have gathered in a certain place, under a certain leader, to be together. With superhuman courage they face up to all those who rise against them. Indeed, they are brave men with a strong spirit, and they are determined not to retreat one inch. They are first-class fighters, fighting the war against the inclination to their last drop of blood, and their only wish is to win the battle for the glory of His name.

However, along with all those contemplations, when they begin to consider themselves—according to their prejudices and their self-interests regarding desires and pursuit of honors—they must unanimously agree and unite against us. Thus, they wholeheartedly and unequivocally resolve that it is better for them not to unite with us. This is so, although among themselves they are very remote and so different from one another that they can never agree on anything. They might even hate each other to such an extent that they cannot bear being in the same room with one another, and all wish to kill each other. Still, against us they all unite.

And since they are biased because of the will to receive in them, and "Bribe blinds the eyes of the wise," they promptly see the opposite of what they thought of us. And after all the praises and virtues that they found in us—that each of us is praiseworthy and honorable—once they have made their resolution, they quickly execute the verdict passionately and zealously, since we spoil their reputation with our views. Thus, on the one hand, they see that truth is on our side; on the other hand, our way is burdensome to them.

To excuse themselves, they have no other choice but to destroy us and obliterate our name from the face of the earth. They toil and strain for that, to disperse us to every direction, and they plot and conspire how to fail us and place stumbling blocks on our way, using all sorts of means—legitimate and illegitimate alike, even if these means contradict the human spirit and the spirit of Torah. They do not care because they see that there will be no persistence to their will if we have any domination and expansion of our goal to wholehearted and honest people, for then we will have the power to show them the truth.

And this is bad for them, for it is better for them to do what their hearts wish and at the same time be "the face of the generation"—influential and spiritual leaders. For this, they conspire plots of ruin and destruction for our future and say, "The sooner the better; it is better to degrade them while they are still small, so not a trace of them remains."

Still, we should be very grateful to them for respecting us and for appreciating our view by at least admitting that there is something to be revoked. In other words, they do not ignore us as though we were dust, but at least we are sort of real to them. This is unlike the first kind of people, who give us no thought and believe that what happens around us is not worth *any* attention. They are also not impressed by our weakness of thinking that they are following our actions, which is why we avoid taking certain actions, lest they find them displeasing, and that this often causes us to escape the campaign for fear of the first kind of people.

To be honest, none of them pays us any attention or any thought. Perhaps it is as it is written, "You will flee when no one is pursuing you." Therefore, we should be glad about such people as the second kind, for at least they joke, mock, despise, and slander us. In other words, at least we have a reality in the world and it is not so easy for them to resolve to obliterate our name from the face of the earth.

3) The third kind are people who wish for our well-being and our favor. However, they are very few, as in "Two is a plural." And I call them by initials, BShMA, meaning B..., Sh..., M..., and A... In the holy tongue [Hebrew], they are called *Bosem* [perfume], and in translation [Aramaic], *BoSMA*, for translation is considered *Achoraim* [posterior]. In other words, they should be rewarded with

the light of *Panim* [anterior light], that all their actions will be in *Kedusha* [holiness], which is called "the holy tongue."

And what should I do when I see that I wish to describe and to picture our loved ones who are in Tiberias? At that time, I feel that Tiberias is a bustling city, and the above-mentioned third kind that are clothed in two bodies are mingled in a whirlpool, roaming among all the wishes and whims that are clothed in other bodies, meaning the first and second kinds. And then it is hard for me to find them because it is as though they are in a big stack of straw and hay, and how can one find two precious pearls, two wheats, which vanish in the vast majority? And although the rule is that even one person out of a thousand counts, they should still endure and cry out as a crane, which are truly lively creatures.

From this we can understand the allegory that our sages present, that the straw and hay and wheat deliberate for whom the field was sown. The argument of the straw and the hay seems so correct that they cannot be persuaded, and at times there is fear that the wheat will surrender under the rule of the straw and the hay. The straw and the hay argue, "We are the majority, and you, wheat, are as nothing compared to our numbers. We are of higher status and we were born before you came into the world. In other words, while you were still nonexistent, we were already grown and handsome, and our greatness could be seen by all. From afar, we dazzle the eye with the beauty that we give to the whole field. But you, wheat, are so tiny and indistinguishable that only through special attention can one see you, when one comes near. This must be due to your incompetence. But we give a place and a shelter for people who are weary and lost on the road, and have no place to rest their heads. We take them in our midst and cover them from winds and from evil beasts so they will not be seen. But who can enjoy you?"

But when it was time to harvest, everyone knew for whom the field was sown, since the straw and the hay are only fit for being animal food; they have no hope of being greater than their current measure of greatness. Wheat, however, after a few corrections, when it is broken, sifted, mixed with wine and oil, and placed in the oven, is placed on a table of kings and is worthy of serving as an offering to the Lord. And all the merit that can be attributed to the straw and the hay is their service to the wheat, which they nurtured and fed.

In other words, they took nourishment from the earth and transferred the nourishment to the wheat. It was a burden and a load to them that the wheat was riding the backs of the straw and the hay, and their value is the same as a servant who serves the king or a maid who serves her mistress.

But prior to harvest time, before the conclusion, it was impossible to clarify the truthfulness and sincerity of reality itself. Rather, each was to his own, arguing according to his own sensation. And being considerate with the truth without noticing if this might cause some lowness and unpleasantness is not such a simple task, except when one can analyze each element into many details until the truthfulness and justness of the matter are brought to light. And this requires being rewarded from above with not being trapped in the net of self-love and being carried away in the flow of the collective.

From all the above-said, it is hard for me to find you when you are on your own, without any mixture of desires and views, since everyone is hiding you, as described in the wheat allegory.

However, I have found a tactic similar to the harvest-time that was mentioned earlier. Only at night, after midnight, when the night-breeze blows and scatters the stack of straw and hay, and everyone lies flat over the field like carcasses, that is, sleeping in their beds, the two wheats break free and pour out their hearts before their Father in heaven. They enter the flame of the fire of Torah until the morning light, when it is prayer time. At that time, their souls come out as they speak the words of the living God. I believe that this is the right time for entertaining with the precious pearls that glow as flames of fire to be mingled with the whole of Israel with the help of the Rock of his Redeemer, and may the Creator give.

Let me write a few more words concerning love. It is known that there is no light without a *Kli* [vessel], meaning that each pleasure must have a clothing in which the light of pleasure might clothe. For example, when a person wishes to gain some respect, to be honored in the eyes of people, his first move is his clothes. In other words, he must dress in honorable attire, as our sages said, "Rabbi Yohanan called his garments 'My honorers.'"

Thus, one must give a certain measure of toil until he obtains the honorable garment, and even after he has acquired the garment, he must keep it from any harm and damage. That is, each day he must dust it, and if it is stained or becomes dirty, he must clean it and iron it.

But most important, he must keep it from the most dangerous saboteur—the clothes moth! In Yiddish, it is called "a Mol," which is a tiny mosquito that can't be seen. The first amendment is that it must not come in contact with old clothes. And there is also a wonderful remedy called "naphthalene," which keeps it from the damagers, called "Mols." And when he has this garment, he is ready to receive the light of the pleasure that is clothed in honorable apparel.

It is similar with love. To be rewarded with the light of love, one must find clothing in which the light might clothe. And the same rules of keeping apply to that apparel: avoiding the "dust" of slander, and especially the sabotaging mosquito known as Mol [in Yiddish, Moil means "mouth," so there is a pun here], which are people of good appearance, who speak beautifully. You'd think that they have already "circumcised" themselves in the covenants of forbidden couplings and slander, and from the uncircumcised heart, but deep within them is the saboteur that can harm you, and you cannot guard yourselves from it because it is all handsome and beautiful.

This is why this mosquito is so tiny that without special attention it is impossible to detect this harm-doer, which comes from those circumcised ones who can spoil this precious garment. Indeed, it is known that this mol does more damage to wool [Hebrew: *TzeMeR*] garments, meaning the letters *MeReTz* [Hebrew: energy], which spoil the energy for the work. And *Yatush* [mosquito] comes from

"*VaYitosh* [and he forsake] the God who made him," or in Aramaic, "And he ceased worshipping the God that he served."

Ordinarily, one who has a precious wool garment must avoid contact with old clothes. In other words, he must avoid contact with "old adherents" who spoil the energy because they are no longer competent for the work, so all their words are only to lessen the energy. And even one with strong garments of love, who is like a tree—meaning he is self-asserted—that mol should still be watched. If that mol gets into the wood, it can do harm, too, as we see that wood decays and disintegrates because a mol enters it.

And the only medicine is Naphthalene, from the word, *Naftoley*, which Onkelos interprets as *Tefilah* [prayer], meaning to pray to the Creator that this damager will not be permitted into his garment.

One should be careful with an honorable garment, for if there are rooster feathers on it, they should be removed. Also, one mustn't enter a place where there are rooster feathers while wearing these clothes. In a garment of the light of love it is interpreted as *Notzot* [feathers], from the word *Nitzim* [quarreling], as in cockfights. This refers to the singing and chanting of people who are still in exile from the path of truth and are enslaved to self-love. All the singing and the praise that they show during their Torah and prayer only inflict quarrels in your soul until you begin to make war in your views—on whose side is truth and justice. This spoils and ruins your garment, which can inhabit love. Therefore, you must be careful and avoid places where there are rooster feathers, so that afterwards you will not have to work on cleaning yourselves up from those feathers.

We can see that for people who strain to acquire the light of honors, if they do not keep their clothes properly when they go outside, the external ones immediately cling to their clothes when they see that it is not proper clothing, suitable for honoring people. In other words, people will see that he is accepting their authority over him and that he is so enslaved to those people who are standing outside, he is compelled to make great efforts to obtain the clothes but also to keep them. Even the mode, meaning the design and manner of wearing, must be precisely according to the liking of those people under whom he stands. Thus, it is precisely those from whom he wishes to receive respect that he must worship with great toil to be favored by them, so they will impart upon him the light of the pleasure that is dressed in clothes of honors.

And if, God forbid, he did not serve them sufficiently, this could yield unpleasant outcomes. That is, not only will they not give him the respect he wants from them, but on the contrary, they will all degrade him, humiliate him, and make him feel low and inferior. And that sensation of inferiority will first make him sad, then idle, and then he will feel that the whole world has grown dark on him until he sees no hope for obtaining pleasure in life. Then, he finds only one counsel—to go home, lie in his bed, and plead bitterly that his prayer will be granted—meaning that the angel of sleep, which is one sixtieth of death, will impart him with the light of the pleasure of sleep. This is the only pleasure he can hope for.

And if, alas, the angel of sleep has no mercy on him and he finds no remedy for himself, then, for the bitterness of his soul, he has no other choice but to take pleasure in a cure that is popular among the desperate who seek relief for their sadness. They fight with the inclination that wishes for one's persistence, overcome it, and extend pleasure from the angel called "suicide." That is, they feel that only this angel can deliver them from their melancholy. Evidently, it is impossible to obtain pleasures from the angel just mentioned without terrible torments and a mighty and awful emotional struggle.

Hence, "The eyes of the wise are in his head," and he knows and sees ahead of time what he can acquire and what he might obtain if he doesn't keep the laws and conditions of his contemporaries. That is, he must surrender and assume everything that the external people demand of him, or they will promptly punish him in this world. In other words, reward and punishment are revealed in this world and do not require faith above reason.

From this we can deduce the boundless care and watchfulness, and the great and special attention required to obtain the clothing that clothes the light of love—a garment that is made of such a fine and delicate fabric—lest the outer ones grip and ruin this precious garment, which has literally been bought by so much sweat and blood.

And now let me to clarify to you how and in what way I begin to obtain that clothing of love: The order of making a proper garment is to first, weave a piece of cloth. In other words, we take threads and place them together in a warp and weft manner [crisscross]. Through the warp and weft, a piece of clothing is woven.

Therefore, I take a thread of warp into a thread of weft. A *Nima* [Aramaic: "thread" as well as "say"] comes from the words "Say a word about it." *Shti* [weft] comes from the word *Tashi* [forgetfulness], as in "You forgot the Rock who begot you." In other words, I begin to act with the power of my memory and soon remember that my friends spoke unfavorably about me, that these words made them do bad things to me, and this saying [also "warp"] wears out the friendship, the camaraderie, and the brotherhood.

Afterwards, a thread of *Erev* [weft] comes to my mind, meaning I heard that my friend spoke favorably about me, which made him do good things, which are *Arevim* [pleasant] and sweet to my taste. That is, I hear and see that my friend has left all his engagements and thinks and acts only in my favor so that I will have pleasant pleasures. And these two threads create a mixture in me, and I don't know which way to decide, saying, "Is truth on the side of the warp or on the side of the weft?"

It is known that everything that exists in our world is in a form of positive and negative—right and left, true and false, light and dark, Israel and the nations, holy and secular, impurity and purity, and bad and good. This is so because it is impossible to detect a good taste without tasting the bitter taste of the bad. This is the meaning of what our sages said, "To avenge the wicked and to give a good reward to the righteous."

The word *Para* [avenge] comes from the verse, "*Para* [let loose] the hair on the head of the woman." In other words, it is possible to receive help from the wicked in order to discover the real flavor and sensation of the good reward of the righteous.

For this reason, when weaving the garment, I stand bewildered and await the verdict that will eject the poverty of mind that is clothed within me. And since I am now engaged in weaving a garment of love, to place the light of pleasure there, I am already biased and an interested party. For this reason, I decide according to the words of the weft, as the Torah implied to us that "Bribe blinds the eyes of the wise."

Thus, I no longer care if the truth is what it is; rather, I care about the goal that I desire at this minute, during the weaving of the garment of love. In that state, I have a deciding line in the middle, meaning the goal is the very thing that always decides between right and left.

And once I have acquired this above-mentioned clothing, sparks of love promptly begin to shine within me. The heart begins to long to unite with my friends, and it seems to me that my eyes see my friends, my ears hear their voices, my mouth speaks to them, the hands embrace, the feet dance in a circle, in love and joy together with them, and I transcend my corporeal boundaries. I forget the vast distance between my friends and me, and the outstretched land for many miles will not stand between us.

It is as though my friends are standing right within my heart and see all that is happening there, and I become ashamed of my petty acts against my friends. Then, I simply exit the corporeal vessels and it seems to me that there is no reality in the world except my friends and I. After that, even the "I" is cancelled and is immersed, mingled in my friends, until I stand and declare that there is no reality in the world—only the friends.

I must be brief because the holiday is approaching.

Your friend, Baruch Shalom HaLevi

Letter No. 9

August 5, 1955, London

To the friends, may they live forever,

"'And it shall come to pass that because,' *Mitzvot* [commandments] that one tramples with one's feet" (*Yalkut* [Collection]).

Baal HaSulam interpreted that it means faith, which a person slights and tramples with his feet.

To understand this more clearly, let us clarify what our sages said (*Tanhuma*), and these are their words: "And it shall come to pass that because," meaning that the verse, 'Why should I fear in days of adversity, the iniquity of my foes surrounds me" (p 49). Blessed be the name of the Creator, who has given Torah to Israel, in whom there are 613 *Mitzvot* [commandments], in which there are light trifle ones and serious ones. Because there are light *Mitzvot* among them, with which people are not meticulous, but rather cast under their feet, meaning that they are light, hence David feared the Day of Judgment and said, "Lord, I do not fear the serious *Mitzvot* in the Torah, for they are serious. What I fear are the light *Mitzvot*, lest I have broken one of them—whether I observed or did not observe—for it was light. And you said, 'Be careful with a light *Mitzva* [commandment] as with a serious one.'" This is why he said, "Why should I fear in days of adversity," and it is written, "Your servant is also cautious with them because of the majority," thus far their words.

We should ask, "It is known that it is easier to keep light *Mitzvot* than serious *Mitzvot*, where easy means they are easy to do, and serious means that it is hard to do. Therefore, why is he afraid that he has broken *Mitzvot* that are easy to do more than *Mitzvot* that are hard to do?" Afterwards, the Midrash explains that it is because he feared the light matters. This is why he ends with "Your servant is also cautious with them because of the majority," that he needed vigilance and care in order to keep the light matters more than the serious ones.

We should understand that concerning light and serious, the world determines what it regards as light and what it regards as serious. And since the world clings to externality, the world knows that what we should watch most are the actions, for they are apparent to all. That is, each one can weigh and measure how many deeds he has done during the day, and how many hours he engaged in the study of Torah. And when his friend sees that another is performing several *Mitzvot* and sits several hours studying Torah, he respects and appreciates him. And when, God forbid, he does not see that his friend is doing good deeds, he sees that his friend is in a lowly state, far from the Torah and work, since he can see only what is apparent. This is why actions are regarded as serious *Mitzvot*.

It seems true that they are serious because the whole matter of *Kedusha* [holiness] is in "We shall do and we shall hear," for the most important is the act, as only the act brings one to hearing, which is called *Lishma* [for her sake], since from *Lo Lishma* [not for her sake] we come to *Lishma*, and without actions it is impossible to achieve any degree.

For this reason, people determined that the most important is the act, and this is the most serious. For this they have determined that the thought, meaning the intention, is regarded as light and lowly, meaning unworthy of time and effort, for the most important is the act.

And although it is true that the most important is the act, it is only for the purpose of *Segula* [remedy/virtue/power]. That is, the prime advice for achieving *Lishma* is the act, but because of it people have left the desired goal, which is to work for the Creator, for engagement in Torah and *Mitzvot* has the power to purify the body so as to achieve *Lishma*. However, they have left the purpose and the goal, and turned the work into purpose, and this is what they regard as very serious.

They have made the thought, which is the intention for it to be *Lishma*, into a "light" matter. This means that only one who engages in Torah and *Mitzvot*—and does not take interest in having the intention *Lishma*—is regarded by them as a light transgression, unworthy of troubling oneself. Even if one exerts oneself, no one will see how much he has toiled in order to be respected, for the majority follows only the way of *Lo Lishma*.

In order for the world to follow the way of *Lo Lishma* in the beginning of the work, it was necessary that they would not see the truth, meaning that they would not notice it at all, for it is a trifling and is not worth the toil. Otherwise, if one would see the seriousness of the matter right at the beginning of the work, as our sages said, "He who learns *Lo Lishma* would be better off to have been miscarried," who would want to begin the work?

And since there is no other way to enter *Lishma* other than specifically coming from *Lo Lishma* to *Lishma*, there was a need to hide the truth and say that the act is the most serious, and the thought mattered little.

The meaning of "light" should be interpreted to mean "slightness," that it is not very important, whereas "serious" means something important. We should also understand that it is from the world fleeting, contemptible, and shameful. That is, when a person begins to work on this intention in the work, he finds it contemptible because the main goal should be to be rewarded with faith, and it is man's nature to value the intellect and not what is above the intellect.

By this we should interpret the Midrash that David said, "What I fear are the light *Mitzvot*, lest I have broken one of them—whether I observed or did not observe—for it was light. And you said, 'Be careful with a light *Mitzva* [commandment] as with a serious one.'" We should understand what "whether I observed or did not observe" means. Should he not know if he observed? Why does he not remember?

As said above, the lightness is on the intention of *Lishma*. In that respect, he cannot know for certain if the intention was for the Creator, since with serious *Mitzvot*, meaning with actions, I know that I was careful because there is the majority's opinion that actions must be observed.

But there is no majority opinion over the intention because the world is not careful to make the aim for the Creator. This is why he feared that his intention might not be appropriate. And in that regard the Midrash concludes, "Your servant is also cautious with them because of the majority." That is, through fear—he feared of being drawn after the collective, who believe that it is not such a great iniquity if the intention is not right, but rather "I have made me keeping and vigilance on "because," on the intention, since the view of the majority is that it is regarded as "because"—he was therefore rewarded with *Lishma* permanently over all the works, so that even past deeds will be corrected in him.

This is the meaning of, "'And it shall come to pass that because' are commandments that one tramples with one's feet," meaning that the view of the majority is that it is not such a great prohibition and iniquity to be careful with keeping the intention *Lishma*. It is about this work that man becomes "transgressed and repeated," and this is called "trampling with one's feet," and he does not notice it because the view of the majority assists him.

However, we should know that it is the correction of the world that he will not see the truth, for not every person is capable of walking on the path of truth, as our sages said, "one comes out to teach." For this reason, one is not shown one's true state in the ways of the Lord, meaning to be able to engage in Torah and *Mitzvot*, and think that one's intention is only for the Creator, as our sages said, "one does not see one's own fault." This is why one always sentences oneself to a scale of merit.

But one who is accustomed to the work and wishes to see the truth in order to walk in it, and his wish is only to correct his actions, then according to his desire for the truth, exactly to that extent is he shown his true level from above—how far he is from the work of *Lishma*. From this he is compelled to be in lowliness because he (sees) the bad in him more than all of his contemporaries, since the whole world does not see the truth, how they are placed under the governance of evil and have not begun the work for the Creator. But he does see that he cannot do anything for the Creator and therefore feels that he is separated from the Creator.

He feels as though he is dead because he is separated from The Life of Lives. And because he feels the taste of death, he is in utter lowliness, since there is none who is lower than the dead. At that time he cries out, "I am better off dead than alive," for at least he would not blemish the Torah and *Mitzvot*, meaning use holy things for his own good, as then he would feel that he is using the holy names for secular needs.

For this reason, to the extent that he is walking on the path of truth he naturally becomes lowly. Hence, one who is proud, it is a sign that he has not yet been rewarded with seeing the truth, and there is certainly no greater lowliness than this because he is submerged from head to toe under the governance of falsehood.

Some smarties pride themselves on seeing the truth. That is, even though they see about themselves that they are entirely dedicated to the governance of evil and are powerless to do anything for the Creator, and see that they are worse than their contemporaries, they still take pride in it and say, "We have the virtue of seeing the truth, while others do not see the truth of how they are placed under the governance of evil. They rejoice and delight in the work of Torah and *Mitzvot* even though it is not really for the Creator, whereas I see the truth." This is why they are proud of it and feel no lowliness.

However, this is similar to a group of sick people who were admitted into the hospital, and the doctors determined that they all had cancer, God forbid. The doctor disclosed this to one person and said, "Know, my son, what I can do for you, since you have cancer." That man was anxious as it is because he knew his days were numbered and he was sentenced to death, and all he could do was pray to the Creator. But the other people, to whom the doctor did not disclose that they had cancer, rejoiced and enjoyed themselves, and the minute the illness stopped disturbing them they thought that they would soon leave the hospital and go home to have a feast with their friends because they felt that they were completely healthy.

In such a case, the man who knows he has cancer will not even consider being proud and say that he is more important than they are, meaning that he has more vitality and joy because he knows that he has cancer. We evidently see that one who knows he has this illness cares for nothing and takes interest in nothing because he has but one concern—how to make the cancer go away from him.

He cannot partake in the joy of the rest of the patients, who do not know they have this illness and the reason why the doctor has released them from the hospital is not that they are healthy, but because the doctor has no cure for them. But they think that the reason they were released from the hospital is that they are healthy.

It is the same in the work of the Creator. Anyone who sees that the evil within him is in full force, and has been disclosed the truth from above—that there is no cure for his illness and only the Creator can help him, as our sages said, "Man's inclination overcomes him everyday, and were it not for the Creator, he would not have been able to overcome it—cannot be proud of having been disclosed the truth, contrary to others, as in the just-mentioned allegory.

It follows that the lowliness that one feels testifies to the extent to which he is walking on the path of truth. Only then, when seeing the truth, is there room for real prayer from the bottom of the heart, for only then can he say, "Lord, if You do not help me, I see no tactic that can help me exit self love and be rewarded with powers of bestowal and faith in the Creator."

Therefore, the order is that one must begin the work in *Lo Lishma* and then try to be rewarded with walking on the path of truth and to achieve *Lishma*.

This is the matter that is said about Jacob, and as RASHI interpreted, that he prepared himself for a gift, for prayer, and for war. We should ask by intimation: "Why should Jacob give a present to the Esau within him, and why should one give a present to the evil within him?"

As said above, the beginning of the work is in *Lo Lishma*. That is, when beginning to work the holy work, we promise the body that this work will give it many good things, that the body will enjoy by engaging in Torah and *Mitzvot*. We tell it that it will achieve *Lo Lishma* in general, meaning that each body has different passions: one craves money, another craves respect, etc., and this is called a "present." Afterwards comes a prayer, when beginning to pray to the Creator to reveal to him the truth and to see his real situation—how remote he is from the work of *Lishma*. At that time begins a war, meaning that we do not want to give the body any reward for its work in Torah and *Mitzvot*.

Finally, one is pitied from above and is given the present of having faith and being granted with being the King's servant, feeling that this is all that is worth living for—to able to say as our sages said, "One hour of repentance and good deeds in this world is better than all of the life in the next world."

What follows from all the above is the act, and this is called a "serious matter," and it is called *Lo Lishma*. Afterwards one should be careful with light matters, meaning with the intention *Lishma*. The sign of it is lowliness because one who sees one's lowliness sees that he is treading the path leading to the work *Lishma*. This gives one room for real prayer from the bottom of the heart, when he sees that no one will help him but the Creator himself, as Baal HaSulam interpreted concerning the redemption from Egypt, "I, and not a messenger," for everyone saw that only the Creator Himself redeemed them from the governance of evil.

And when rewarded with the work *Lishma* there is certainly nothing to be proud of because then one sees that it is only God's gift, and not "my power and the might of my hand," and there is no foreign hand that can help him. Therefore, he feels his lowliness—how serving the king is an immeasurable pleasure, and without His help he would not agree to it. Indeed, there is no greater lowliness than this.

May the Creator help us be rewarded with serving the king on the path of truth.

Baruch Shalom HaLevi Ashlag

Son of my father, Baal HaSulam

Letter No. 10

August 24, 1955

To the friends, may they live long,

I am very surprised that I have not received a word from anyone. I thought I would receive the work of each and every one, meaning that each one would elaborate on his deeds, as in, "For I will see Your heavens, the works of Your fingers." "Your heavens" means works for the Creator. They are recognized by the "works of Your fingers," meaning by each one trying to work to raise the *Shechina* [Divinity] from the dust, to keep, "Each one pointed with his finger and said, 'Behold, This is our God,'" etc.

We should know that work is in the right, which is as it is written, "Be whole with the Lord your God." That is, a person needs to walk in wholeness, meaning believe that the Creator is whole and deficient. This can be felt only by "The right [side] of the Lord is exalted," namely in greatness of the Creator—that we must always picture the greatness of the Creator.

As for man, in everything he does, he is serving the king. And every *Mitzva* [commandment] that one does gives contentment to the Creator. When one prays, the Creator hears the prayers and praises that the person sings and praises the Creator.

We should also picture that there are several people in the world to whom the Creator did not give the opportunity to serve Him and please Him, but rather pushed them away. And even when they perform some *Mitzva*, they do not remember or believe that the Creator sees and hears, accepts and regards the works of the lower ones. The Creator pushes them away by not giving them an opportunity to think, do, or believe.

To those whom the Creator wishes to bring near, He gives good thoughts, meaning to remember while performing the *Mitzva* that he is doing it for the Creator, or simply that when blessing, "That all was made by His word," he is speaking out of habit, and during the act pays no attention to the fact that he is speaking to the Creator. Or even more, he is not given an opportunity even to bless out of habit.

And if one imagines that the Creator has given him an opportunity to do a *Mitzva* in order to bring contentment to his maker even once a month, and to serve the king even once a month, they should be satisfied. Abayeh said, "Therefore, it should be said while standing." "Standing" means the full level. That is, a person needs to speak upright and be happy if he is given an opportunity to serve the king, while others are not. At that time the Creator is whole, meaning that we must say that the name of the Creator, meaning the name, "Good and Does Good," appears and shines to a person in utter wholeness, as well as that the person is whole, meaning that he has another merit in Torah and *Mitzvot* [commandments] and good deeds.

This is so because as much as one does in order to be serving the king, he still does not deserve it. One should (know) that there are many people in the world to whom the Creator did not allow to do anything for His name.

However, we should also walk on the left line, meaning criticize if this is true, if one's faith is whole, if the things he does are in utter purity and holiness without any ulterior motives, if the name, "Good and Does Good," is swallowed in the organs, etc.

At that time the left line is disputed with the right line because he sees that if he calculates sincerely, it is all to the contrary. Then there is a dispute between the lines—between right and left. And if one does not work in the middle line, the left revokes the right and he becomes one whose "knowledge is greater than deeds," meaning that he criticizes more than the good deeds that he does.

It follows that he falls to Hell, which extends from the left line. And there is Hell of the fire of lust, or snow that is chilled by work and he desires only to be in a state of rest, and idleness, and sleep, etc. This requires overcoming and prayer for the Creator's mercy from above so he may extend the middle line, meaning subdue the left line under the right. That is, he says that although the criticism mandates otherwise, he goes above reason.

By that the middle line improves the right line, for before he extended the left line and was walking on the right, he thought that reason, too, mandates the labor in the work of the Creator. But now that he has extended the left line, when he subdues toward the right, it is evident that he has chosen the right even though he has another view, from the left.

This is why we should remember as we walk to extend the work of the left—to keep the intention only to show that even though there is left, he nevertheless chooses the right. This is why we should divide the times of work and not mix one with the other.

I wrote the *Achoraim* [posterior] of the three lines, and when we are rewarded, we extend the three lines in *Panim* [anterior].

May you be granted good writing and signing,

From me, your friend, Baruch Shalom

Son of my father, Yehuda HaLevi Ashlag

Letter No. 11

September 8, 1955

To the friends, may the Lord be upon you,

◆ ◆ ◆ And perhaps this is the meaning of what we say at the *Mussaf* service [additional to the regular service] of *Rosh Hashanah* [beginning of the Jewish year], "Happy is the man who does not forget You, and a man who exerts in You." We should understand, if one always remembers the Creator, what other effort is there?

In "Assistance of Our Father" [part of the service], before the Eighteen Prayer, we say, "Happy is a man who hears Your commandments, and places You Torah [teaching/law] and Your words on his heart." We should understand, 1) he should have said, "Who observes Your commandments, 2) what is "Torah" and what are "words," 3) What is the connection between placing the Torah and the heart; it should have said, "on the mind."

Our sages said about "Kingship, Memories, Horns": "Kingship, so you will make Me king over you. Memories, so that your memory shall come before Me. But why the *Shofar* [horn]?" We should understand the meaning of memories, since there is no forgetting before the throne, so how can it be said, "So that your memory shall come before Me"? Also, if we blow then the Creator remembers us; how can this be said? In corporeality, the sound awakens a person who is asleep, but how can this be said about the Creator?

However, all these verses and saying of our sages advise us how to cling to Him, since our only flaw is that we do not feel His greatness. When we begin to criticize as in, "What is this work," we want to promptly receive everything as *Ohr Pnimi* [Inner Light]. And you know that the Inner Light shines specifically when there are *Masach* and *Ohr Hozer* [Reflected Light], meaning clean *Kelim*. But *Behina Dalet* receives from the *Ohr Makif* [Surrounding Light], since *Ohr Makif* shines from afar, as it is written in *Tree of Life*.

This means that even if a person is still remote from the Creator and does not have equivalence of form, he can receive from the Surrounding Light. The ARI wrote that the Surrounding Light is greater than the Inner Light. That is, when can one receive when he is still remote? Only when he increases the greatness and importance of the Surrounding Light, meaning the exaltedness of the Creator and the importance of the light of Torah. Then he can receive illumination from afar.

We must believe that all the beauty of Creation is in the internality of the Torah. But faith requires great efforts. This is the meaning of, "Happy is the man who does not forget You." How is one rewarded with this? By "exerting in You."

There are two meanings to the "You": 1) You, meaning the Creator; 2) In the Creator who is clothed in the twenty-two letters of the Torah.

Also, "Happy is a man who hears Your commandments," meaning rewarded with hearing. It advises us how to be rewarded through "Your Torah and Your words."

In other words, he believes that the whole Torah is the words of the Creator, meaning that "You" is clothed in the twenty-two letters of the Torah. We need to pay attention to this, as you know what Baal HaSulam said, that the mind only serves the man, but the man is primarily the heart.

This is the meaning of "kingship," that you will crown Me over you." That is, an act that will inspire us so that we take upon ourselves the burden of the Kingdom of Heaven. But we see that promptly after the reception we forget about the reception. At that time we are advised, "so that your memory shall come before Me," meaning before the Creator. That is, all the memory we have should work only to remember the Creator. This means that memories are like kingships, meaning that we need to be inspired.

And with what? With the *Shofar* [horn]. You probably know that the ARI interprets *Shofar* to mean the *Shofar* of *Ima*, *Shofar* of *Bina*. *Shofar* means beauty, and Baal HaSulam explains that beauty is *Hochma* that extends from *Bina* that has returned to being *Hochma*. By a person believing that all the beauty and importance are in *Hochma*, in which all the pleasures are included, and all that is missing is corrections, so a person wants to remember good things, since human nature is to forget only bad things.

Therefore, we must believe that everything has been prepared for us, and we will be rewarded with remembering and not forgetting the Creator for even a minute, and we will be awarded good writing and signing.

From me

Letter No. 12

October 10, 1955, London

To my friend,

Yesterday, I received your letter intended for the people of Gateshead. In the meantime, I am passing your letter to the friends in London, and I would mainly like to get them to answer your letter so there will be correspondence between you. If this succeeds, it will bring great benefit both in corporeality and in spirituality.

I am writing to you the content of the talk that I gave on a weekday of the festival of *Sukkot* before the students of the late Rav Desler concerning the "shadow of faith": We have to know that "shadow," meaning concealment, is the *Kli* [vessel] to be rewarded with the light of faith.

By that I have interpreted the words of our sages about the verse, "so that your generations may know that I had the sons of Israel live in *Sukkot* [huts]." They were clouds of glory, according to the words of Rabbi Eliezer. Rabbi Akiva says they were actual *Sukkot*. And I asked, "How can there be such a fundamental dispute between them, where one says, actual *Sukkot*, meaning corporeal huts, and the other says a spiritual *Sukkah*, of clouds of glory?"

However, both are the words of the living God, and there is no dispute here whatsoever. Rather, one says that the main thing is to mention the *Kelim* [vessels], and the other the lights. Actual *Sukkot* means actual concealments, from the word "thatch," which is called "shade." Rabbi Eliezer says that we must mention the lights, called "seven clouds of glory," which is regarded as faith. Both discernments coincided at the time of the exodus from Egypt. Therefore, when we set ourselves straight, we are rewarded with the light. However, we must not think that there is no delight or pleasure when working *Lishma* [for Her sake].

I told them an allegory about that: We must know that the world was created with a desire to receive. Therefore, as soon as a baby is born, it wants to enjoy through its final day—such as for us to play with it. And when it grows, it wants only delight and pleasure.

We must know that pleasure is a spiritual thing. We cannot grasp the pleasure; it is light, and there is a rule that there is no light without a *Kli*. Therefore, each pleasure must come within some clothing.

For this reason, we determine that each delight and pleasure is truth, since each pleasure extends from the light, and the only difference between man and beast is only in the clothing, meaning in the *Kelim*. And certainly, the light dresses according to the value of the *Kli*. However, this is in particular. In general, there is no difference between a great man and a small man but only in the clothing.

Just as we see that when a little girl is playing with a doll, the pleasure she feels is real, and if we, the parents, want her to leave the doll and go eat, the girl thinks that she has cruel parents, meaner than the neighbors, since the neighbors don't interrupt her playing and her parents do. We also see that if there is a six month old baby in the house and he is crying, and we say to the girl, "Why are you playing with the doll and kissing it? It's a false baby, come and play with a real baby," she refuses, even though we are certain this is a true clothing.

And if we can say to the girl, "Why are you enjoying playing with a real baby?" she will have no answer. But if we tell her, "You see how the baby's mother is playing with him?" or "Even other people are playing with the boy and kissing him, and it will never happen that a grownup will play with a doll and kiss it." At that time she will probably reply that the real pleasure is actually in the doll, meaning in a false clothing, and the reason why grownups kiss and play with real babies is only that they have no desire for pleasure, but I want to enjoy my life, so I must be happy with the doll." It is indeed so, but a person who is still not sufficiently developed cannot derive pleasure from true clothing although there is pleasure there. It is likewise with the case of from *Lo Lishma* and *Lishma*.

This allegory contains the answer to our friend's letter...

Baruch Shalom HaLevi Ashlag

Letter No. 12b

October 1955

To the friends, may they live long,

I have no news and I hope that the Creator will make my way successful.

I am writing to you a summary of the talk I gave to the students of Rav Desler concerning the *Sukkah* [a hut on the festival of *Sukkot*], called "shadow of faith."

A *Sukkah* means thatch, which is the waste of barn and winery. A thatch is called "shade," and shade is called "concealment of the face." In order not to have the bread of shame, we have room for work, meaning that we can engage in Torah and *Mitzvot* although we feel no flavor or vitality. Naturally, afterwards we can receive the vitality and not blemish the gift, meaning that the gift will not be blemished due to the shame that is present in the receiver.

And before we can receive the vitality of the Torah, we must receive vitality form corporeal things because without vitality it is impossible to live. This is why the Creator has prepared for us reception of vitality from corporeality. This means that vitality is called "light" and "pleasure," and pleasure is spirituality. It is a rule that there is no light without a *Kli* [vessel], meaning there is no such thing as pleasure without clothing. For this reason, the whole difference is not in the pleasure, called "light," but in the clothing, meaning in the *Kli*, since there is a clothing of falsehood, and clothing of truth.

This is similar to a five-year-old girl playing with a doll. The girl is playing with the doll as though the doll is a real child with feelings. And although the doll does not respond, she talks to it. At the same time, if there is a six month old baby in the house, and he is crying, and the five year old girl is told, "Go play with the real baby and we will benefit as well because the baby will not cry," she will refuse completely. That is, she cannot derive pleasure from a clothing of truth, but from a clothing of falsehood. But as for the pleasure, we see that the girl is feeling real pleasure.

But when the girl has grown to be eighteen, she must derive pleasure from a clothing of truth. Likewise, before we grow up, we derive pleasure specifically from *Lo Lishma* [not for Her sake], regarded as "clothing of falsehood." This is called "shadow," "concealment," and then there is room for work, and we derive vitality from false things. Afterwards, when we are rewarded, we receive the light of faith.

Letter No. 13

October 20, 1955, London

To all the students, may the Lord be upon you.

I received the letter of Rabbi ... and ... and I will answer all the questions in general, including the questions of Rabbi... It is written in the *Gemarah*, "A sage stood before Rabbi Yohanan, 'All who engage in Torah and good deeds, and buries his sons, all of his iniquities are forgiven'" (*Berachot 5b*). This means that as a person is obliged to engage in Torah and good deeds, he is obliged to bury his sons. Otherwise, all of his iniquities are not forgiven. I wonder, can this be?

We should interpret this according to our way. All the work we have is only to turn the reception to be in order to bestow. This is against our nature and desire. However, we were given the remedy of Torah and *Mitzvot*, by which we obtain the power and might to subdue our bodies, so that all of our intentions will be for the Creator. This is the meaning of engaging in Torah through the light in it, as well as to engage in good deeds, which is the meaning of loving others. By those two we can exit reception and be rewarded with bestowal.

In that regard, the accuser argues, "Go and see what people do. Since the day I understood, and all the great ones and famous ones in our generation do not concur that we should do these works. And also what I learned did not teach me that one must be a true servant of the Creator in concealment. That is, that the good deeds that they do are hidden from people. Meaning, even if one does good deeds and engages in Torah and *Mitzvot* (because they do not see), people say that it neither work nor Torah, and this is not the way."

It turns out that as much as a person engages in Torah and *Mitzvot*, they do not see anything because they do not like it. It follows that this is called "concealment."

It is said about that, "Buries his sons." That is, he must bury all the concepts and perceptions he received and saw from his environment, which contradict the true path of the Creator. In other words, he should place all those perceptions in the ground. But those perceptions, too, will be revived at the end of correction. This means that when he is rewarded with *Lishma* [for her sake] and subdues his inclination, there will be vitality in them.

In other words, to the extent that they had caused him labor and work, and according to the effort, they deserve vitality and gratitude, for having obstructed his work for the Creator. But for now, they cannot be toyed with, meaning with the concepts and perceptions that interrupt him from the true work of the Creator. Rather, they must be buried. At that time, all of his iniquities are forgiven, where iniquity means the first iniquity, namely faith above reason.

We should always try to make the fall due to the obstructers will take very long, but immediately grow stronger, trust the Creator, and pray from the bottom of the heart. Meaning, when one has fallen into a deep pit, "I call upon you oh Lord."

By that we understand the words of our sages in *Berachot*, "Abba Benyamin says, 'Two things I regretted all my life: my prayer, that it will be before my bed.'" They interpreted in the *Gemarah* to mean "next to my bed." "...and for my bed to be placed between north and south." We should understand why is it so difficult to do this, that he had to regret it.

According to the above we understand that bed means down, falling, from the words, "fell down." Therefore, he did not regret the fall, since the path of the Creator is to have falls and ascents. Rather, what did he regret? That it is not next to his bed. Meaning, when he falls down, he wants to immediately grow stronger and pray to the Creator to help him.

Also, if he must fall, which is down, it should not be to the east or to the west, which is the face and back, said about *Hochma*, but for his bed to be placed between north and south, which is right and left, which is *Hassadim*. That is, that the fall must be on the desire to receive in the heart, and not in the mind, which is regarded as *Hochma* [wisdom], since the *Klipa* [shell] against the mind is called, "Pondering the beginning." But the heart sins only in the "what."

And I shall end with the *Gemarah*, "The residents of Yehuda were meticulous with their words, and their Torah was true. The residents of the Galilee were not meticulous with their words, and their Torah was untrue" (*Iruvin* 4:53). In other words, they made sure that everything they said in Torah and *Mitzvot* will be in the holy tongue, meaning, with words of bestowal. Whereas the residents of the Galilee were not meticulous, and said that they could engage in Torah and *Mitzvot* in order to receive, to be proficient in Mishnah.

We can also say that the Torah of the residents of Yehuda, who learned from one teacher, was true, and the Torah of the residents of the Galilee, who did not learn from one teacher, was untrue. We should explain that there is no difference between the first explanation and the second explanation. Meaning one who has one teacher, namely, he is meticulous with the holy tongue, meaning, words of bestowal and concealment, and one who wants to learn in the rest of the tongues, meaning in the language of reception. It follows that he has two teachers—one from reception and one is Baal HaSulam, which is the language of bestowal.

It is my hope that the Creator will help us to be able to trust the Lord, and He will deliver us from all the darkness and we will be rewarded with cleaving onto Him, once and for all.

Regards to all of you,

     Baruch Shalom HaLevi Ashlag, son of Baal HaSulam

Letter No. 14

November 21, 1955, London

To the students, may they live long,

I see that you are behaving with me with eye for an eye, meaning that if I don't reply to your letter right away, then you believe that you have already excused yourselves, and you can no longer write me. Indeed, you are right; it is all my fault that the correspondence is not so frequent. I pray that He will give me the knowledge to correct all of my faults.

Yesterday I gave a talk before I went back to Israel, to the group of students of Rabbi Dessler. I told him the verse, "Raba said, 'One should know in one's heart if he is a complete righteous.'" I said that repentance means that a person should return back to his origin.

That is, since the essence of creation, which is called "man," is the will to receive, and the Creator is the giver, and when a person returns to his root it is called "repentance." How is repentance? It is as Maimonides says, "Until He who knows the mysteries will testify that he will not turn back to folly." That testimony appears in a person only once he has repented. Then he attains the upper pleasantness, meaning that the Creator places His *Shechina* [Divinity] on him. A person who has repented means that he was rewarded with *Dvekut* [adhesion].

This is the meaning of, "One should know in one's heart, in one's soul," meaning if he wants to know if he has already repented, he has the scrutiny if he's already been rewarded with the pleasantness of the Creator. This is the sign that he has repented, meaning that he's already working in order to bestow (See in the *Introduction to Talmud Eser Sefirot*).

This is the meaning of "Seek peace and pursue it." The whole dispute is only from the will to receive, and "seek peace" can be in the will to bestow. This is the meaning of what is written, "And Israel sowed in that land, and he found a hundred gates," meaning one-hundred percent. This is precisely the quality of Isaac who had received from Abraham, as it is written, "And Abraham gave Isaac all that he had."

And RASHI interprets the Midrash, "Rabbi Yehuda says, 'This is *Gevura* [strength or might],' And Rabbi Nehemia says, 'This is blessing.'" But they both referred to the same thing. Rabbi Yehuda speaks from the perspective of the work, that He showed him the place of work, which is precisely by overcoming, and Rabbi Nehemia speaks of the reward, where specifically by overcoming, one is rewarded with the blessing, and the blessing is one-hundred percent. By being rewarded with repentance from love, all one-hundred percent of the work is blessed, even the time of sins.

And one is rewarded with everything only by overcoming, called "strength," and each and every strength that a person elicits joins into a great amount. That is, even if a person overcomes once and gets an alien thought, and says, "But I already know from experience that soon I will not have this desire for the work, so what will I get now if I overcome it a little?'" At that time, he must reply that many pennies join into a great amount, meaning to the general account, whether to the root of his soul or to the public.

Perhaps this is the meaning of "The gates of tears were not locked." *Shaarei* [gates] comes from the words, *Se'arot* ["hair," or "storms"], which is overcoming. "Tears" comes from the word "tearing," meaning that there is a mixture with other desires, and only in the middle of the desires there is a brief moment of a desire

Letter No. 14

to overcome toward love and fear of heaven. "...not locked," but rather that moment joins into a great amount. When the amount is full, the person begins to feel the spiritual clothing.

This is the meaning of the importance of tears, meaning that even if he is in the lowest state and has base desires, but still has the strength to overcome, meaning that from the point in his heart he yearns and craves the Creator, then that force is very important. Thus, even when a person is in exile, when his point in the heart is placed under other governances, called "Divinity [*Shechina*] in exile" for that person, for one moment he overcomes and sanctifies the Creator. And even though he is already certain, because of all of his experiences, that afterwards he will fall again, it is still very important that a person can say the truth openly.

This is similar to a person standing among criminals who are swearing and cursing the work of the Creator. And among them there are some who lecture eloquently and let you understand that there is no point to serving the Creator. But still there is someone there who cannot explain the value and the essence of the work so well, but he can make a few objections, meaning that he utters protests that what they're saying is not true. It is good that he disagrees, even though he is not as eloquent as the swearers. This is called the "gates of tears", and it is called "Many pennies join into a great amount."

Let us hope that the Creator will open our eyes and delight our hearts with "Say unto Zion, your God is King."

Letter No. 15

December 3, 1955

How could Jacob love Rachel more than Leah because she was beautiful? We know the words of our sages, "Who marries a woman for beauty?"

Answer: The Torah teaches us the ways of the Creator. There are two discernments in the work: 1) *Hochma*, 2), *Hassadim*. *Hochma* means, seeing and knowing, and it is called the "revealed world." And there is a concealed world called "Leah." This is the meaning of, "Leah's eyes were soft," which is *Hassadim* and faith above reason.

This is also the meaning of matter of Jacob and Laban. Jacob is called, "serving the Creator," and Laban is called the "Creator," who is the Emanator (the Holy ARI, in *Tree of Life*, Gate *Akudim* [tied] interprets that Laban is called the "upper whiteness," namely the Emanator). He has two daughters, meaning two degrees: Leah, called the "concealed world," and Rachel, called the "revealed world."

The purpose of creation is to do good to His creations. It is on the revealed world. And the concealed world, which is called Leah, is called the "light of *Dvekut* [adhesion]."

"And Jacob loved Rachel," meaning, he wanted to extend the light of the purpose of creation. But Laban said that first he must receive Leah, which is the light of *Dvekut*, called "light of *Hassadim*."

"And the Lord so saw that Leah was hated," meaning that Jacob was not pleased with Leah, so the Creator gave him multiplication specifically from Leah. That is, he showed him that specifically through light of *Dvekut* we are awarded with multiplication in Torah and work.

But at the same time, we need the correction of Rachel, meaning to extend the light of the purpose of creation, regarded as *Hochma*. For that, Rachel told him, "Give me sons, and if not, I will die." This means that Jacob had to prepare all the required corrections for Rachel, so he would have multiplication at the degree of the revealed world, as well. This is so because if he does not have offspring, he will have no vitality in this work, and he will have to leave that degree. This is regarded as, "And if not, I will die," meaning that he had to extend *Hassadim* into *Hochma*.

This is the meaning of, "And God remembered Rachel." Our sages said, "the" [a word added only in Hebrew], meaning thanks to Leah, meaning by extending *Hassadim* into *Hochma*. That is, we can extend the revealed world on the basis of *Hassadim*.

May the Lord help us walk in the ways of the Lord with faith.

Letter No. 16

December 21, 1955

Let a driven leaf heal and let them say that I am in the delegation of their Maker, flying among flyers, The Great Tamarisk, to whom the Upper One assists, our glorified teacher, Rav...

I received your letter, and may the Creator illuminate that our way is the right way and we will strain our memory for the day of memorial. Then we will be granted the light of memory, which is good for cleansing the material air, and we will breathe the air of holiness, which is the true and eternal life.

I would like to add to what you wrote as follows, "I am certain that if I had met the greatest agnostic, etc.

We know that there is a custom, applied all over the world, that it is not good for a highly skilled professional to be among poorly skilled workers and learn from their actions. For example, when a cobbler is among unskillful cobblers, they let him understand that it is not worthwhile to make a good shoe, but do it however it comes out, and it is not worthwhile to make a good and handsome shoe.

Or a tailor, if he is skillful, when he is among unskillful tailors, they let him understand that it is not worthwhile to strain to make the clothing neat, tidy, and fitting its owner. Hence, he should be wary of being in contact with them.

But when a builder is among tailors, he cannot learn from their bad actions because there is no connection between them. However, within the same profession, each one should watch himself and be in contact only with pure-hearted people.

According to the above, with any person that you consider a servant of the Creator, you should be watchful and see if he is a skilled professional, meaning wishes his work to be clean and pure and intended for His Name. At the very least, he should know that he is not a good worker and seek advice in his soul by which to be a skillful worker, and not an ordinary worker who aims only for the reward.

But a good, skillful worker is one who does not consider the reward, but enjoys his work. If, for example, a skillful tailor knows that the clothing fits its owner at every point, it gives him spiritual pleasure, more than the money he receives.

Thus, with people who are not from your profession, it is not important if you are among them, since you engage in building and they engage in tanning. But with people who engage in Torah but are not meticulous about keeping the clothing fit for its owner, they only have a mind that is against the Torah, opposite from the view of Torah. And here you must always be watchful... and keep a good distance away from those people, as it were a bowshot. And this is not so with ordinary people.

- Hence, since you have no contact with the people of Mizrahi, you do not need such a careful watch.
- But from the people of Agudat Israel, you do need to keep away.
- And with Hassidim, you need even greater vigilance.
- And with people who were close to my father (Baal HaSulam) you need to keep a very watchful eye.

And this is the reason: In the world of *Nekudim*, *Melech ha Daat*, the level of *Keter*, which is the first *Melech* [king], fell lower than all the *Melachim* [kings] during the breaking. This is so because while the coarser is also higher when it has a *Masach*, it is the worst when losing the *Masach*. For this reason, it fell lower than all the *Melachim*.

And we can interpret these words. When they walk in the path of the Creator, they have a twofold will to receive: for corporeality and for spirituality. Hence, those who were close to Baal HaSulam, while they were learning, had a *Masach* and *Aviut* [coarseness]. But now that they are not surrendering and have no interest in having a *Masach*, their whole work is to become "handsome Jews" or "Rebbes" [great rabbis].

Thus, this is *Aviut* without a *Masach*, and they naturally give off what they do. And as for me, I have no trust in them, and there is no one to hold them down. I am being brief because I do not wish to have them in my thoughts, for you know the rule: "One is where one thinks."

To understand the matter more clearly, I shall give you a brief example: It is known that between each two degrees there is a medium made of both discernments together.

- Between the still and the vegetative, there is a medium called "corals."
- Between the vegetative and the animate, there is the stone of the field, which is an animal that is tied to the earth by its navel and nourishes off it.
- And between the animate and the speaking, there is the monkey.

Hence, there is a question: What is the medium between truth and falsehood? What is the point that is made of both discernments together?

Before I clarify, I shall add another rule: It is known that it is impossible to see a small object and it is easier to see a large object. Hence, when a person commits few lies, he cannot see the truth—that he is walking on a false path. Rather, he says that he is walking on the path of truth. But there is no greater lie than that. And the reason is that he does not have enough lies to see his true state.

But when a person has acquired many lies, the lies grow in him to the extent that he can see them if he wishes. Thus, now that he sees the lies—that he is walking on a false path—he sees his true state. In other words, he sees the truth in his soul and how to turn to the right path.

It follows that this point, which is a point of truth—that he is treading a false path—is the medium between truth and falsehood. This is the bridge that connects truth and falsehood. This point is also the end of the lie, and from here on begins the path of truth.

Thus, we can see that to be rewarded with *Lishma* [for Her sake], we first need to prepare the biggest *Lo Lishma* [not for Her sake], and then we can achieve *Lishma*. And similarly, *Lo Lishma* is called a "lie" and *Lishma* is called "truth."

When the lie is small and the *Mitzvot* and good deeds are few, he has a small *Lo Lishma*, and then he cannot see the truth. Hence, in that state, he says that he is walking on the good and true path, meaning working *Lishma*.

But when he engages in Torah all day and all night in *Lo Lishma*, then he can see the truth, since by the accumulation of lies, his lie increases and he sees that he is indeed walking on a false path.

And then he begins to correct his actions. In other words, he feels that everything he does is only *Lo Lishma*. From this point, one passes to the path of truth, to *Lishma*. Only here, at this point, does the issue of "from *Lo Lishma* one comes to *Lishma*" begin. But prior to that, he argues that he is working *Lishma*, and how can he change his state and his ways?

Hence, if a person is idle in the work, he cannot see the truth, that he is immersed in falsehood. But by increasing Torah in order to bestow contentment upon his Maker, one can then see the truth: that he is walking on a false path, called *Lo Lishma*. And this is the middle point between truth and falsehood. Hence, we must be strong and confident on our way, so every day will be as new to us, as we need to always renew our foundations, and then we shall march forward.

Your friend, Baruch Shalom HaLevi Ashlag

Letter No. 17

January 18, 1956

Hello and all the best to my friend, who is tied to the shackles of my heart...

A response to your letter from December 29, 1955, to which until now I had no time to reply due to being burdened with my daughter's wedding.

And regarding the first question, "Why did Jacob, our father, bless the sons through an angel?" It is explained in the writings of the ARI that *NRN de Tzadikim* [righteous] are the internality of the three worlds, *Beria, Yetzira, Assiya*. The origin of the souls is from the world of *Beria*, the *Ruach* extends from the world of *Yetzira*, and *Nefesh* is from the world of *Assiya*. And all the bestowals extend from the world of *Atzilut*, called "He, His life and His essence are one."

In the world of *Atzilut*, the ten *Sefirot* over there divide into three discernments: 1, *Keter*; 2, *Hochma* and *Bina*; 3, *ZA* and *Malchut*.

They are regarded as *Shoresh*, meaning *Keter*, *Mochin*, meaning *Hochma* and *Bina*, and the recipients of the *Mochin*, meaning *ZA* and *Malchut*, called "male" and "female," Israel and Leah, Jacob and Rachel. The *ZON* receive the *Mochin* for the souls of the righteous, who are the internality of the three worlds *BYA*.

Letter No. 17

The operator and transmitter of the upper abundance is Angel *Matat*, See in *The Zohar* (*Vayetze*, p 36 and in the *Sulam* [Ladder commentary], item 71, that he wrote there). Angel *Matat* is called the "minister of the world," whose name is as the name of his rav. At one time he is called by the name *HaVaYaH* and another time by the name *Shadai*, since he performs two operations.

1. He receives the *Hochma* and gives to *BYA*, and then he is called *Shadai*, as in, "He said to His world, 'enough,' spread no more,'" referring to the abundance of *Hochma*, as there was a *Tzimtzum* [restriction] on receiving the *Hochma* in the *Kelim* [vessels] of the will to receive. Therefore, the Emanator brought back the left leg of the *Tav* back up, and because of it, the leg of the *Tav* is thick because He brought the left leg back up so it would not illuminate into the *Klipot* [shells] (see the "Introduction of the Book of Zohar," p 26, and in the *Sulam*, item 23).

2. The second discernment of Angel *Matat* is when he also has *Hassadim* to bestow upon the lower ones. At that time his name is as the name of his rav which is *HaVaYaH*, and *Matat* is completed and is called by the name of its master, *HaVaYaH*.

When Jacob blessed his sons, he had to extend the blessing according to the order of the degree, until the abundance would be extended to the lower ones. Therefore, he extended the abundance for the sons up to Angel *Matat*, and from *Matat* the abundance would flow to the sons. This is why Jacob blessed his sons through Angel *Matat*, who is the bestower and the transmitter of the abundance from the world of *Atzilut* to *NRN de Tzadikim* and to the three worlds *BYA*, and this is why he said, "The redeeming angel will bless me."

By that you will understand your second question regarding "my name in the midst of Him," which Maimonides wrote, "for My name is included in the midst of Him." You asked, "What does it mean that his name is as the name of his Rav?" since we have no attainment in His essence, but only in the revealed.

The thing is that a joint name means that each name indicates an attainment, because that which we do not attain we do not define by name. And any attainment in spirituality is precisely when there is a connection between the attained and the attaining. This is called "shared by the attaining and the attained together." Then we can say that there is the disclosure of a name, a form, and a specific limitation over the abundance. But, in attaining without an attained you cannot speak of any form or limitation, and no attainment is applied to it. This is regarded as "There is no thought or perception in him at all," and as "essence without substance" (See in the "Preface to the Book of Zohar," p 50, item 12).

This is the meaning of His name, meaning what we attain through Angel Matat, is as the name of his rav which is also specifically a disclosure, meaning that Matat gives the ZON, who are the recipients of the *Mochin de Atzilut*, where there are two discernments—*Hochma* and *Bina*—that appear to the lower ones in the form of *Hassadim* and *Hochma*.

When Matat gives *Hochma*, he is called by the name of his rav, by the name *Shadai*. And when he gives *Hassadim* as well, then the name of his rav is *HaVaYaH*. And then Matat is called "the elder of his home who rules over all that he has," where the angel Matat is the minister of the world and rules the world, meaning that through him the abundance extends to the worlds *BYA*, and are included with the *NRN de Tzadikim*.

This is the meaning of "My name is in the midst of Him," meaning that Matat's giving the names of Matat refers to the form of the abundance that consists of two forms, which are *Hochma* and *Hassadim*, that these names operate in Matat according to the measure of the name of the rav that he extends.

And regarding your third question, why the Holy Torah elaborates in the introduction of Ephraim to Menashe, we can explain this according to the rule that we have in the work of the Creator, that the goal must always be before him, and to know what is his role in life, and to which final point a person should come so he can say that he has achieved peace and quiet.

This is so because only when the final goal is revealed before him can a person prepare himself with all the means and activate the forces at his disposal. Were it not for this, he would not know how to balance his forces and the keeping, because the real means required in order to have as keeping in the ways that involve dangers, when he does not know the full force of the lurking enemy, if he does not know who is the real enemy that should be subdued. Therefore, when beginning to speak of the orders of the work, and of having blessing in the work, the goal should be of utmost importance.

Also, it is known that when beginning to walk on the path of work, one begins from light to heavy. At first we learn and do the easiest things to understand and to do, and then what is a little more difficult, etc., until we are accustomed and experienced in the ways of the war of the inclination. At that time we attack the fiercest attacks.

It turns out that we have two things that we should put one before the other. Joseph's view was that we should mainly speak of the ways of the work according to the order, meaning from easy to hard. And Jacob's view was that first and foremost we have to speak of the goal.

Drafts and Appendices to This Letter

1) Regarding your third question, "Why the Holy Torah so elaborates in the introduction Ephraim to Menashe: It is known that preceding one to the other depends on the importance of the matter. Regarding the work of the Creator, we must know what is important, meaning to give the main emphasis on the main point, being the goal.

...It is written in *The Zohar* (*Yayechi* 4:14, and in the *Sulam*, item 41) that there are two great and important ministers. One minister is from Ephraim, whose quality is to keep Israel in exile and to have them multiply there. The other minister is from Menashe, therefore his quality is to make them forgotten in exile.

He explains there that there are two kinds of judgements: 1) judgments from *Rachamim*, called *Malchut* in *Bina*, and one from *Malchut* in *Malchut* called "judgements that come from *Malchut*." He explains there that each minister consists of both discernments.

...He explains there that the minister of Menashe consists of *Rachamim* [mercy], and judgement in mercy, and the minister of *Ephraim* consists of mercy, and judgement in judgement, called *Malchut*.

It follows that Jacob blessed them, meaning that the judgement would be mitigated, and by that would be the redemption. And since the order of the work is in mercy and then judgement, for it is known that there are four discernments: 1) receiving in order to receive; 2) bestowing in order to receive; 3) bestowing in order to bestow; 4) receiving in order to bestow.

The first two discernments are not really according to the way of Torah, but according to the Torah *Lishma* [for Her sake], beginning with bestowing in order to bestow, and this is called the "quality of mercy." The second discernment of Torah *Lishma* is called "receiving in order to bestow," and this is called the "quality of judgement.?

This is why Joseph wanted to bless them on the order of the work, where first comes the quality of mercy, called Menashe, and then the quality of Ephraim, called judgement, but Jacob blessed according to the order of importance, meaning that the complete correction is the quality of judgement to be corrected, which is called "the darkness shines as light." Jacob's view was that although we begin to work with the quality of mercy, the goal should be revealed before him—that the purpose is to achieve the end of correction, and afterwards begin to work according to the order, meaning with the quality of mercy.

2) Angel: The *Shechina* [divinity] is called an angel, as it is written, "Behold! I send an angel before you." It is called an angel because the *Shechina* works through Matat. This is so during the exile, but

at the time of redemption he is in *Dvekut* [adhesion] with the king called ZA (*Vayechi* p 18, items 53, 23).

3) See in the portion, *Vayetze* (p 36, item 71 in the *Sulam*), where he explains what is written in the corrections [*Tikkunim*] (*Tikkun* no. 70, p 119) about the verse, "and the animals ran to and fro." "To" is Nuriel, and "fro" is Matat. He interprets there in the *Sulam* that "to" means *Hochma* and "fro" means *Hassadim*. Since he already has *Hochma*, he is going to receive *Hassadim*. It turns out that he already has the complete *Hochma* and *Hassadim* together. This is why Matat is called the "minister of the world," since there is wholeness in him for the lower ones in the three worlds BYA where the NRN de Tzadikim are found, who are called there the "internality of BYA."

This is the meaning of "the elder of his home rules all that he has," meaning that he has *Hochma* and *Hassadim*. In ruling the world, he is with the name *Shadai*, which is the first discernment of "and fro," meaning from the *Sefira Hochma*, which is left, and this is the meaning of the name *Shadai*. Afterwards he goes up, which is the second discernment of "and fro." This means that he returns to the name *HaVaYaH* which is *Hassadim*, and he called by the name of his master *HaVaYaH*.

Letter No. 18

May 11, 1956, Manchester

To the friends, may they live long:

I have received the letters of... and the rest of the friends are idle in their writing, since they think that there can't be any profits from correspondence, because they doubt that there can be any profits from correspondence. This brings up the question, "What can bring profits?" Some think that they already have answers to all their questions. In that case, what need is there for questions, because the answers are already placed in a box for them, and all they need is to do what they already know.

Or one who implies that he still needs to correct his bad qualities, so what does he mean by that? Does he think to notify me that he regrets this day and night, meaning that for him it is as in, "And my sin is ever before me," meaning that he is always worried and concerned about this, and other concerns do not occupy him? If this was his intention, I would enjoy it very much.

Still, it is written, "A concern in one's heart let him speak of it with others." And since the festival of Shavuot is approaching, and we need much preparation to be rewarded with the giving of the Torah, I will bring here some words in the name of my father.

Letter No. 18

This matter is brought in the article, "The *Arvut*" ["Mutual Guarantee"], and these are its words, "Now if you obey My voice indeed and you will be My virtue from among all the nations, for all the earth is Mine and you will be a kingdom of priests and a holy nation." I will not elaborate on the questions, but the main thing that is explained there is that through the people of Israel, who are more capable than all the nations to approach the Creator, He will then bestow the abundance upon the rest of the nations.

Therefore, know my friends that since we were together with Baal HaSulam we are more capable of approaching the Creator, but we need to listen to his voice and to keep his covenant, for the voice of the living ARI [Baal HaSulam] will certainly not stop from us. As we were near him, he is certainly speaking on our behalf, and his voice is heard when he comes into the holy place. When a person approaches *Kedusha* [holiness], his voice is heard and we are certain to succeed.

This is the meaning of "For the sake of my brothers and friends I will say, 'let peace be in you.'" This means that precisely because of the brotherhood and friendship "I will speak peace." Otherwise they would be speaking in disputes and quarrels.

The interpreters interpreted that "I will say, let peace be in you'" refers to Jerusalem. We should understand according to our way. Jerusalem is called the "heart of the world," and in the soul, Jerusalem is called the "heart of man," meaning man's desire is called Jerusalem, and there is a dispute there, meaning the desires of the nations of the world, from which man is made, and there are desires of Israel there and each wants to rule over the other.

It turns out that within the heart, called Jerusalem, desires quarrel and collide with one another and at that time no one rules. Naturally no one can acquire his wholeness. This is the meaning of what Rabba said, "I beg of you, do not inherit the gate of Hell." That is, there is sufferings from both the corporeal desires and from the spiritual desires.

This is applied to students who begin to enter the work of the Creator. Since none can show his full force, they are as broken vessels, meaning desires that come from the shattering, in which sparks of holiness were mingled called sparks of bestowal within the *Klipot* [shells] which are called "sparks of reception."

But, "For the sake of my brothers and friends," meaning because the purpose of creation was to do good to His creations, and in a place of hatred it is inappropriate for the light of the Creator, called "light of love," to appear. "I will say, 'let peace be in you,'" where "in you" means that inside the heart there will be peace. It is as in, "The Creator desires to dwell in the lower ones," meaning to be with the lower ones in love, brotherhood, and friendship, for the lower ones to attain the light of the Creator, as it is written "I will listen to what God will speak, for He will speak peace onto His people and onto His pious ones and let them not turn back to folly."

Meaning when we hear the voice of the Creator speaking to the heart, as in "He who comes to purify is aided," and it was interpreted in the holy *Zohar* that he is aided by a holy soul, meaning that the heart hears the voice of the Creator and then specifically the voice of holiness receives the governance over all the desires, meaning the desire to bestow. And naturally, they will not turn back to folly, meaning he will not sin again because all the desires of reception have surrendered under the desire to bestow.

At that time all the good pleasantness appears on the heart, for then there is room in the heart for the instilling of the *Shechina* [Divinity], and the gentleness and pleasantness, and flavor and friendship spread, and fill up all of man's organs.

This applies specifically when hearing the voice of the Creator. At that time the whole body surrenders and enslaves itself to holiness. At that time the body becomes a slave serving the holiness. But when not rewarded with hearing the voice of the Creator, we see otherwise, as the verse says, "You give us as flock for food" (Psalms 44), meaning all the desires of holiness are as food swallowed by the will to receive.

"His enemies take their spoil for themselves," meaning that the will to receive takes all the energy that was intended for holiness; it takes it for itself, meaning if sometimes one can engage in Torah and work, it takes from that all the energy and we work without any rhyme or reason. "And you scattered us among the nations," meaning that all the forces of bestowal were scattered under the governance of reception, which are called "nations."

"You sell your people cheaply," meaning that even though there is no pleasure in the work of reception, still. If we have to perform an act of bestowal, there is no energy because they are the rulers. "And have not profited by their sale" means that we need not enjoy while doing corporeal things, but even when there is a glimpse of hope that there might be some benefit for the receiver then there is already energy to work. And it is likewise to the contrary: If there is any shadow of hope that some *Mitzva* [good deed] will come out of it, then the receiver is in control.

The concealment is so great that anything that is Lo *Lishma* [not for Her sake] can be done, and something that is *Lishma* [for Her sake] is so loathsome and base and despicable that he rejects that thought outward with all his might because man's nature cannot tolerate something lowly.

This is the meaning of, "You make us a reproach to our neighbors, a scoffing and derision to those around us." That is, the will to receive called the "nations that live near us," meaning in the heart, these nations mock and deride the work of *Lishma* with all kinds of mockery until we are powerless against them.

It follows that all of one's efforts are to be favored by the Creator and to try to hear the voice of the Creator who said, "For the sake of my brothers and friends I will say, 'let peace be in you.'" The voice of the Creator that we were rewarded with hearing while being together with the voice of the living ARI, he is certainly exerting on our behalf.

All we need is to be standing guard so we will know our approaching bad situation, so we do not ask the Creator for luxuries, but simply a life of holiness and "he who comes to purify is aided."

By that we will understand the words, "A cane and a loaf tied to each other were given from heaven." We should ask, "Do they not contradict one another?"

The thing is that a "cane" means suffering. A cane is only to tyrannize, which is suffering, and a "loaf" is pleasure. This means that a person is rewarded with two things together, meaning feeling the taste of suffering while working Lo *Lishma*, meaning for purpose of receiving, and tastes pleasure when engaging for the purpose of bestowal, and then the words "Let them not turn back to folly," will come true.

Signing with a blessing and may we be rewarded with the reception of the Torah.

Baruch Shalom HaLevi Ashlag
Son of Baal HaSulam

Letter No. 19

May 15, 1956, Manchester

To my friend,

I received your letter and enjoyed what you wrote regarding what is explained in the introduction to the *Sulam* [Ladder commentary], and I will only fill in after you. I will present the above matter as a question: It is written in the writings of the ARI that there is a reality of worlds, and that *Zivugim de Hakaa* [pl. of *Zivug de Hakaa*] occur there, as well as *Masachim* [screens], *Hitpashtut* [expansion] and *Histalkut* [departure], *Ohr Pnimi*, and *Ohr Makif*. Does this relate to themselves, meaning that this *Sefira* wants this and another wants that? That is, do they have choice and feeling as do people in this world, or are they still, emotionless, like the world that we are in?

For example, the earth yields fruits and receives energy from the rain, the wind, and the sun. If it lacks some of the energy it must receive, it does not yield and does not impart or produce any products. Then people cannot enjoy it, and could even starve to death if the earth does not yield its produce.

But by man's plowing, sowing, and harvesting and gathering, it behaves toward people in the same manner—if man serves the earth, the earth serves man.

At the same time, we know, and this is the accepted view, that the earth does not feel or has free choice. Rather, it simply follows the conditions it was given by nature, which the Creator has sealed and imprinted in it, and this is how it works best.

But we call this "still," meaning that it does not move of its own accord because it has no desire. Likewise, the sun and all the hosts of heaven, all follow nature's directives and have no choice of their own that you can say that they are expecting reward or punishment. Rather, all their actions result from nation, where however the Creator desires them to work, so they work.

This is also what we should understand concerning the upper worlds. Everything was created only to serve man, where by the help that he receives from our world, where we exist, he also receives help from the upper world in order to achieve the goal for which he was created, namely to be rewarded with *Dvekut* [adhesion] with the Creator and receive the tower filled with good things that the Creator has contemplated in his favor.

And when one is rewarded with that, it is considered that he has achieved the completeness of the thought of creation, as in, "The Creator desired to dwell in the lower ones," and "*Shechina* [Divinity] in the lower ones—a high need," since this is His will, and man in this world should strive only to do His will—to receive all the delight and pleasure because so is His will.

According to the famous rule, that there is no thought or perception in His essence at all, it follows that everything that appears to the souls on the degrees from world to world is only in the expanding light, meaning to the extent that the Creator wishes to be known—by revealing to them a measure of light from the upper world. This is considered that the upper light spreads to the lower ones, meaning that the lower ones attain Him to the extent that He wanted them to attain His greatness.

The measures of attainment change from time to time because it depends on the ability of the lower ones. Whether great or small—to that extent the light appears. Also, every measure of attainment has its own name because the *Sefirot* are called "covers." The cover comes off and the *Sefira* [sin. for *Sefirot*] begins to illuminate according to man's work.

Before the world was created there was no *Tzimtzum* [restriction]. But for the lower ones to be able to receive, there had to be this concealment, and with every measure of work *Lishma* [for Her sake], the concealment comes off and the light shines accordingly. As the earth yields fruits in this world only after work, there is no disclosure of light without qualification on the part of the lower one.

And if you wish to say, "What are the *Sefirot* and degrees themselves?" We say that this is unattainable because our attainment is only with respect to His desire to do good to His creations. Therefore, one should attain only that which is related to man's attainment, meaning a person's impression from the upper light that appears through the *Sefira* to the creatures, but not the *Sefira* itself.

The multiplication of *Sefirot* is only according to the attainment of the lower ones, depending on their attainment, and each one has a special skill according to one's labor. Besides that, everything is equal because there are no changes in spirituality. This is why we say about the *Sefirot* themselves that they are regarded as "there is no thought or perception in Him at all."

They ascribed a name for each *Sefira* because all those who attained the light of the Creator through their work wanted all those who follow them to benefit from their discoveries, too. Therefore, they named each and every attainment, so they might understand the intentions and attainments they had attained. This would create a common language between them.

As we learned in the revealed, every innovation that one makes in the Torah, he can pass on to posterity. It is likewise in the upper world—we should accept the innovations that the previous ones had discovered, so they will be able to walk on the path of success and not be stopped midway because he thinks that the state he is in is already perfection. For this reason, we have no attainment in all those names and *Partzufim* in and of themselves, for it is all spirituality and

Godliness, and it is written, "I the Lord did not change." Instead, everything is with respect to the attaining individual.

This is similar to ten people standing and looking at an airplane flying from afar. To the onlookers, the plane seems like a tiny dot. But some of the people have binoculars that magnify the plane several times in size. However, each of them has a different set of binoculars—one has binoculars that magnify significantly, and for another, it magnifies less. It follows that one sees the plane as four meters long, another says it is three, and yet another says it is only two meters long. They are all reporting what they are actually seeing, but still there are differences between them. Yet, the differences make no change in the plane itself, for all the changes are only in the eyes of the perceivers.

It is likewise in spirituality. All the changes are only according to the measure of qualification of the lower ones. And by that we can understand what is written, that the soul is part of God above. It means that what the soul attains is Godliness, but it can only attain a part. Therefore, although it attains Godliness, because it depends on the qualification of the lower ones, it can only attain a part. However, the part that it attains causes no changes in Godliness, just as with the above-mentioned plane.

This is why we say that the lower ones can attain only the expanding light, which is the part that the Creator wanted them to attain. For this reason, there is no difference between the expanding light and His essence, except in that one attains only the part that the Creator wanted him to attain, as with the example of the plane.

This will clarify the questions you have asked.

Your friend

Letter No. 20

June 15, 1956, Manchester

To the students, may they live long,

I recently received letters from... and I will reply to all the letters in a general and abstract manner. This means that even the elder in the group will be able to receive satisfactory answers, even to those questions he did not put in writing. I still remember how Baal HaSulam taught him how to write, and I am certain he remembers it.

Baal HaSulam explained writing in regard to what we say, "Remember us to life, O King who desires life, and write us in the book of the living." Writing is always with black ink over white paper. "White" is the time of Torah and work, and "black" time is the evil and lowliness that a person feels about himself. This blackness should be surrounded by white around each and every letter. In other words, it is impossible to see the situation as it truly is, except by the hours that one gives for Torah and work, for the light in it reforms him.

Therefore, specifically by the multiplication, meaning the right, one comes to a state of left, called "blackness." At that time it is considered that the writing is as it should be. But mere blackness, when a person does not exert extensively in Torah and *Mitzvot* [commandments] and says about himself that he is bad, that bad extends from the place of the *Klipot* [shells], and there is no room for this in the single authority.

We should always be careful not to invert the order of times of right and left. It is as our sages said about the verse, "The eyes of the Lord your God are always upon her from the beginning of the year to the end of the year, etc., at times favorably, and at times unfavorably." "At times favorably," how so? When Israel were complete wicked in the beginning of the year, and were sentenced few rains, but in the end they repented. It is impossible to add, since the sentence has already been given, but the Creator brings them down on time on the soil that needs them. Everything is according to the soil. "At times unfavorably," how so? Israel were complete righteous in the beginning of the year and were sentenced many rains, but in the end they went astray. It is impossible to lessen, since the sentence has already been given, but the Creator brings them done not in their time on a soil that does not need them (*Rosh Hashanah*, 17b).

I interpret this in two ways: 1) An answer to the friends who say that when they were born they were given little strength from above, meaning a limited mind that is neither keen nor understanding or with good memory or energy and a strong and encompassing view. Rather, they speak badly about their mental capacities and tell themselves that this is probably due to a sin in the previous incarnation, and the Creator has sentenced them to come down with little corporeal powers, since in the beginning of the year, meaning when they were created, they were sentenced to this.

However, they have to know that if they repent, those few rains, meaning the few mental capacities, come down to the earth. That is, they use all the energy they have positively, and this is enough for the measure that the earth, meaning the heart, to yield its crop—multiplication in Torah and *Mitzvot*.

If they are not rewarded, even if they were sentenced to many rains but then went astray, all the corporeal capacities, called "many rains," are brought down not in the time when the earth needs them. That is, they use all their energy and wit not for the land of holiness, but for a desert, where there are bad animals. But for the earth that will yield crops there are no rains at all. There they can see about those great ones that in regard to pure and clean work they have no wit, and no energy or power.

Also, one should put one's mind and heart only for the rains to go where they are needed. This is a sufficient measure so it can yield its crop, and this is called "at times favorably."

This explains what our sages depicted, "at times favorably," precisely when they were complete wicked in the beginning of the year. Why did they not say that they were righteous and remained righteous? Rather, whatever powers one's mind is given, he can always say that they are small. They explained about this that even with complete wicked in the beginning of their creation, meaning in the beginning of the year, who are sentenced to few rains, it is still enough for the earth, meaning his desires, to yield fruits of *Kedusha* [holiness].

I elaborated on this to rebuff the excuses that some of the smarty friends use to explain their actions.

Another meaning is that if a person is not rewarded with correcting his works so they are pure, even though he is given some vitality of holiness—which he can use to feel a bit of wholeness in himself, so he can praise and thank the Creator for bringing him a little closer to His work—this force must illuminate for him during the keeping of Torah and *Mitzvot*, since one must not enter the king's home wearing rags.

If he is not rewarded, he feels wholeness when engaging in idle things such as eating and drinking and other such things. But when he approaches the keeping of Torah and *Mitzvot*, he feels his lowliness. It follows that specifically at the king's gate he wears the sack of lowliness, and therefore cannot yield blessed fruits because the cursed does not cling to the blessed.

Rather, it should be to the contrary—precisely when he performs the *Mitzvot*, he should feel whole. By that he qualifies himself for the Creator to instill His *Shechina* on him, and is rewarded with the delightfulness and sweetness of the upper pleasantness. Finally, he is pitied from above and he attaches himself to His eternity.

But the main thing is to strengthen ourselves in the matters of faith precisely where the "who" and "what" questions arise.

By this we will understand what RASHI says about the verse, "This is the statute of the law." These are his words: "Since Satan and the nations of the world count Israel, saying, 'What is this commandment, and what is the point about it?' He wrote a statute about it: 'It is a decree before Me and you have no permission to doubt it.'" This means that this is why its reasoning is not written.

But it would seem logical that it should be the opposite, meaning that when there is no one to ask, there is no need for a reason. But when someone asks, there should be a reasoning there. However, the meaning of the statute of the law refers to faith, and this is precisely where there are questions, there the answer should be above reason.

With this you will also understand what they said, "Let the mother come and wipe her son clean." What is the connection between the red cow and the calf? Is it because of the word-play, where he it says "cow" and here it says "calf," that this is the only connection? But as mentioned above, the sin with the calf is as it is written in the "Introduction of the Book of Zohar," *MI-ELEH* [who are these], as it is said, "These are your gods, O Israel," meaning knowing and not *MI*, called *Hassadim* [mercies], which is faith. This is the reason for the story about the cow, which is faith above reason, and by that you will atone for the sin of the calf.

Your friend Baruch Shalom
Son of Baal HaSulam

Letter No. 21

July 7, 1956, Manchester

To the students, may the live long,

I am surprised that I am not receiving mails from you each week; I thought you would replace the legwork that was in you while I was in Israel, when you walked to study Torah, with handwork, meaning that you would write letters, but you have still not come to this. The only one among you who excels is... for he does not wait for my written reply but does what he must. I suppose he has the full understanding of how he should behave.

And Rabbi... sometimes thinks that his questions should be presented in writing, and sometimes thinks that it is enough to present them in thought. However, he should know that it is actions that we need, for there is "thought, speech, and action" (and the action should be placed inside the thought), and the thought should be placed inside the act. "Speech" comes from the words, "One speaker per generation," meaning a leader, for we need the thought to become an action, for everything has its own correction.

Rabbi... began to write but stopped, and from Rabbi... I have not had the privilege of receiving even the silhouette of a letter. As for Rabbi... when I was in Israel I received from him a letter once every two weeks or so. I am sure he has good memory because last year he sent a letter to London and the address was unclear so the letter returned to him. Perhaps he fears that by the time he troubles himself with writing and sending, it will return to him. It turns out that according to his view, his effort will have been in vain, and this might be a good enough reason for him.

But the truth is not so, as people say, "No pain, no gain." It is also possible that he trusts his loyal friend since he excuses him by his friend making the *Kiddush* [blessing at the beginning of a festive meal] and he replies [Amen] to his blessing. And Rabbi... must be taking the path of concealment, and I need say no more. And to... who has still to come up with excuses, but knows himself and trusts that when he begins to think of excuses he will certainly find some. And as for the elder in the group, our Teacher, Rabbi... he needs love of friends, meaning for someone to write for him.

And yet, we must exert, move forward, and with the Creator's help reach the desired goal. And the most important thing required of us is the prayer. We need to understand why the prayer was given to us. Could the Creator not give us abundance without prayer? However, Baal HaSulam said that everything is tasteless unless there is a desire and an appetite for it, called "craving."

When a person begins to walk on the path of work, and prepares his *Kelim* [vessels] to receive the gift from the Creator, the Creator gives him room to increase his desire. This is done specifically through prayer. The rejections and concealment one receives from Him, and the efforts that one makes to move forward each time—while seeing that he is going backwards—intensify the need for the Creator's salvation.

So is the nature—he craves and each time imagines that he is already marching on the highway. And suddenly, he looks back to the place from which he came, and then leaves the highway and reconnects with the uneducated people and follows them. When he sees that he is among the uneducated, meaning in heresy, he begins to crave faith once more. And then through prayer the craving grows and expands until it reaches a level when the Creator says that his

Kelim are now ready to receive the salvation. Then one is rewarded with the Creator hearing the prayer.

But in truth, each prayer that a person prays is on the path of correction, since each prayer adds its share, meaning expands the vessels of reception. This is the meaning of "the Creator yearns for the prayer of the righteous," meaning that through prayer, man's desires expand, and each prayer that he prays and sees that he has still not been answered makes him need the Creator, for he feels in his organs that only the Creator Himself can help.

It follows from all the above that even on the lowest states there is room for prayer that the Creator will deliver him from his lowliness. But when a person feels his lowliness and escapes the campaign, it means that for all the rejections he had received in order to grow closer to Him, he has grown farther. Therefore, this requires a special heart to overcome in prayer.

But the main thing we need to know is that each person has a point in the heart that gives the strength to work. But when we take that strength and use it to work in the ordinary way, meaning "automatically," then he has no more energy to work for the main purpose, for the body knows that it has already worked in Torah and *Mitzvot* and has no more energy to do more things.

We must know that we must not add in actions, whether in *Mitzvot* that are done out of habit, or *Mitzvot* that are done out of faith. This is so because one who is truly righteous will not make more than four *Tzitziot* [fringes] to his garment, and will not wear the *Tefillin* or put up two *Mezuzot* [pl. of *Mezuzah*] on the doorpost and so forth.

Only in the intention is there a difference in *who* is the obligator—the environment or the faith, meaning the habits he has absorbed from the environment or because of the commandment of the Creator. This is the meaning of "A prayer for the poor when he is wrapped and pours out his words before the Lord."

It is known from the holy books that the prayer of the poor is accepted above. We need to know what is a prayer of the poor.

This is explained in the verse, "A prayer for the poor when he is wrapped." What does he want? To pour out his words before the Creator, for all the words to be only before the Creator and not before the environment.

There is a rule that a person always works only for the cause, or that the environment is his cause to work. It follows that he is working before the environment and not before the Creator. One should resent this. Why should it not be before the Creator? He should ask the Creator to have mercy on him.

This is the meaning of what is written in *The Zohar*: "A prayer for the poor." *The Zohar* interprets, "As I am resentful, so man should resent his receiving all his vitality from the environment. But when he begins to work in faith, he has no vitality at all and the work becomes as loathsome to him as a carcass.

Baal HaSulam said about this what the dove said to Noah: "I would rather have my food as bitter as olives then let them be from the hand of man." It is so because the primary goal is only to draw closer to Him, and the truth will show its way, meaning if his faith as appropriate.

Therefore, when one wishes to achieve Torah and *Mitzvot Lishma* [for Her sake] but has no vitality in it, it is a sign that he has no faith in the Creator, and how can he work when he does not believe in Him? Therefore, this is the only point on which we must make every effort that one has acquired from the point in the heart, since each point in the heart gives strength to work, but if this force is used to serve the environment...

By that you will understand the words of our sages, "Any wise disciple without knowledge, a carcass is better than him." We should understand this: If he has no knowledge, why is he called "a wise disciple"? He is a wise disciple in that he learned from the environment, but he does not have the "knowledge" that is called *Dvekut* [adhesion] with the Creator. He sees that if he does not take strength for work from the environment but from the intention to bestow, then his work becomes as loathsome as a carcass in his eyes, since "such is the way of Torah—lead a life of sorrow." It means that he feels sorrow in his work and not contentment, as was said about the dove, who said, "'I would rather have my food as bitter as olives," etc.

Indeed, why are they bitter? It is because the work *Lishma* is against nature, which is reception in both mind and heart. Before a person reveals his prayer, the Creator cannot save him, as it is said, "It is a time of trouble for Jacob, and he will be saved from it," for only then does he receive the craving for the Creator. This is regarded as "If the Creator does not help him, he cannot overcome it," as it is against nature.

But when the environment gives him the food, meaning he feels reception in Torah and work, he naturally has vitality. At that time he does not need the Creator and has no demand to receive knowledge, which is "and know this day and respond to your heart." These are the answers to the heart when a person is rewarded with *Dvekut* with the Creator.

This is the meaning of "a student in whom there is no knowledge, a carcass is better than him." That is, it is better for him to take upon himself the work that is as loathsome to him as a lifeless carcass. This is also the meaning of "Skin a carcass on the street but do not need people," meaning that if you are on the street, namely in the environment, take for yourself a simple work and do not rely on people, meaning to receive the nourishment and sustenance from the environment, called "people."

This is also the meaning of "Make your Sabbath a weekday but do not need people." That is, the settling of the heart will be as a weekday. Even though you feel no sanctity, meaning a settling on the heart when you have no vitality, but do not rely on people to give you nourishments. Rather, every time there is no vitality, turn to the Creator to have mercy on us and deliver us from darkness to light, from enslavement in the body to redemption.

A person should insist on going in the way of the Creator as much as he can, and not follow the ways of the environment. This is the meaning of what our sages said, "Every wise disciple who is not as hard as steel is not a wise disciple." We should examine this: If he is a wise disciple, meaning even if he is proficient in the Mishnah and Gemarah and observes *Mitzvot*, why is he not regarded as a wise disciple if he is not as hard as steel? However, as mentioned above, he should be standing as steel and not take strength from the environment, and then one comes to a state of "And children of Israel sighed from the work."

The main advice for this is prayer. Each one of you should dedicate time for prayer, especially those who served the Great Tree [Baal HaSulam], and may his merit help us follow his path of work, which he had established for us.

"Righteous are greater in their death than in their life." This means that the righteous are great in their death, meaning when a person feels the righteous when he is alive, meaning sees the righteous' greatness. This is so because when he sees smallness in the righteous, it is in one's favor, for sometimes a person must disclose his own prayer seeing that he has remained alone in the world, as it is written, "And no man shall climb with you on the mountain." That is, when a person must climb to the mountain of the Lord, he does not see anyone from whom he can receive support. ... heard this matter Baal HaSulam.

On another way, meaning outside the path of faith, it is called "holy still." As Baal HaSulam said, "still" means general movement. That is, the earth as a whole moves, but to the individual still item there is no movement and no sensation of the truth. Individual movement is called "vegetative." This is awarded specifically to those who follow the path of truth, as it is written, "There is none who reads justly and there is no faithful sentence. Chaos is certain and a vain word yields labor (and yields falsehood)."

The explanation of the above words, with the above words we can somewhat understand what is explained in *TES* [*Talmud Eser Sefirot* [*The Study of the Ten Sefirot*]], that there are three states, called *Holam, Shuruk, Hirik. Holam* is called "bottom *Hey* in the *Eynaim*

[eyes]," and the *Kelim* of the upper one being in the lower one. This means that when the lower one sees that the holy *Shechina* is in the dust, meaning that there is a blocking on the *Eynaim*, which are open Providence (and not faith).

That is, the upper one has restricted Himself and shows His *Katnut* [infancy/smallness] so that the lower one may take upon itself the choice. This is so because specifically during concealment there is room for choice. But with revealed Providence, when one sees the greatness of the upper one, it is called "knowing" and not "faith," and then there is no work. It follows from this that the upper one degraded Himself and lowered Himself for the sake of the lower one. And then there is choice in the lower one, for then there can be slander.

And when the lower one takes this work upon himself, through prayer, labor, and faith, all three go together, and in general only in the form of faith. Then he is rewarded with seeing the *Gadlut* [adulthood/greatness] of the upper one, and this is called "the upper one raising his *AHP* from the lower one," meaning that he was with the lower one and appeared in the form of the lower one (as in, "A student who is exiled, his teacher is exiled with him." Baal HaSulam interpreted that if a person is in *Katnut*, then wherever he looks, whether at the Creator or at friends, everything has the form of a lower one in his eyes).

And when the Creator hears the prayer of the lower one, the upper one raises his *AHP* by lowering the bottom *Hey* from the *Eynaim*, which is open Providence, and then he sees that the upper one is in *Gadlut*. It follows that the lower one ascends through the upper one—if he sees that the upper one is great then he becomes great. This is specifically by the *AHP* being with the lower one, meaning that the lower one regretted the upper one being in *Katnut*. This is called "*Shechina* [Divinity] in the dust," and it is called *Shuruk*.

However, this causes the loss of the lower one's place for work, and then the lower one does not want to receive all of his *Gadlut*, regarded as *GAR de Hochma*. At that time the upper one diminishes himself because of the lower one, which is considered that the upper one is mingled with the lower one, the *GE* of the lower one. At that time the lower one causes the upper one to diminish himself into *Hirik* once more. This is regarded as the cause being the lower one, that the lower one can receive this knowledge only as *ZAT*, which is regarded as being in a clothing of *Hassadim*. In other words, to the extent that he can walk on the path of faith he receives knowledge, and not more. Otherwise he would have no room for choice.

I do not intend to interpret any further unless someone writes for more interpretation. Then he should write me the questions, and if I am rewarded, I will be able to answer him.

From your friend who awaits redemption

Baruch Shalom HaLevi
Son of Baal HaSulam

Letter No. 22

July 7, 1956, Manchester

To my friend,

I read your letter where you announce that you have dark times and bright times. Know, my friend, that such is the way of Torah, as it was said, "You will lead a life of sorrow."

There are three kinds of life: 1) The life of the wicked is called "death." 2) The life of those who follow the ways of the Creator is called "a life of sorrow." 3) The life of the righteous, meaning those who have already been rewarded with Torah, who taste real life, as our sages said, "For one who learns Torah *Lishma* [for Her sake], the whole world is worthwhile."

Therefore, if you are writing that you have a life of sorrow, it is a sign you are walking on the path of Torah. That is, you have darkness and brightness because such is the way of writing Torah—black on white. However, you need to strive to have black fire over white fire, meaning that everything you feel will be a burning flame.

As for asking that I will write you the order of the work, know that as soon as you begin to work you will remember everything that you have heard from me and from Baal HaSulam. The fact that you are forgetting is for your own good, and only during the work, the

Torah that you need appears before you. Nevertheless, I will write a few things for you.

As soon as a person opens his eyes he is already used to take a book or say the blessings or say, "I am thankful..." Everything requires prior preparation, meaning not to go by rote. Rather, when beginning to say, "I thank," we should know who obligates me to say this—is it habit or is there a reason why I should say, "I thank." Thanking should be said where there is a dispute, as our sages said, "Rabbi Yehoshua Letan thanks" (*Ketubot* 16). Specifically when there is black can you speak of white. At that time you must see the real reason, who is the obligator.

It is better for you to know for certain that your obligator, meaning the reason for working wholeheartedly, is that you heard from Baal HaSulam that one must walk in the path of faith and believe that the Creator hears the prayer, and that the Creator longs for the prayer of the righteous, meaning those who want to be righteous but cannot, due to the evil within them, and ask of the Creator to send them help from above.

Our sages said, "If the Creator does not help him, he will not defeat it," and "He who comes to purify is aided," and as it is written in the holy *Zohar*, "With what? With a holy soul."

The Creator wishes for us to receive the Torah. Therefore, we must feel a lack for the Torah, for luxuries are not given from above, only necessities, for one feels the need only for what is really necessary (because there is no [light] without a *Kli* [vessel], meaning desire). But with luxuries, a person does not feel a lack—that he needs the Creator.

The main benefit is for a person to need the Creator, meaning the giver of the Torah. Therefore, when a person feels his lowliness, it is a reason for him to need the Creator. But when he feels that he can help himself—that he does not need the Creator—he is separated.

The main thing to be rewarded is *Dvekut* [adhesion] with the Creator, for this is the essence of the correction on our part, when a person begins to believe in the Creator, for this is the main thing.

This is only indication if a person is walking on the real path. When he sees his true state, then he should say, "I thank," although common sense gives no reason to say "I thank."

And concerning the four hours we spoke of, you must keep them, meaning arrange the work. That is, 1) the exile of the *Shechina* [Divinity]. It means that the *Shechina* is in the dust and everyone seeing that Providence is in concealment, and it is hidden that the Creator is the doer of good. The Creator is the one who makes that concealment, so that Torah and *Mitzvot* [commandments/good deeds/corrections] will taste like dust, to give a person room for choice.

This is so because only where there is choice there is faith. But where there is knowing, meaning open Providence, there is no room for choice, meaning faith. It follows that it is man who has caused all that, since before one is rewarded with faith, complete faith, the holy *Shechina* must seem to him as dust. One should regret this, and this is the meaning of "If he is rewarded, he sentences himself..."

2) If this is true. Man's purpose is only to benefit the Creator, meaning, if not for this goal, he does not want to live in the world and exist only for himself. And to examine the real state, without any compromises, only to see the truth, if he sees that the body has considerations that it is worthwhile to exist for itself, meaning to please itself, then there is room for prayer to the Creator. That is, then he sees his lowliness.

3) Engage in words of Torah. This will be specifically in wholeness, as Baal HaSulam said, "The cursed does not cling to the blessed." Therefore, while engaging in Torah, one should draw light, and then is the time for wholeness.

We must believe what our sages said, "From Mattanah to Nahaliel." The Torah is called *Mattanah* [gift]. That is, the fact that a person is permitted to learn and pray, and observe *Mitzvot* even one minute a day, that, too, is a gift from the Creator, for there are several billions in the world to whom the Creator did not give the chance to be able to think of the Creator for even one minute a year. Therefore, while engaging in the Torah, one must be glad, for only through joy is one rewarded with drawing the light of Torah.

The Torah is divided into two times: 1) Simple learning, as one learns in order to simply understand the matter. 2) Scrutinizing as much as possible, so the Creator will help you understand the internality of things. By scrutinizing the matter in order to understand, you make for yourself *Kelim* [vessels] in which you will be able to receive the internality. This is also how you should divide the prayer.

May the Creator open our eyes and we will be rewarded with the Creator's teaching—how to come out from enslavement to redemption.

Your friend, Baruch Shalom HaLevi
Son of Baal HaSulam

Letter No. 23

August 1956, Manchester

To the friends, may they live forever,

I would like to be closer to the friends with the approaching of the new year. We need to strengthen ourselves with confidence that we will be rewarded with the general redemption, that the name of the glory of His kingdom will be revealed over all the earth, and those who are far will hear and come. That is, those who felt they were far from work in pure holiness will be rewarded with hearing, at which time there is unification of doing and hearing, as it is written, "Raises the poor from the dust, lifts the wretched from the refuse."

It is known that there are two general discernments: 1) mind, 2) heart. When a person tastes the taste of dust in his work, as in, "A snake, all that it eats is dust," meaning that the taste of Torah and *Mitzvot* is only that of dust, the reason is that he is poor, that he lacks faith. Also, he falls into a state of "heart," when the will to receive is for worldly lusts, called "refuse" [garbage], and then he is wretched.

When he regrets it, meaning prays and cries out to the Creator to help him in his plight, what does he yell? "Raise the poor from the dust," since I am poor and taste the taste of dust, and I am wretched and lying in the refuse, and all because of the concealment of the face that is in the world. At that time we ask of the Creator to deliver us from slavery to freedom.

This is the meaning of one who prays, prays next to the pole. In the *Sulam* [Ladder commentary], he interprets that the pole means *AHP* of the upper one that fell into the *GE* of the lower one. When the upper one raises his *AHP*, the *GE* of the lower one rise, as well. It is also written that precisely through the pole the souls rise from world to world, and this is the connection between upper and lower.

We can interpret this according to our way, meaning that through the fall of the *Kelim* [vessels] of the upper one to the place of lower one, meaning that if the lower one feels the *Katnut* [smallness] of the upper one, this is the meaning of "Israel that have exiled, the *Shechina* [Divinity] is with them." That is, the *Shechina* is also in exile with them, and it is called "*Shechina* in the dust," namely that the Torah and work taste like dust.

When a person regrets the exile of the *Shechina*, meaning when the *Shechina* is not in exile, but hides for Israel and agrees that the lower one will speak of the upper one everything he is meant to say, and the lower one speaks this way because he feels this way.

When he regrets it and prays from the bottom of the heart to raise the *Shechina* from the dust, by that the upper one reveals himself to the lower one in his full *Gadlut* [greatness]. At that time the lower one, too, ascends.

It follows that this is the above-mentioned pole, meaning specifically through that pole the prayers rise from world to world, meaning from revealing to more brightness. This is why we need to pray specifically next to this pole.

By that we will understand why *Rosh Hashanah* [beginning of the year] and *Yom Kippur* are regarded as good days [festivals] although they are judgment. Judgment relates primarily to the wholeness that appears on those times. There is fear that the outer ones might come into self-reception in mind and heart. This is why we must increase the awakening for repentance.

Letter No. 23

Repentance means returning the desire to receive into being a desire to bestow. By this we return to adhesion with the upper source and are awarded eternal *Dvekut* [adhesion]. At that time we can receive the wholeness that appears on the terrible days [ten days of repentance between *Rosh Hashanah* and *Yom Kippur*] because the nourishments are allotted on *Rosh Hashanah* [the beginning of the year], meaning that the light of *Hochma* and wholeness and clarity appears.

However, we must prepare *Kelim* [vessels] that will be ready to receive, meaning the light of *Hassadim* that we must draw. This is the repentance and awakening of the Rachamim, as in "As He is merciful, be you merciful," since then we will be able to receive all the wholeness in purity.

This is the reason why it is considered a good day, due to the appearance of the wholeness. This is also the meaning of "Blow the *Shofar* [festive horn] at the new moon, at the full moon, on our festive day." The word *Shofar* comes from the word, *Shapru* [improve] *Maaseichem* [your works], since now there is a cover for the moon, meaning concealment.

I could not elaborate due to the approaching of the festival, and I wish you good writing and signing.

From your friend who sends you regards and all the best,

Baruch Shalom HaLevi Ashlag

Letter No. 24

November 7, 1956, Manchester

Hello and all the best.

To my friend,

In response to your letter from October 27 regarding your first question about having to stand guard and evoke the love in the hearts of the friends, which you find unbecoming, I actually see that as necessary for you. You know what Baal HaSulam said, that from between man and man one learns how to behave between man and the Creator.

This is so because the upper light is in complete rest, and it is necessary to always evoke the love, "Until the love of our wedding pleases." In other words, you are being shown from above that on this way, you must always evoke the love of His name, since everyone awaits your awakening.

That is, as you see that in love of friends you have the rights as you see it, meaning as it is being shown to you from above, you are the evoker (although the truth is not necessarily so; if you ask the friends, I am not so sure they agree with your evidence that it is only you who desires them and not the other way around).

This is the meaning of "A judge has only what his eyes see." That is, as far as judgment goes, you must judge only by your evidence.

This is why it is being shown to you from above that you have to keep awakening the love of the Creator in this way, that you must always stand guard, all day and all night, when you feel a state of day or feel a state of night.

We say to the Creator, "Yours is the day, and Yours is also the night." Thus, the night, too, the darkness of night, comes from the Creator to man's favor, too, as it is written, "Day to day utters speech, and night to night expresses knowledge" ([See the *Sulam* Commentary, Part 1, Item 103).

It follows that you must evoke the heart of the friends until the flame rises by itself, as our sages said about it, "When you light up the candles." By that, you will be rewarded with awakening the love of the Creator upon us.

And regarding your second question about your always having to evoke the heart of the friends, who, after they have already been rewarded with seeing the importance of the study, etc., still do not respect the lessons—that, too, stands to your merit.

In other words, you had to see for yourself that the Creator has given you His proximity several times already. There have already been several times when you felt that you had no other concern in the world but to remain adhered to Him forever, for you are unworthy of serving the King even in the simplest of works because why should you be more privileged than your contemporaries?

And yet, you wait for the Creator to awaken you to work, meaning to have an awakening from above, and then you will begin to study the lessons.

Namely, just as you must awaken the students, you are saying that the Creator should awaken you. That is, if the Creator gives you a reason and good taste in the work, you will agree to work. But before that, you cannot. Then, you are shown from above how low and inferior you consider the students to be.

And regarding the third question, about keeping the party with great exaggeration, it is so because this is how people behave when they are afraid that the baby will leave the house alone at night. They tell him, "There is a bear outside and other wild beasts," since the baby cannot understand any other way. In other words, if he were to know the truth, that there is no lion or bear outside, but it is best for the baby to go to sleep, and most importantly, to remain indoors, the baby wouldn't be able to accept the truth.

Therefore, you should know my brother, that to accept the path of truth and the words of truth of Baal HaSulam, there aren't many people who can hear the words of truth, for you are only seeing many kids. And what can I tell you while you are in kindergarten, and you are impressed by them, writing to me that they are cheerful and gay? Indeed, so is the way of babies—to be cheerful and gay. But it is known that a baby is not taken seriously when crying or when happy because its excitement and feelings are about unimportant matters.

And when you see that the baby is crying during service, you are impressed, and when he is glad and dances, you are impressed, and you write that you envy the children for being cheerful and dancing. And what do you want? To be a baby all over again? You should know, my brother, that your childhood days are over, since before you walked into Baal HaSulam's room, you were dancing, just as they are.

And may the Creator assist us in the corporeal and in the spiritual.

Your friend, Baruch Shalom HaLevi Ashlag
Son of Baal HaSulam

Letter No. 25

November 23, 1956, Manchester

To the friends, may they live long,

I received a few letters from...

I would be very happy if I could be with you, but what can you do that time causes? However, there are *Mitzvot* [commandments] we can keep, which time does not cause, meaning things that transcend time. For himself, man is limited by time and place. But when one strives to adhere to the Creator, he must equalize with Him, meaning be above place and above time.

It is known that a place is called *Kli* [vessel], meaning a certain will to receive. "Above place" means that one does not want one's labor to be only for "one's place," but for "Blessed be the place," who is the place of the world [referring to the Creator], meaning that all the labor should be only to bestow, and above time, for time relates only to reason. A person's reason always makes him understand that now is not the right time to accept His work for His sake. But it is in that regard that we must always go above time. That is, do not say that the early days were better than these, but we always need renewal of powers, meaning the foundations on which to build all the work until we are rewarded with permanent instilling of the *Shechina* [Divinity].

Also, we must always walk on two paths that deny one another, meaning in deficiency and in wholeness, which is prayer and praise and gratitude.

See in *The Zohar* (*Vayeshev*, and p 12 in the *Sulam* commentary): "This is why that body and the purifying soul broke, and this is why the Creator makes that righteous suffer torments and pains in this world, and he will be cleaned from everything and will be rewarded with life in the next world. It is written about that, 'The Lord tests the righteous,' indeed" (the *Sulam* commentary on *The Zohar*, *Vayeshev*, item 36, p 12). In item 38: "And when the moon is blemished," meaning when the soul emerges when the moon is flawed, the soul blemishes the body.

It is written in the *Sulam*: "How can it be said that the soul blemishes the body?" He explains that the blemish of the soul extends from the diminution in *Bina*. *Malchut* takes that diminution, as in "Mother lent her clothes to her daughter," and the bodies become fit to receive the *Gadlut* [adulthood/greatness], too. Thus, the flaw that the souls cause in the bodies is in order to correct the body and qualify it to receive the light of *Gadlut*, thus far his words.

To understand this during the preparation period for entering the king's palace, we can interpret that the body in its own way is whole. That is, it feels no deficiency about itself, as one feels if there is any corporeal lack. Then one does not sit idly in despair, but the sense of lack evokes in a person tricks and tactics, and one never falls into despair. This is precisely to the extent of the sensation of the lack. That is, if he regards the thing he craves as luxury, the sensation of deficiency is not so strong with luxuries and one easily gives up.

However, it is not because it is difficult to obtain that he accepts the situation and gives us, saying, "I did what I could and I have no idea how to get what I want," and for this he turns his mind elsewhere. Rather, it is because what he is asking for is superfluous to him, and with redundancies there is no sensation of lack as there is for necessity. Indeed, when it comes to necessity, a person never accepts the situation and always seeks advice and tactics to obtain the necessity, meaning that man's driving force, which does not let him give up, and each time it is renewed, is only the power of deficiency.

This depends on the measure of the deficiency, which in turn depends on the measure of suffering. A great need means that if he does not obtain what he wants he will feel great suffering, and a small need is if it does not pain him if he does not get what he wants, but if he gets it he will feel more complete.

Concerning necessity and redundancy, each person determines this measure by himself. Our sages said about that, that if one is accustomed to living with a necessity of a servant running before him, he must be provided this, and there is a story about Hillel who was running before him. Thus, each person can determine what is necessary.

This is the meaning of the soul blemishing the body. It means that when a person does not have a soul, he has a complete body. That is, he does not feel it necessary to work in purity. But by engaging in Torah and *Mitzvot*, the light in it reforms him. That is, the light in it, meaning the soul that one attains, breaks the body, meaning that the body breaks when it sees that it is incomplete.

This means that previously he knew that he had to engage in purity in order to attain wholeness, which is regarded as luxury, and one can give up luxuries. But when the body breaks, meaning that he sees that he is deficient—meaning sees the lack that there is in the upper *Behina* [discernment] called *Bina*, referring to Providence—there awakens in him a motivating power that will not rest until he is pitied from above and is awarded the face of the *Shechina* [Divinity].

May the Creator help us assume the burden of the kingdom of heaven above place and above time, to cling to His eternity.

Your friend, Baruch Shalom HaLevi Ashlag
Son of Baal HaSulam

Letter No. 26

December 7, 1956, Manchester

Hello and all the best to my friend, the dearest of men, pursuing righteousness and mercy, and crowned with virtues.

This morning, I received your letter together with twenty gerah, which is a shekel. I will write you something concerning Hanukah according to what I heard from Baal HaSulam, an explanation about what our sages said, "What is Hanukah? *Hanu Ko* [parked thus far (here)]." He said about this that there are two degrees: 1) *Ko*, 2) "This." Our sages said, "All the prophets prophesied in *Ko*, and Moses prophesied in "This." Hanukah is regarded as *Ko*.

The explanation of the words of Baal HaSulam is with an allegory: When soldiers go to war and fight for some time, afterwards they are given a vacation in a retreat with plenty of good food and drink. The commander's intention is to replenish their strength so they will not be tired and will be able to fight once more. But one who is unaware will think that they are given a vacation because the war is over. But the truth is that the war is not over, and this vacation is to give them strength and courage to go to the front once more.

So is the matter with Hanukah. This is the meaning of *Hanu* [parked], where the parking was not because of wholeness, meaning an illuminating mirror. Rather, the parking was *Ko* [here/thus far], meaning incomplete, which is a mirror that does not illuminate. In other words, the war of the inclination is still not over, but we have to come to the real completeness. This is the meaning of *Hanu-Ko*, parking as in *Ko*, meaning receiving the upper bestowal so they would have more strength to go forward in the war of the inclination.

What extends from this is that when one walks on the path of the Creator, he is given many awakenings from above—in the middle of the prayer or while studying Torah, or while performing a *Mitzva* [commandment]. This awakening enters the heart and he begins to feel that flavor and grace of holiness.

However, one should know that he was given this abundance only so as to gain new strength and be able to grow stronger in the work, that he will engage in the battle of the war of the inclination. Then, each time he is given a temporary rest, meaning upper abundance, for when the awakening from above comes to a person, it seems to him that there is no longer any war, for at that time he begins to feel the beauty and glory of holiness, and the lowliness of corporeal matters, until he resolves to work only for the Creator.

But since a person did not really finish his work, the awakening that he was given is taken away from him, and he soon falls into his previous state, where he feels grace and beauty only in corporeal things, and regards matters of sanctity as redundant. At that time he engages in Torah and *Mitzvot* only out of compulsion and coercion, and not because of the desire and joy as when he had the awakening.

That awakening is the Hanukah candle. Therefore, if he is smart, he should always exert until he is helped from above to be rewarded with real wholeness.

Let us hope that the Creator will open our eyes and delight our hearts forever.

From your friend, who wishes you and your family all the best,

Baruch Shalom HaLevi Ashlag

Son of Baal HaSulam

Letter No. 27

December 18, 1956, Manchester

To the friends, may they live forever,

It has been a very long time since I received letters from you, except for... and a short letter from...

We must renew our work each day, meaning forget the past. That is, if we did not succeed before, we must start anew. It is like a merchant: If he had a business that did not succeed, he closes that business and promptly starts a new one, hopeful that although he did not succeed in the previous business, he will certainly succeed in the new one.

So are we. Although in the past we did not succeed, in the future we are certain to succeed. But we will not stay idle because without doing any business it is impossible to succeed. Rather, we must believe that it will certainly be drawn upon us and we will be rewarded with the light of His law, which is the true law, that truth will protect us and we will draw the light of His law, and will be granted with clinging to His name forever.

Our sages said, "Rabbi Yohanan said, 'Jacob our father did not die. He asks, 'Was it in vain that the mummifiers mummified and the undertakers buried?'" Rather, I call the verse, 'Fear not, O Jacob My servant,' declares the Lord, 'And do not dread, O Israel, for

I will save you from afar, and your descendants from the land of their captivity." As his descendants are alive, so he is alive." RASHI interprets that only among the living can you speak of captivity, but with regard to the dead, you cannot speak of captivity (*Taanit* 5b).

The interpreters asked:

1. The question still stands. The Maharsha interprets that the body dies and the soul exists, so why did specifically Jacob not die? He explains that since Abraham and Isaac died in the land of Israel, but Jacob died abroad, and so we need to be told that Jacob, too, did not die.

   I will interpret this according to our way, and this will reconcile the famous question about the verse, "So they sent a message to Joseph, saying, 'Your father charged before he died, saying, 'Thus you shall say to Joseph, 'Please forgive, I beg you, the transgression of your brothers.'"''

This is perplexing:

2. Where do we find that Jacob commanded such a thing before his death? And there is also the question of the Midrash about the verse, "And he called his son, Joseph," and commanded him the burial.

3. Why did he not command Reuben, who was the elder, or Judah, who was a king?

And the interpreters asked:

4. About Jacob telling Joseph—"deal with me with mercy and truth," meaning mercies performed with the dead—no reward and recompense is given for the mercy. But afterwards he says to Joseph, "But I gave you one portion more than to your brothers." RASHI interprets that since you exert and trouble yourself with my burial, it is no longer true mercy.

Another perplexity:

5. Joseph said to him, "I will do as you say." The "I" is redundant [in Hebrew the word "I" is repeated twice in

this verse]. He should have said, "I will do as you say" [with a single "I"].

To understand the above we must understand the quality of truth, which is the quality of Jacob. It is written, "Let truth be given to Jacob." Baal HaSulam interpreted the matter of truth (presented in the *Sulam*, in the "Introduction of the Book of Zohar," item 175), that two factions of angels slandered Creation, and two advocated it.

The angels of truth said that the world is all lies, meaning that the world is called "will to receive," and truth is the desire to bestow contentment upon one's maker, which is *Dvekut* [adhesion]. How can they achieve this? The angels of mercy said, "He does mercy," and through the mercy they will achieve *Dvekut*. See there the whole matter of "And cast the earth to the ground," meaning that from *Lo Lishma* [not for Her sake] we will be rewarded with *Lishma* [for Her sake] and will achieve the quality of truth.

Jacob, who is the quality of truth, commanded before his death, meaning gave a will to Joseph to do true mercy, meaning that by that he will be awarded the quality of truth, meaning that he will be entirely to bestow. This was so to all of his sons, but he commanded specifically Joseph, meaning that after his death Joseph will not get even for the selling of Joseph by his brothers.

And although Joseph sees that his brothers blemished by selling, he must still engage only with the quality of truth, meaning to bestow, and correcting the flaw is for the Creator alone. This matter of correction was later corrected with the ten slain of the kingship (as explained in several places).

Joseph replied, "I will do as you say," meaning that my self will be as you say—that I will walk only in the way of bestowal. This reconciles why he said specifically to Joseph, and why he used specifically the word "I."

This also explains the second question we asked, "Where do we find that Jacob commanded Joseph before his death, meaning that before his death he said specifically to Joseph to follow the path of truth, which is only to bestow, and therefore you must not get even for the sale?"

And also, once Joseph has taken it upon himself and said, "I will do as you say," meaning bestow, by later telling him, "I gave you one portion more than to your brothers," he does not spoil the truth by receiving the gift now, since now he is regarded as receiving in order to bestow, for he has no need for himself, but all his actions are in Torah and *Mitzvot* in order to bestow.

This explains the fourth question: After the acceptance of the truth, he could reward him, but it would still be considered pure bestowal. This is why Rabbi Yohanan said that Jacob did not die. It means that the quality of Jacob did not die because he bequeathed his quality to his sons. This is why Rabbi Yohanan said specifically Jacob, since truth is the most important; if there is truth, one is rewarded with Abraham and Isaac, who are *Hassadim* and *Gevurot*.

It follows from all the above that Jacob did not die, but his law, the law of truth, will shine for us and we will be rewarded with following in his footsteps and with growing stronger with more exertion. We must not heed the view of the landlords, who bring us sparks of despair, but say as our sages say, "The Son of David comes only inadvertently." That is, redemption, called "the Son of David," comes specifically by distracting the mind of landlords.

This is the meaning of RASHI's interpretation that life is only in captivity, meaning that only when one is regarded as "alive" does he feel that he is captive and must break free from the prison. But when a person is dead, he does not feel that he is captive.

Jacob's quality will shine for us out of captivity, as it is written, "And your descendants from the land of their captivity," meaning that all the desires for work are captive. This is also the meaning of "Fear not, my servant Jacob ... for I will save you from afar." Although they were in utter remoteness from the Creator, the

Creator promises us that He will save us, as our sages said, "If the Creator does not help him, he will not prevail over it."

Therefore, we must understand how our helper is mighty, as it is written, "The Lord is a man of war." And as for the salvation of the mighty one, he does not mind whether he should help a lot or little. But rather, "I will save you from afar." Even when we are in utter remoteness, He will save us.

Let us hope that from this day forth, meaning each and every moment, we will be rewarded with eternal wholeness and to cling to the truth.

From your friend, Baruch Shalom HaLevi Ashlag
Son of Baal HaSulam

Letter No. 28

January 2, 1957, Manchester

To my friend,

I read your letter from the month of *Tevet* (December 1956) and I will answer in brief and in general.

I have already written you that there are mitigated judgments. To understand this in the preparation to entering the Creator's palace is that sometimes a person feels that he is in a state of lowliness, meaning that he has neither Torah nor work, and also thoughts of worldly vanities and so forth. At that time one becomes despaired saying, "'And I to serve my master' must have been said about someone else."

Rather, to people of high degrees, who have been born with good and upright qualities and a good mind, and desire and craving to persist with the study of Torah, and their only engagement since their arrival in the world, their minds and hearts are only about Torah and work. But a man of my value, I belong in the cowshed, and the verse, "For it is not a vain thing for you, for it is your life and the length of your days," was not said about me.

Sometimes there is mitigation during the awakening of the lowliness, and a person sees that "I did not know how immersed I was in transient things and my idle matters. I did not pay attention to being as one should be. And the psalm that is said, 'Will be glorified in me for He desires me,' I too should be saying that psalm because all of Israel have a part in the next world, as in 'He stood and concealed it for the righteous in the future.'

"But now that I am far from the whole thing, I must not despair and only trust the Creator, that 'You hear the prayer of every mouth.' 'Every' means that even though my mouth is not as proper as it should be, the thirteen qualities of mercy are bound to awaken on me, as well.

"From this day forth, I hope to be going forward, though I have already said this many times and in the end remained in my lowliness." At that time he replies that there are "world," "year," "soul," and these three must be united in same time, place, and soul together.

For this reason, he says, "It is now certainly the time for me to come out of all these bad states, and 'one who comes to purify is aided,'" and he promptly begins the work with renewed vigor and strength.

Even during the negotiation he does not feel suffering from the lowliness, that he sees he has been in this lowliness all his life. On the contrary, during the negotiation he feels pleasantness and elation because now the greatness he will later be awarded shines for him. This is considered that the surrounding light shines to him from afar.

That is, although he is still far from the king's palace, meaning he has not yet been rewarded with purifying his *Kelim* [vessels] so as to be for the Creator, he nonetheless has illumination from the light that is destined to clothe in him. It follows that the state of lowliness does not pain him, but on the contrary, gives him pleasure.

This is regarded as "mitigation of the judgments," meaning that that situation is not so bad. It is so because he is not looking back to the past, but ahead, to the light he is destined to obtain. It follows that he is attached to the Creator in terms of the surrounding light.

However, the two above states are also difficult—for a person to be able to judge and scrutinize himself regarding which state he should accept and follow. Usually, when a person is still uneducated in the ways of the work, he is like a shadow. Sometimes he is shown from above a state of despair, and sometimes he is shown from above a mitigation of the lowliness.

But anyhow, if one cannot choose for oneself what he must take, he should still believe that the state of despair is the truth. Instead, he should say that he is still not qualified in the work but is still in the catapult, meaning being thrown from above from state to state.

And if the person falls into the first state, called "despair," then he really is dead. And sometimes a person puts himself to death, meaning goes to a place where there is danger. This is called "putting himself in a dangerous place." For the most part, the environment causes such a state called "death." And then, "the dead are free," since a dead person becomes liberated from the *Mitzvot* [commandments]. That is, he says that all the *Mitzvot* he had taken upon himself from his teachers were useless, so he has no reason to pursue them.

The advice for this is only to return to an environment of living people, meaning people who are still pursuing the *Mitzvot* they have assumed from their teachers. And although in that state he cannot believe that there are people in his group who are alive, rather it seems to him that the world has darkened and wherever he looks there are only heaps of bones surrounding him, there is one thing where he can exert and see—if his group is nonetheless pursuing with the commandments of his teacher.

Sometimes one is not even allowed from above to see even this. At that time he sees before him a cunning person, that he cannot deceive himself that he is walking on the straight path, and seeing that his works are undesirable torments him.

This is not so with the group. Either they do not see their real situation or they do not even have the time to see their lowliness, so they lead a tranquil life and are at peace. But (I) lead a life of pain.

At such a time a person sometimes craves to enjoy worldly vanities, but that, too, cannot satisfy him. And although he sees that others do enjoy life, and why was he sentenced to be unable to be satisfied like others? He walks around and sees people running about each to his work, or shop, or seminary, and none of them seem to be in any pain and suffering. Instead, they are all merry and joyful. So why can't I find reason for satisfaction with honor and provision?

In other words, even people who have less than he does are still not tormented by life so much as to say that they are not enjoying life. But as for me, I feel that life is tasteless, meaning that all the corporeal pleasures cannot please me enough to satisfy me.

I am not saying that if corporeal pleasures do not give me as much pleasure as I want I will give them up, for even something that is not worth a dime you do not throw outside. But the concern is that I am not feeling as much pleasure as they do, so I will be as satisfied as others.

In truth, if we were to draw (this) and say that corporeal pleasures contain forty percent pleasure, that could be satisfactory to people who settle for forty percent. But to people who have tasted a spiritual taste, of whom we can say that they had had a sixty percent pleasure, they find it difficult to get used to living on food that contains only forty percent. This is why they are all merry and joyful, and he lives a life of pain, since he needs sixty percent pleasure. However, he does not throw away the pleasure, even if it contains only one percent.

This is why "Anyone who is greedy is angry." That is, even though they receive as much pleasure as others, he is angry. That is, he wants to find the amount of sixty percent pleasure that he was used to in the spiritual flavors. But to begin with, you can only enjoy a tiny light in corporeality, as it is written in the holy *Zohar*, meaning a very limited amount of pleasure. Therefore, even when he dies, meaning when he has lost the taste of spiritual life, when he remembers that he is used to tasting the flavor of a higher percentage than there is in corporeal pleasures, he is afflicted and dissatisfied.

Letter No. 28

This is the meaning of "The maggot is as hard to the dead as the needle to the living flesh." That is, when he is dead, but remembers the taste of pleasure he had had while being spiritually elated, called "maggot," "as a needle to the living flesh," meaning when he was alive and all his pleasures were in Torah and work, and he felt the flavor of the work of devotion in order to bestow contentment upon his maker. And if some sin awakened in him, meaning a craving of the will to receive, it pained him.

This is the meaning of "as a needle to the living flesh," meaning when he was attached to life. But now that he remembers the maggot he is regarded as dead, and is afflicted, too.

However, it is a rule that the dead are forgotten from the heart. That is, he forgets that he was alive once, and that now he is in a state of death. They are washed by the flow of life of the general public and no longer live a life of sorrow. In other words, they come to a state where they forget everything.

At that time he comes to the state of "the dead are free," meaning he is freed from all the commandments he had received from his teacher, and comes to a state of forgetfulness, forgetting even that he once possessed some works. Instead, it seems to him that he has been in this state his whole life, and forgets to make even that calculation, but simply flows on with the currents of the world.

It therefore follows that there are several states before one comes to grip the pipeline of life that sustains all the souls:

1. He forgets to make a scrutiny as to his current state.
2. He scrutinizes and sees that he is dead, and remembers the time of maggot. At that time he feels a life of pain, as it is written, "As a needle to the living flesh." However, he falls into despair.
4. He scrutinizes and sees that he is dead, but the light of confidence shines for him and he grows stronger, deciding that henceforth he will walk in the ways of work as in mitigation.

5. During the work, when he works under the commandment of the mind and heart as much as he can, as in "Whatever you can do with your hand and strength, that do," at that time it feels tasteful to study Kabbalah, although he does not understand the content of the spiritual matter. Still, the study shines for him with the light in it. He also feels the flavor of working above reason, and feels the remoteness that the will to receive causes him, and he craves to engage only in work of bestowal until the Creator pities him and greets him, as it is written, "I will hear what God will say, for He will speak peace to His people and to His followers, and let them not turn back to folly."

Indeed, we should understand a heavy question—that we have been granted with hearing the words of the living God from the mouth of the living ARI, Baal HaSulam, and saw that nothing was hidden from him, and each time we were awarded with surrendering before him with our hearts and souls we felt that we were in spiritual air, above all the vanities of this world, how is it that we have remained in our current state, each according to his degree, where each of us should have been at a higher degree than he is in now?

This matter is revealed in the Torah. I have already explained to you the meaning of Israel's exit from the hands of Pharaoh, and why if the Creator wanted to bring Israel out of Egypt, He had to have Pharaoh's consent, since he is almighty. I explained that Pharaoh is the body, and the body needs to "love the Lord with all your heart," etc., and love cannot be forced.

For this reason, we should ask, "It is known that the work should be above reason, so why did the Creator show Pharaoh the signs?" Another question: "I have hardened his heart that I may place these signs of Mine within him." It makes sense to argue that He has denied him the choice. That is, besides the fact that the inclination in a man's heart is evil from his youth, he continually added him with hardening of the heart, so he had no way to choose the good and reject the bad.

Indeed, we should understand it the way Baal HaSulam had taught us: The foundation of our work should be in order to bestow. However, when there is a sign, it is difficult to work *Lishma* [for her sake], and the main thing is "that I may place these signs of Mine within him." That is, specifically above reason, it is difficult to work *Lishma*.

But the main thing is that where there is a question of "who," there is room for connection with "these," and by the two of them, God appears there, since "These" without "who" cannot be, as explained (in the "Introduction of the Book of Zohar," in the *Sulam* commentary).

And most importantly, we need the letters of Torah to appear, for the "the uneducated are not pious," meaning that it is specifically one who is learned in Torah that we need. Otherwise it is regarded as "one who gives his daughter to an uneducated, it is as though he puts her in the lion's mouth." Put differently, if he is illiterate in Torah, it is certain death. Also, Torah is called the middle line—containing both things together, meaning "who" and "these," which together make up the name *Elokim* [God].

Accordingly, if a person begins to enter the work on the path of truth and begins to taste flavor in the work, then it is possible to fail with the will to receive. That is, he already has a basis for engaging in Torah and work because he feels it as more palatable than all the vanities of this world.

In that state he no longer needs faith above reason because the sensation of pleasure is a clear sign to him that it is worthwhile to be a servant of the Creator. But if he is not given flavor in the work, he will not be able to continue with the work because it is difficult to begin with work that is above reason. Rather one begins in *Lo Lishma* [not for her sake] and then arrives at *Lishma*.

The order is as we teach infants to walk: We hold their hands and lead them (again). When they begin to walk we leave them alone. In the beginning they fall, so we help them again, and they fall again. So is the order until one can walk unassisted. This is regarded as being above to work *Lishma*.

Then, when he is awarded many things, he already knows how to conduct himself so as to be in order to bestow, even though he is receiving many things because he is learned in the Torah, meaning that he constantly engages in the Torah—to make all his intentions for the Creator. This is the beginning of the time when he is shown the secrets of Torah, which is the abundance poured upon the servants of the Creator.

With the above we will understand the matter of the hardening of the heart, which the Creator had promised Moses. That is, after all the miracles and wonders, meaning even if we receive several kinds of *Gadlut* [greatness/adulthood], both in terms of elation and in terms of innovations in the Torah, although in the act it will give us huge inspiration, to the point where we decide that there is none else besides Him and we should dedicate ourselves only to serving the Creator.

Therefore, do not think that this will cancel the room for work with respect to what the person must discover, for the person will promptly be annulled before his teachers and there will be no room for choice, meaning what one should (discover) choose.

In that regard, the Creator promised, "I can do something that you cannot understand that such a thing will be in reality. That is, if I have hardened his heart," since the Creator gives the hardening of the heart because promptly after all the evident signs he forgets everything and has to start his work anew. "And if you ask 'Why I need all those signs if he forgets them?' but the time when he has a clear sign that it is worthwhile to be the Creator's servant is called 'support.'" And it is not attributed to him, but only to the supporter. But alongside this he accustoms himself to walk, as with the allegory of the infant.

Therefore, even though we were rewarded with hearing the words of the living God from the *Shechina* [Divinity] that was speaking out of the mouth of Baal HaSulam, the choice still remains with us. Thus, although he had revealed to us many revelations, it was only in order to guide us so we might walk unaided.

Hence, for each innovation he had revealed to us in the Torah, which brought us elation and great confidence to dedicate our lives only for the sake of the Creator, there promptly came a hardening of the heart, as in "for I have hardened his heart," so we would later be able to make our own choice, as this is called "labor without support."

His intention was to bring us to the desired wholeness. This is why each one remains in a state that is unsuitable for a student of his, and we need to strengthen ourselves, as it is written in my previous letter, that Jacob the patriarch did not die, meaning that his quality of truth lives forever. And when the verse, "And fear not, my servant Jacob, says the Lord, neither be frightened, Israel, for I will save you from afar and your seed from the land of their captivity."

That is, even if we are in complete remoteness, the salvation of the Lord is as the wink of an eye, and we will be rewarded with coming to the truth, meaning to bestow contentment upon the maker. Amen, may it be so.

Your friend, Baruch Shalom HaLevi Ashlag
Son of Baal HaSulam

Letter No. 29

January 17, 1957, Manchester

To the friends, may they live forever,

Some time ago, I wrote you a letter but still received no reply if it has reached you. And except for ... you are all slacking in your letters to me. This must be a matter of "an act that time causes," and I'll say no more.

Concerning *Rosh Hashanah* [beginning of the year] for the trees, which is on the 15th of *Shevat*, in the *Masechet* [Talmud tractate] of *Rosh Hashanah* (p 14), "On the first of *Shevat*, what is the reason? Rabbi Hoshia said, 'it is because most of the rains of the year have passed.'" It was written in the Tosfot that the above reason is also according to Beit Hillel, who concur with the 15th of *Shevat*, since by then the majority of the rainy days have passed, and it is the time of crouching (the last third of the rainy season), and the resin is abundant in the trees, and the fruits have ripened.

In the *Masechet* of *Rosh Hashanah* (p 11), it is said, "One who comes out on a *Nissan* (Hebrew month) day and sees blooming trees and says, 'Blessed is He who did not deprive His world of anything, and created in it good creations and good trees with which to delight people.'"

Letter No. 29

We should understand:

1. What does, "He did not deprive His world," mean? Are blooming trees a proof that nothing is missing?
2. "Created good creations"—what proof is this that creations are good?
3. The connection between man and tree;
4. It is known that if the majority of the rainy days have passed it is the sign of the beginning of the year. This reason is both according to Beit Shamai and according to Beit Hillel.

First we need to understand the meaning of *Rosh Hashanah* in the work. It is known that *Rosh Hashanah* is the time of judgment, when people are sentenced favorably or to the contrary. *Rosh* [head] is regarded a root from which the branches emerge. The branches always extend according to the essence of the root, for a root of oranges will not bring out branches of apples.

According to the root and the *Rosh* that a person establishes for himself at first, so he continues his life. The root is the foundation upon which the whole construction is built.

The judgment that a person is judged in the beginning of the year means that the person himself is the judge and the executer, since the person himself is the judge, the arbiter, the plaintiff, and the witness. It is as our sages said, "There is a judgment below; there is no judgment above."

"Rains" mean vitality and pleasure by which the tree bears fruits. Man's main work is during the winter days, on the long nights of *Tevet*. From *Tishrey*—which is the general beginning of the year—to *Shevat*, the majority of the rainy days have passed, meaning that a person has already received vitality and pleasure from Torah and work. At that time a person sentences himself if he should continue throughout the year only with Torah and work, or to the contrary.

"If he has one advocating angel over him out of a thousand, to testify to one's integrity," meaning if he has merit, then a person is notified of his integrity, meaning that he will walk on the right path. At that time "out of a thousand," as in "I will teach you wisdom." Then, after the deliberation, he is acquitted in the judgment, meaning that he has taken upon himself to henceforth engage only in pure things, called "bestowal," both for the Creator and for people.

But this is true only if merits are the majority, meaning that until now the majority of vitality he has received was from matters of bestowal. At that time he decides that it is worth continuing, and then it is considered that he has been declared innocent.

But if he did not receive the majority of vitality from spiritual matters, but derived all of his vitality from corporeal matters, and if he has merit, called an "advocating angel," then he is also declared innocent. That is, he decides to continue for the rest of the year only with matters of bestowal.

If the majority are iniquities, meaning that after all the works and labors, he still received the majority of vitality from matters of the will to receive for himself—the root of all iniquities and sins—then he is declared guilty.

That is, he takes upon himself to henceforth proceed only as the do the rest of the world, meaning with matters that are only for reception for oneself. This is man's guilt, since matters that are in reception for oneself detain a person from achieving one's eternal perfection and be awarded the sublime pleasures. This is regarded as "condemning oneself," when one decides to continue the rest of his days only with matters that are condemning for the soul.

This is why the Tosfot write, "since by then the majority of the rain-days have passed," etc., "and the resin is abundant in the trees, and the fruits have ripened." That is, if he has passed the majority of the long nights of the winter days in Torah and work, and the resin is abundant in the trees, and he knows and feels that a fire is burning in his heart, as in "Her flames are flames of fire, the fire of the Lord," he decides to continue on this path. This is the meaning of "and the fruits have ripened," meaning that henceforth he will be rewarded with fruits.

For this reason, the 15th of *Shevat* is called "the beginning of the year" [*Rosh Hashanah*], when a person has already calculated whether to continue in the work or to the contrary, for by now he knows from which discernment he can draw life—from matters of self-reception or matters of bestowing contentment upon his maker. He knows that all his work is only to obtain the desire to bestow, since the Creator has prepared for us desire to receive the pleasures at the time of creation, for He desires to do good to His creations and created the will to receive.

Creation, too, would have remained a desire to receive, meaning that if we received the abundance of spirituality and eternity in our will to receive, the pleasures would have been incomplete from the perspective of the branch that wishes to resemble the root. This is why there is the bread of shame. This would leave Creation deficient.

For this reason, the Creator has prepared for us a correction called *Tzimtzum* [restriction]. That is, where there is will to receive, a person feels concealment, as it is written in the introduction to the *Sulam* [Ladder commentary], that although the life that is clothed in the body extends existence from existence, its original root is still not apparent due to the *Tzimtzum*.

And through adapting to Torah and work we are rewarded with the correction called "reception in order to bestow," by which we are rewarded with *Dvekut* [adhesion] with Him. It follows that by this, everything becomes completed. This is the meaning of "who did not deprive His world of anything," referring to the correction of bestowal, as will be written below.

Now we will explain the connection between trees and people, which our sages connected. It is written, "For man is the tree of the field." That is, all the works applied to trees in order to make them fit for bearing fruit apply also to man. Until a person is ready to bear fruit, he must endure all the works applied to trees.

The fruits are man's final goal, and once, at a 15th of *Shevat* meal, Baal HaSulam explained why there is the matter of eating fruits. He said that it is because this is the whole difference between *Kedusha* [holiness] and *Sitra Achra* [other side], as it is written in *The Zohar*: "Another god is infertile and does not bear fruit," as he interprets in the *Sulam*. That is, their source runs dry and they wither until they are completely shut. But those who advance in *Kedusha* are rewarded with blessing in their works, "Which yields its fruit in its season and its leaf does not wither" ("Introduction to the Book of Zohar," item 23).

This is why the people of Israel make an indication of it, to show that the main thing is the fruits. And the fruits of holiness are by being rewarded with the revelation of His Godliness, and he becomes as a never ending fountain, advancing from degree to degree until he is rewarded and says, "He will be glorified in me, for He desires me, and He will be to me a gazelle's crown."

The works that apply to trees were also given to man, to qualify him. In *Sheviit* (Chapter 2, 42) he brings things that are required for tending to trees, and from this we learn concerning man's work.

Fertilizing—providing them with fertilizer. Likewise, man needs to add fertilizer to himself, which is waste—indecent qualities in a person. However, one should not bring the fertilizer from outside, as is done with trees, but should bring the fertilizer from concealment to disclosure, meaning into his senses, so he will feel the measure of the lowliness of his indecent qualities. Otherwise one cannot correct one's actions.

Hoeing—digging at the base of the trees. Likewise, man should dig and search his purpose, namely what is the purpose for which he has come into this world.

Removing calluses—cutting off the calluses, which are flaws that appear in the tree. A callus is something that is outside one's body. There are several things that a person does and which are seen outward, by people. That is, during the prayer, or when he speaks words of piousness to his friend, by which his friend sees his work that is outside his body. These must be cut out and cancelled. Instead, "Be humble with the Lord your God."

That is, when a person performs some work for the Creator, the sign is if he seeks to conceal it from people. This is a mark that his aim is true. If not, it is to the contrary—he is craving only to disclose to people, and he is purifying the body outwards with poor excuses. But when he is aiming for the Creator, he naturally wants to cover the matter.

Removing the leaves from the tree to make it easier on it. Likewise, man has leaves which precede the fruits, meaning that the fruits emerge on the leaves. This is the meaning of coming from *Lo Lishma* [not for her sake] to *Lishma* [for her sake]. The *Lo Lishma* is called "leaves," and the fruits are the *Lishma*.

However, these leaves should be removed in order to make it easier on the tree to achieve *Lishma*. Otherwise, if one does not remove the *Lo Lishma* he will remain in the state of *Lo Lishma*. Afterwards, when rewarded with *Lishma*, it is written, "Its leave will not wither." Rather, all the works that were in *Lo Lishma* eventually enter *Kedusha* [holiness].

And there is a higher interpretation, as it is written in the *Sulam* ("Introduction to the Book of Zohar," item 2), that "leaves" are the forces of judgment in the *Masach* [screen], meaning the *Tzimtzum* that was on the will to receive that no abundance would illuminate, but that there would be darkness. By this the *Masach* is born. It follows that the force of the judgment of the departure of the light brings him to make a *Masach* by which he receives the strength to receive in order to bestow.

Also, during the preparation, prior to being awarded entrance to the Creator's palace, one should grow accustomed to the powers of overcoming the desires for self-reception. The way is to begin with small things, which do not give him that much delight and pleasure and are easier to relinquish and say about them, "Were it not a *Mitzva* to engage in these matters, I wouldn't do them."

Afterwards he adds until he accustoms himself to relinquish even the most important things for him. Even with things that touch his soul he can say that were it not a *Mitzva*, he would not engage in them. All this is required for him to be strong and trained in war, and then he is awarded entrance to the Creator's palace to be among God's servants.

The force that compels him to keep himself from all the things, so he will not be immersed in desires of self-reception, is the force of judgment, which rules and keeps him from failing in the above. This is so because when he has self-interest, the vitality and abundance promptly depart from him. Therefore, he determines and decides and keeps the *Masach* that he will receive specifically in order to bestow.

It is likewise in the manners of preparation: the above-mentioned force of judgment shows its power and its actions are apparent until one decides once and for all never to breach the laws of Torah. But until one arrives at that final resolution, as an unbreakable law, one is in a state of "back and forth," regarded as a catapult, until one comes to fear the punishment of the above-mentioned force of judgment.

Allegorically, even when one feels elated and thinks that he will never fall, if he fails with self interest, in mind or in heart, the power of judgment promptly rules over him and the spiritual vitality departs from him. That is, he is denied of all the desire and fancy that he had in Torah and work, and he falls into the authority of the *Sitra Achra*, who governs him. He has no tactic or strength to overcome her and he follows her like sheep to the slaughter. She forces him to crave and derive vitality from the lowest desires of reception in reality, meaning such base things that ordinary God fearing people will never want.

The reason for this is that he was used to receiving spiritual vitality, and he finds nothing tasteful about the ordinary trivialities of this world. So until he receives some reward instead of the spiritual vitality that he possessed—when he derived emotional satisfaction from them—he craves the lowest of the worldly matters, perhaps there he will be able to satisfy his soul.

At that time, he is suspicious of every transgression in the Torah, since the power of judgment pushes him into the *Sitra Achra*, and the desire to receive sees to filling oneself with pleasure so he will have vitality to fill up for the *Sitra Achra*, called "the root of the will to receive for oneself alone." For this reason, he descends to the place of lowliness, perhaps there he will find what he seeks.

But it is questionable whether he finds what he is seeking. And yet, he pokes through the trash like chickens pecking through the trash. At the beginning of the fall he still remembers the spiritual state that he had, meaning that a *Reshimo* [recollection] still remains in him. At that time he still knows that now he is considered dead, meaning doing all the lowly things, whether in thought or in action, too, in a place where he feels no shame from people.

And yet, he knows that this is not man's purpose, and it is lowliness. He intellectually understands that he must overcome this time of descent, although he knows and sees and feels, he is lying like the dead, hopeless, and tied with ropes of *Aviut* [thickness/will to receive] under the authority of the *Sitra Achra*.

The memory that he remembers seems to him like a good dream that he will never be able to dream again. This is what he knows and feels (he is absolutely certain that it is impossible to continue the spiritual state that he had then). In other words, he does not have the strength of devotion and faith above reason as before. For this reason, this *Reshimo* brings him nothing but suffering because he is utterly incapable of escaping his current state.

And because it is human nature to forget the suffering, for it is our nature to forget the dead, meaning that if he remembers his spiritual time, he sees that now he is dead, so he comes into an even greater descent. That is, he forgets his good state and believes that he has always been in the current state of self-reception, and never desired the work of the Creator, meaning that the words, "And you who cling," were certainly not said about him. Instead, all his vitality comes only from corporeal matters.

And if he sometimes remembers that he had a spiritual state, he excuses himself that even then it was probably not genuine, but an imitation. And most importantly, he does not need to come out of that state.

But if he finally thinks, "What shall become of the correction of the soul?" He excuses himself that he will correct it in the next life, but not now. And then he comes into an even greater descent, meaning that he forgets to think for even one moment about everything that is happening with him. Instead, he is without any calculations, flowing with the currents of the world and having fun like everyone else.

This is the meaning of "descending and inciting" a person toward self-reception. And "ascending and slandering" means that he has broken the laws of Torah and takes his soul, and remains without any vitality.

This continues until he is pitied from heaven and is made to somehow fall into a good environment of books or authors, and he suddenly begins to feel again "the voice of my beloved is knocking."

Sometimes it can be to the contrary, that he comes into a lowlier environment and by observing their lowliness he suddenly begins to feel the herald, "Return, O [mischievous] sons." Then he promptly musters strength and is reminded of the ways and laws he had received and heard, and he becomes elated once again and promptly exits all the lowliness and is revived.

At that time he already feels that he has the power to overcome by powers of devotion, and he begins to choose the good once more, and loathe the bad. Only then is he the judge of choice and good counsels and upright conducts, and has the strength to go forward.

But during the death, meaning when his dead is lying before him, no condolences are accepted, as it is written, "The dead are free," for when a person dies he becomes free of *Mitzvot* and no advice can help him.

And if he fails with self interest once more, the quality of judgment hits him once again and he is placed in the catapult until the living, meaning the time when he is alive "will put it into his heart" to beware and guard himself with all kinds of caution so he does not fall again into the authority of the *Sitra Achra*.

That fear from the force of judgment continues until it is carved in his heart that he will determine his conduct steadfast, as it is written, "And he saw the Kenite, and took up his discourse and said, 'Your seat is firm.'" RASHI interpreted (that wicked Balaam said), "I wonder from where you have been granted this, for you were with him in the counsel, 'Let us deal wisely with them,' and now you have settled in the firm and strong of Israel."

In other words, the *Sitra Achra* comes to him with the argument, "What is the matter with you? You always walked with me concerning matters of self reception, and now you have set up your state firm to not move an inch from your spiritual place." This is called "fear of punishment," when he observes the laws of Torah for fear of punishment of the power of judgment.

This is the meaning of removing, as in "He asks it and he answers it," meaning ascents and descents. Through the questions and answers one determines the real form of the work of the Creator.

Dusting—the exposed roots are covered with dust.

The "root" is regarded as "thought," which is the root of the action. If the thoughts are revealed, meaning that one looks in every place and spies on every place, both on the ways and conducts one has received from one's teachers, whether they are true, then one needs to struggle with these thoughts, as in "And a man strove with him"—said about Esau's minister—and accept them above reason.

This is the meaning of "and be dusting in the dust of their feet." This means that although you have spies who say, "We will not go up," and although their spies, meaning the thoughts of the students, bring up dust, meaning that it seems to them that their teachers' words are as valuable as dust, he should still take his teachers' words above reason.

Here I will offer an example: Baal HaSulam promised us that by walking in his path and following his guidance we will be rewarded with His eternity, to cling unto Him, and to enter the King's palace. Although we all feel that we have not the properly pure qualities to be the King's servant. Still, "The Lord is near to the broken-hearted," since all the indecent qualities that are inherently within us, the Creator has planted them in us and has created us with all the lowliness.

Baal HaSulam said, "The Lord is high and the low will see," since the Creator loves the truth. For this reason, the Creator brings near those who are truly low. Sometimes we come to a state of despair and feel that we will rise from our current condition, meaning during the contemplation. It was said about this, "dusting," meaning that we must fight these thoughts.

Smoking under the tree—to kill the worms that grow in it. It is written about the manna, "[they] left part of it until morning, and it bred worms and became foul." Baal HaSulam interpreted the manna to mean faith. It is known that each day we must renew the faith.

This is the meaning of "gather each day," meaning even if it is still day for him, he should renew the foundation of the work, meaning the purpose of the work. One has to know that his being in a state of "day" is only the result of faith, since if one follows the path of faith he is rewarded with the clothing of *Shechina* [Divinity], each according to his measure of faith.

This means that the day is not his goal, but he can use the day in order to testify to faith. That is, he will say, "Now I see that I have been walking in the path of faith because the result I have is that of a day. It follows that I must grow stronger in the root."

Baal HaSulam interpreted "the shepherds of Abraham's cattle" similarly: He gives nourishments to Abraham's possessions, meaning to the quality of faith, as his quality is the "father of faith." But, receive the quality of faith as the goal and the essence. Otherwise he will be regarded as "bowing to the sun."

While the foundation is only faith, one is in a state of poverty and lowliness, as it is written, "and I am a worm." In other words, *Anochi* [me/selfish], regarded as faith, causes him to feel that he is a worm because his whole work is above reason, and because he is above reason he cannot feel pride.

But if he does not renew the faith, but rather, as it is written, "[they] left," and he toys with his day and makes it the essence, then "it bred worms." Where he should have been a "worm," he "bred" [in Hebrew *Yaram* means both "bred" and "was haughty"], meaning was proud, since he felt he was higher than everyone.

All this is because he works within reason. From this he comes to "bred," meaning pride, and his pride spreads afar until it comes to the measure of "and became foul," as army men say, "pride smells from afar."

The advice for this is as the Mishnah tells us, "smoking." The smoke comes by burning, meaning that each day he burns his work from yesterday and only today he begins to get in to the joy of a holy war—to bring out the land of Israel from under the authority of reception and admit the point into a state where he feels that the wings of the *Shechina* [Divinity] cover him, as it is written, "Who shields him all the day, and he dwells between His shoulders."

In other words, precisely when assuming the path of faith, regarded as a burden that is carried on the shoulders, one is rewarded with the *Shechina*. It is as Baal HaSulam said, that each day we must give to the Creator everything that he has been through, whether *Mitzvot* or transgressions, and begin anew. This is also the meaning of "smoking," for the smoke blocks the eyes, called "the mind's eyes," which is one's within reason.

Stoning means removing the stones. These are the understandings that he has within reason, which belong to the stony heart. That is, when he feels day, and feels zest and emotions in the work, he says, "Now I see that it is worthwhile to be a servant of the Creator because I find pleasure and vitality in it." It follows that he already has support, meaning that from all those supports he gets many stones and has a whole building within reason.

These are truly stumbling blocks. It is as Pharaoh said, "See upon the birth stool; if it is a boy, then you shall put him to death." That is, where you have pleasure, called "stones," do not receive it into the stony heart, called "reception." "If it is a boy," meaning that bestowal has awakened to you from that, as in "the shepherds of Abraham's cattle," then "put him to death," meaning destroy these thoughts.

"But if it is a girl," meaning *Nukva* [female], receiving everything into the will to receive, whether in mind or in heart, "then she shall live." This is what Pharaoh advised to receive as vitality and foundation. But the path of Torah is to remove these views and thoughts.

Cutting out means chopping off and cutting out the dry branches from the tree. That is, everyone one has acquired from the environment by habit, commandments, and dry laws, should be cut off, meaning forget the laws of overseas. It is so because the land of Israel is called *Lishma*, and what one takes from the environment is only *Lo Lishma*.

Trimming, means that when there are many fresh twigs it is customary to cut off some of them and put them aside. That is, even the laws and wisdoms that are truly moist, if they are too many, meaning that his knowledge is more than his works," then he must not use a lot of knowledge and scrutiny because the majority appears primarily in actions, for each act testifies to the quality of its operator.

We learn from all the above that people are akin to trees. This is the meaning of "One who comes out on a Nissan [Hebrew month] day and sees a blooming tree," meaning that the trees have already begun to show their strength, meaning that it is already apparent that they want to impart fruits to man's benefit. To benefit means to bestow, as it is written, "My heart overflows with a goodly matter, meaning "I say, 'My works are for the king,'" which is good.

And since the trees are blooming, namely giving, they are called "good trees." Clearly, at that time there are also good people, meaning that they, too, do things in order to bestow contentment upon their maker. Otherwise the trees, too, would not be imparting their fruits, as our sages said, "The whole world is nourished for Hanina, my son." Because there are righteous, who are giving, they act so that the trees will give.

This is the meaning of "did not deprive His world of anything." It means that He has prepared for us the engagement in Torah and *Mitzvot* by which we will achieve perfection, called "reception in order to bestow." It follows that besides creating the will to receive, He has promptly prepared the correction of the bread of shame so there would be completeness in the benefit.

Thus, one must give oneself an account each day, renew his work in overcoming, and forget the past. Instead, he should be very confident that from this day forth he will succeed in achieving permanent and eternal *Dvekut* [adhesion].

May the Creator help us with all our troubles and redeem our souls, and we will be saved in corporeality and spirituality, Amen may this be so.

Your friend, Baruch Shalom HaLevi Ashlag
Son of Baal HaSulam

Letter No. 30

March 28, 1957, Manchester

To my friend,

I received your letter from Purim and enjoyed it, since you are the only one who writes me some details about what is happening there, and I will answer your questions.

Regarding where the children should learn, a seminary of *Hassidim* is preferable, since in a seminary of *Hassidim* you are at least safer with fear of heaven, whereas in the rest of the seminaries you should fear the friends in this regard.

As for buying a part of *The Zohar*, I am not interested in this. Although I have my hidden reasons, there is one reason I can disclose to you. When you do something, you need to benefit either in corporeality or in spirituality. Here, as far as corporeality and making money are concerned, there are other good deals in the world, and I avoid them because I have no desire to engage in business. As far as spirituality is concerned, meaning that I will have a part in the *Sulam* [commentary] of *The Zohar*, I already have a big part in these books because the Torah has awarded me with two parts. By the law of Torah, there are only four heirs, and I deserve two portions... so I have no need to buy, meaning

Letter No. 30

to give money so as to be given what I deserve. But I have my hidden reasons.

Please try to give me every detail of what is happening there.

Blessings for the *Kashrut* of the festival,

Baruch Shalom HaLevi Ashlag

Letter No. 31

1957, Manchester

To the friends, may they live forever,

It's been a long time since I have written you. I have been waiting for demand to come from you. In the meantime, I will write you an article that I heard from Baal HaSulam in 1948 at a Purim meal at his pure table.

We should understand several precisions concerning the *Megillah* [Purim story]:

1. It is written, "After these things the king promoted Haman." We should understand what is "After these things." After Mordechai saved the king, the king should have promoted Mordechai. But what was eventually written? That he promoted Haman.

2. When Ester said to the king, "We have been sold, I and my people," the king asked, "Who is he, and where is he" (not "this is he"). This means that the king did not know of anything. But it is written that the king said to Haman, "The silver is given to you, and the people also, to do with them as you please." Thus, we see that the king did know of the sale.

3. Concerning "according to the desires of each person," our sages said, "Raba said, 'to do according to the desires of

Mordechai and Haman'" (*Megillah*, 12). But it is known that where it says only "king," it is the King of the world, so how can it be that the Creator do according to the will of a wicked?

4. It is written, "And Mordechai knew all that was done." This means that only Mordechai knew. But it is written before that, "And the city of Shushan was perplexed." Thus, the whole city of Shushan knew about it.

5. Concerning the words, "for a decree which is written in the name of the king and sealed with the king's signet ring may not be revoked," how did he later write a second decree that revokes the first decree?

6. What does it mean that one must be intoxicated on Purim until one cannot tell between the damned Haman and the blessed Mordechai?

7. What is the meaning of the words of our sages, "'And the drinking was according to the law.' What is 'according to the law'? Rabbi Hanan said in the name of Rabbi Meir, 'According to the law of Torah.' What is the law of Torah? Eating more than drinking."

To understand all the above, we should begin with the matter of Haman and Mordechai, which our sages interpreted, "according to the desires of each person," meaning Haman and Mordechai. Mordechai's desire is called "the law of Torah," which is eating more than drinking. Haman's desire is the opposite: drinking more than eating. We asked, "How can there be a meal according to the will of a wicked? The answer that is written about it is, "no coercion," meaning that the drinking was not compulsory.

This is the same as what our sages said about the verse, "And Moses hid his face for he was afraid to look." And he said, "In return for 'and Moses hid his face,' he was rewarded with 'He beholds the image of the Lord.'" It is so because precisely when he does not need some thing (because he can put a *Masach* [screen] over it) that he can receive it. This is the meaning of "I have helped one who is mighty." That is, precisely one who is mighty and can walk in the ways of the Creator, the Creator helps him.

This is the meaning of "The drinking was according to the law." Why? Because there was "no coercion," for he did not need the drinking. But afterwards, when they began to drink, they were drawn to the drinking, meaning that they were attracted to the drinking and were needy. Then they were in a state of coercion. At that time they revoked Mordechai's way, and this is the meaning of their saying that that generation was sentenced to destruction, for they enjoyed the meal of that wicked.

This means that had they received the drinking without coercion, they would not have revoked Mordechai's will, which is Israel's way. (But) once they took the Creator by coercion, they sentenced themselves to destroy the law of Torah, which is Israel. This is the meaning of "eating more than drinking." Drinking is disclosure of *Hochma*, called "knowing," and eating is called *Ohr Hassadim* [light of *Hassadim*], which is faith.

However, we should scrutinize the matter of Bigtan and Teresh, who wished to assassinate the King of the world, "But the plot became known to Mordechai ... and the matter was investigated and found." The investigating was not a one-time thing, as it was not easy for Mordechai to obtain it. Only after much work was he revealed this matter of the flaw. And once it had been clearly revealed to him, "they were both hanged." That is, when they felt the flaw about it, then they hung, meaning removed these works and desires from the world.

"After these things," meaning after all the labor and toil that Mordechai performed through his scrutiny, the king wanted to reward for the labor of working *Lishma* [for Her sake]. But there is a rule that it is impossible to give to the lower one anything (if) he has no need for it. The desire and need is called a *Kli* [vessel], and there is no light without a *Kli*.

What if the king had asked Mordechai what he should give him? Mordechai was righteous, whose work is only to bestow. He has no desire for any ascension. Rather, he is content with little. But the king desired to extend the *Hochma*, which is disclosed *Mochin* that extend from the left line, while his work was in the right line. What did the king do? He promoted Haman, meaning made the left line important.

This is the meaning of "and (the king]) advanced him and established his authority over all the ministers." He put him in charge, meaning that all the king's servants kneeled and bowed before Haman, since the king commanded that he would be in charge, and everyone accepted it.

Kneeling means acceptance of governance, since they liked Haman's way more than that of Mordechai. Also, all the Jews in Shushan accepted Haman's domination so much that it was difficult for them to understand Mordechai's view, since it is easier to walk in the ways of the Creator by knowing.

It is written that they asked, "Why are you transgressing the king's command?" And since they saw that Mordechai insisted on walking on the path of faith, they were perplexed and did not know who was right. They asked Haman who was right, as it is written, "They told Haman to see whether Mordecai's words would hold, for he had told them he was a Jew." That is, the way of the Jew is eating more than drinking, namely that faith is the most important, and this is the whole foundation.

This was a big interference to Haman that Mordechai disagreed with him, and everyone saw Mordechai's view, who claimed that only he was following the Jewish way, and another way is already regarded as idolatry. This is why Haman said, "Yet all of this is worthless to me each time I see Mordechai the Jew sitting at the king's gate," for Mordechai claimed that only through him is the king's gate.

Now we will understand what we asked, "And Mordechai knew," but it is written, "And the city of Shushan was perplexed," which means that everyone knew. This means that the city of Shushan was perplexed and did not know who was right. But Mordechai knew that if Haman would have control, by this he would wipe out the whole of Israel, meaning the way of Judaism, since Haman's entire grip is on the left line.

This is the meaning of Haman casting lots as it was on *Yom Kippur* [Day of Atonement], as it is written, "One lot for the Lord, and one lot for Azazel." The lot to the Lord is the right, which is *Hassadim*, called "eating," which means faith. The lot to Azazel is really the left line, which is "not good for anything," and "anything" extends from here. This is why there was blocking on the lights, since the left line freezes the lights.

This is the meaning of "cast Pur, which is the lot," meaning he interprets what he had casted and replies that Pur is [pronounced as] *Pi-Ohr* [the opening of light], where through the lot to Azazel, all the lights were blocked. It follows that he dropped all the lights below. Haman thought that "the righteous prepares and the wicked wears," meaning that through the works that Mordechai and those accompanying him were constantly doing, he would take the reward, meaning that Haman would take all the disclosure of lights into his own authority.

All this was because the king gave him charge to extend the light of *Hochma* below. Therefore, when he approached the king in order to destroy the Jews, meaning to revoke Israel's domination, which is *Hassadim*, and establish revealed knowing in the world, the king replied to him, "The silver is given to you, and the people also, to do with them as you please," meaning as Haman pleases, according to his authority, which is left and knowing.

Thus, the whole difference between the first decree and the second decree is in the word "Jews." In the edict (edict is the content that came out from the king, and then there are explanations of the edict, which interpret the meaning of the edict), "to be issued as law in every single state, published to all the peoples so that they should be ready for this day."

It does not say for whom they should be ready. Only Haman explained that edict, as it is written, "and it was written just as

Haman commanded." In the second decree the word "Jews" is written, "An edict to be issued as law in each and single every state was published to all the peoples, so that the Jews would be ready for this day to avenge themselves on their enemies."

Therefore, when Haman came to the king, the king said to him, "The silver," which was prepared in advance, "is given to you." That is, you need not add any action, since "the people also, (is given to you) to do with them as you please." In other words, the people already want to do what is good in your eyes, meaning the people already want to assume your governance. But the king did not tell him to revoke the governance of Mordechai and the Jews. Rather, it was prepared in advance that at this time there would be disclosure of *Hochma*, which is regarded as "which pleases you."

"The edict" was "to be issued as law in every single state, published to all the peoples" means that the law was that it would be revealed, that there would be revealing of *Hochma* to all the nations. However, it was not written that Mordechai and the Jews, namely faith, would be revoked. Rather, the intention was that there would be disclosure of *Hochma*, yet they would prefer *Hassadim* in every place.

Haman said that since now is the time for *Hochma* to be revealed, in order to receive *Hochma*, while Mordechai's argument was that the disclosure is only to show what they are taking; it is not compulsory, namely that they have no other choice because there is no disclosure of *Hochma* here. Rather, they choose *Hassadim* of their own accord.

This is the meaning of what our sages said, "Thus far by coercion; henceforth willingly." It is written about the verse, "observed and received," meaning that the disclosure came now only so they could receive the way of the Jew willingly.

This is why there was a dispute over it between Mordechai and Haman. Haman's argument was that the reason why the Creator is revealing the domination of *Hochma* now is so that the lower ones will receive the *Hochma*. Mordechai claimed that the reason why the Creator is currently giving dominion to the left line is only to include it in the right, meaning that the right is the most important.

It therefore follows that the second letter did not revoke the first letter, but explained and interpreted the first edict. The words, "published to all the peoples," means that it is for the Jews. That is, so the Jews would be able to choose *Hassadim* of their own accord.

This is why it is written in the second letter, "so that the Jews would be ready for this day to avenge themselves on their enemies." He interprets that the reason why *Hochma* is currently in control is to show that they prefer *Hassadim* to *Hochma*. This is called "to avenge themselves on their enemies," for their enemies want specifically *Hochma*, while they reject the *Hochma*.

By that we will understand what we asked about the king asking, "Who is he ... whose heart would desire to do so," since the king said, "The silver is given to you, and the people also, to do with them as you please," since the king gave the order only to reveal *Hochma*. That is, the left was to serve the right, by which it will be seen to all that the right is more important, that this is why they choose *Hassadim*.

This is the meaning of *Megillat* [scroll/book, but also *Gilui*] (disclosure)] Ester [*Hester* (concealment)], which seem to contradict one another. Revealing is because it is revealed to everyone, and Ester means that there is concealment. However, it means that the disclosure is only so as to choose concealment, and specifically by that the lights appear below.

Now we will understand what our sages said, "One must be intoxicated on Purim until one cannot tell between the damned Haman from the blessed Mordechai." The story of Mordechai and Ester took place before the building of the Second Temple. The building of the Temple is the extension of *Hochma*, and then *Malchut* [Kingship] is called the Temple.

This is also the meaning of Mordechai sending Ester to go to the king and plea for her people, and she replied, "All the king's servants ... who is not summoned, he has but one law, that he be put to death... And I have not been summoned to come to the king for thirty days." It means that as it is known that it is forbidden to draw GAR below, and one who draws GAR is sentenced to death, since the left line causes separation from the Life of Lives.

"...unless the king holds out to him the golden scepter so that he may live." Gold is *Hochma* and GAR, meaning that only by the awakening of the upper one can he remain alive, meaning in *Dvekut* [adhesion], but not by the awakening of the lower one. And although Ester, which is *Malchut*, needs *Hochma*, it is only upon the awakening of the upper one. But if she draws GAR she will lose all of her self.

In that regard, Mordechai replied to her, "relief and deliverance will arise for the Jews from another place," by completely revoking the left line, and the Jews will be left with the right line, which is *Hassadim*, "and you and your father's house will perish." Because *Abba* [father] establishes the daughter," she must have *Hochma*. However, it must be by eating more than drinking.

However, if the Jews have no choice, they will have to revoke the left line. It follows that her entire self will be canceled. It is in that regard that she said, "If I perish I perish." If I go, I will perish because I might cause separation. If I do not go, "relief and deliverance will arise for the Jews from another place," meaning in another way, for they will completely revoke the left lie, as Mordechai had commanded her.

This is why she took the path of Mordechai, meaning invited Haman to the feast. That is, she extended the left line as Mordechai had commanded her, then included the left in the right, so that the entire drawing of *Hochma* was promptly with the aim not to receive the *Hochma*, but to prefer the *Hassadim*. In this way, there is disclosure of lights below.

This is the meaning of *Megillat* [the revealing of] Ester [concealment]. Although there is already disclosure, she still takes the concealment [Ester means *Hester* (concealment)].

Let us hope that the merit of Baal HaSulam, whose holy words we were privileged to hear although we have not been rewarded with understanding the depth of the matters that are the most sublime.

Let me bless you with a *Kosher* festival, and may we be granted with salvation in the general salvation.

Your friend, Baruch Shalom HaLevi Ashlag
Son of Baal HaSulam

Letter No. 32

April 12, 1957

To the friends, may they live forever,

It has been awhile since I have received letters from you. Although I've known the excuses for some time, it is also clear to you that the biggest problem is that you have excuses. Let us hope that the Creator will help us.

Since the festival of Passover is approaching, let us talk a little bit about the matter of blood of *Pesach* [Passover] and the blood of circumcision. *Dam* [blood] means *Demama* [silence/stillness], as in, "And Aaron kept silent," and "Be silent for the Lord." That is, he does not ask why he has questions.

To understand the above we should precede with the words of our sages. "Our sages said, 'Those who are offended but do not offend, degraded but do not respond, work out of love and delight in pain, the verse says about them, 'And those who love Him will be like the rising of the sun in its might.'"" RASHI interprets that they perform *Mitzvot* [commandments] out of love for the Creator to not take reward, and not because of fear of calamity (*Gitin* 36b).

This means that when one begins to work with great exertion, more than he has received by upbringing, a demand forms in his heart. Finally, he asks and says that according to the measure of his work and toil in Torah and *Mitzvot* beyond his contemporaries the Creator should have been revealed to him a long time ago, and should have revealed to him the flavors [also reasons] of Torah and *Mitzvot* and played with him, as it is written, "Israel, in whom I glorify Myself," meaning that the Creator plays with the servants of the Creator.

Yet, he sees the opposite—that through all his labor and toil, he went backwards compared to his contemporaries. Thus, instead of hearing the voice of the Creator speaking to him, he hears his own disgrace, as it is written, "With which Your enemies have cursed" (Psalms 89). That is, his is not being treated properly (it follows that all his toil and labor in Torah and work are at risk).

At that time he feels offended, insulted, for he is at a higher degree than his contemporaries. And although at such a time he cannot see any sign of greatness about his contemporaries, he still says to himself, "If others had the work schedule and knowledge in Torah that I have, the Creator would certainly listen to their words and their labor would not be in vain (I mixed two things together here: mind, for those who understand, and also despair, for those who understand).

It is known that truth is the most important, meaning that "All that a judge has is what his eyes see." Therefore, if he sees his true state, with all the thoughts that trouble his mind, he receives from this two things: 1) he feels insulted—that he is not taken into account; 2) subsequently, he comes to the 2nd state, where he hears his offence. For this reason, at that time he feels great torments when he tries to hang on in that state.

This is the meaning of, "Who are offended," who feel offended, meaning that he is not being noticed. "...but do not offend" means that it is as in operator and operation. The operation is that he feels offended. The operator, who works, is called "offend." He says that the Creator's intention is not to insult him, but on the contrary, it is the conduct of the Creator to do good.

Also, he is "degraded but does not respond," meaning that he does not make excuses, as in "Ethiopia quickly stretches out her hands to God" (Psalms 68).

Letter No. 32

The question is "What is the truth?" That is, why did the Creator make him feel such a lowly and painful state? The thing is that when a person begins to work *Lishma* [for Her sake], meaning not for any reward for his labor, and takes upon himself in both mind and heart to be clean, without any self-interest, he is allowed from above to see his state—if his aim is truly *Lishma*. Then, if he survives the test, he is let into the Creator's palace and sits in the shadow of the King.

It follows that only here, in this state, can he discover his true measure of love of the Creator, and not take reward because now he has nothing but pain. This is regarded as the way of the Torah being, "You will lead a life of sorrow." In other words, before one passes the state of "a life of sorrow," when the labor is sufficient to find the Creator, his only grip is the grace of holiness.

It is as Baal HaSulam explained about the words of our sages, "A woman with a bottle full of feces, and everyone is running after her." It is as I have explained to you the explanation that cannot be put in writing. This is regarded as "Ester was greenish, and a thread of grace was drawn upon her," as in, "Her father indeed spat in her face."

Here is where we need help from above, and this is the meaning of the Passover blood and the blood of the circumcision. That is, when we can hang on and keep quiet at the time of Torah, called *Peh-Sach* [*Pesach* (speaking mouth)], and during the performance of the *Mitzvot* implied in the commandment to circumcise, then we are rewarded with coming out of exile and entering redemption, which is the flavors [and reasons] of Torah and *Mitzvot*.

The letter stayed with me and I did not send it. Now, tomorrow I am going to America, meaning on the first of *Iyar* TaShYaZ (May 2, 1957), so I am sending you the letter.

Your friend, Baruch Shalom HaLevi Ashlag

Letter No. 33

April 23, 1957

To the wise Rabbi, the elder of the group,

I received a letter from your grandson... where he asked several questions. And since I normally answer in general and not specifically, though I like the questions to be specific and not general, the general actually contains many details.

That is, the answer is usually more effective for the work on the real path. And then, precisely when the person asking has many details, it is possible for the general to illuminate in many details, which we call "many *Kelim* [vessels]," so I will answer in general.

It is known that the most important is the joy. However, we need to understand the meaning of joy, as it is written, "This joy, what does it do?" Also, why was the praise of the work defined with regard to joy, as it is written, "Because you did not serve [work] ... with joy."

We can understand the meaning of joy from worldly matters (as Baal HaSulam said, that he gives him the conducts of this world only to receive from them letters and vessels for spiritual needs).

We see that people toil all day, some at work and some at commerce, and wait all day for the time when they can return home, have a good meal, and enjoy with their families.

Letter No. 33

Or, one who sails across the sea and suffers the hardships of the job, and longs for the time when he can return home, when he sees that the return to his home approaches, joy begins to fill his heart. At that time the constant longing that he has to reach his goal increases the goal. That is, he feels that it is worthwhile to make every effort only to be able to come home and enjoy. Otherwise, meaning if he did not toil, he would have nothing with which to enjoy because the house would be completely empty and he would not be able to enjoy.

It follows that there are two issues here: 1) a good meal, or one who comes from sailing the ocean and brings a lot of money; 2) the longing to reach the goal. We can say that if we could weigh the pleasure on a scale, we could say that the pleasure of the meal or the pleasure of one who brings money from abroad weighs one kilo, and the craving of one who craves all day to go home and eat his meal can increase the pleasure to the extent that the pleasure will weigh one hundred kilos.

Also, one who yearns to return home with the money he has made abroad, the yearning increases the pleasure immeasurably, and the pleasure grows only according to the measure of the yearning.

In turn, the measure of the yearning grows according to the measure of the labor. That is, one who works hard and toils, to the extent that he is suffering, the pain itself brings him the measure of the yearning to get rid of the suffering and reach his destination. And all the vitality he has while suffering is only from the future, as he feels that soon he will be able to return home.

It turns out that if a person has a good meal or a lot of money but did not toil for them, he can taste only the first level of pleasure, meaning to the extent of one kilo. But one who has toiled and yearns receives pleasure from the second level and will be able to increase the pleasure one hundred or one thousand fold.

We might ask, "And what is the truth," meaning if there is pleasure in the meal and in the money. If he is yearning, what difference does it make if the meal and the money are objects, and how can labor and yearning add to the pleasure?

But as we said above, corporeal possessions and spiritual possessions have one nature. Any pleasure, whether corporeal or spiritual, is called "light." And we have a rule about lights, that we have no attainment. That is, it is impossible to determine its final form unless through the *Kelim*. This means that we determine the shape of the lights according to the quality of the *Kelim*.

And regarding *Kelim* [vessels], it is known that it is regarded as yearning for something. It follows that the *Kelim* increase the light. This means that it is not the light that must be great, but the *Kelim* must be greater. Only if one has many *Kelim*, meaning a strong desire, one feels greater pleasure in the light.

Therefore, even in corporeality, the meal and the money do not determine the measure of the pleasure, but rather the labor and the yearning determine the measure of the pleasure.

By that we will understand the meaning of joy. It is customary that one who begins with the work of the Creator is sent foreign thoughts in the middle of the Torah and prayer. This torments the person. But the torments are only to the extent that one wishes to be rid of them and expel them.

And how does one expel these thoughts? Only through joy. That is, one should be confident that he will eventually reach the desired goal, which is to bestow contentment upon his maker and serve the king.

Also, one should make depictions, meaning imagine how good and how pleasant it is to be in the King's shadow, and behold the pleasantness of the Lord and visit in His palace." It is written that the Creator enjoys with the righteous, and I, too, will certainly reach that degree.

Subsequently, one should look at the foreign thoughts, which cause him this loss of not being able to be among the dwellers of the King's palace, and then he can examine the scrutiny of giving good reward to the righteous and avenging the wicked, meaning the value of light and darkness.

It follows that to the extent that he is suffering from the foreign thoughts, so he delights when he has good thoughts. And if there is a time when he has no foreign thoughts then he is happy. And at a time of lowliness he should receive vitality and joy from the future, meaning that eventually the Creator will have mercy on him and will approach him.

It follows that through the foreign thoughts he increases the meal, meaning the time when he has good thoughts and can praise and thank the Creator for bringing him closer to Him now.

Thus, the foreign thoughts are primarily in order to bring him joy—that he will long for the time when he can serve the King unflawed. This elevates the foreign thoughts—presented in books—where a person must correct the foreign thoughts if they come to him in the middle of the work.

May the Creator help us be rewarded with serving the Creator with gladness and a good heart,

Your friend

Letter No. 34

Eve of *Rosh Hashanah* [Jewish New Year's Eve], September 14, 1957

To the friends, may they live forever.

After I have come close to you in the imaginary corporeal place, let us hope for bringing the hearts closer, as for a long time now we have not had correspondence, and the physical act brings unity, as it is said in *Rosh Hashanah* prayer [Hebrew New Year's Eve service], "And they shall all become one society." In that state, it will be easier "To do Your will wholeheartedly."

This is so because while there is not just one society, it is difficult to work wholeheartedly. Instead, part of the heart remains for its own benefit and not for the benefit of the Creator. It is said about it in *Midrash Tanhuma*, "'You stand today,' as the day at times shines and at times darkens, so it is with you. When it is dark for you, the light of the world will shine for you, as it is said, 'And the Lord shall be unto you an everlasting light.' When? When you are all one society, as it is written, 'Alive everyone of you this day.'

"Usually, if someone takes a pile of branches, can he break them all at once? But if taken one at a time, even a baby can break them. Similarly, you find that Israel will not be redeemed until they are all one society, as it is said, 'In those days and at that time, says the Lord, the children of Israel shall come, they and the sons of

Letter No. 34

Judah together.' Thus, when they are united, they receive the face of Divinity."

I presented the words of the Midrash so that you don't think that the issue of a group, which is love of friends, relates to Hassidism. Rather, it is the teaching of our sages, who saw how necessary was the uniting of hearts into a single group for the reception of the face of Divinity.

Although there is always one of the friends who stands out and yells, "Join your hands for a single group!" and always attributes the negligence to the friends, I still cannot exclude him from among the friends who are negligent in the matter, and this should suffice for the understanding.

Primarily, let us hope that in the new year, *Shin-Tav-Het-Yod* ["May you live" but also the year in the Hebrew calendar, counted in letters (1949-50)], the Creator will give us eternal life, as it is written, "For God has appointed me another seed instead of Abel," etc., and "May you live" shall come true.

The meaning of *Rosh Hashanah* [New Year's Eve] is a new beginning, when a person begins to build a new structure. It is as our sages said, "One should always consider oneself half sinful, half righteous. If he performs a single *Mitzva* [good deed/commandment], happy is he, for he has sentenced himself and the whole world to the side of merit. If he commits one transgression, woe unto him for he has sentenced himself and the whole world to the side of fault."

We should understand what it means that one should always consider oneself fifty-fifty. 1) If he performs one *Mitzva* and sentences to the side of merit, how can he be said to be fifty-fifty again? After all, he has already sentenced and already has a majority of merits. Conversely, if he committed one transgression, how can it later be said that he is fifty-fifty? 2) How can it be said that he is fifty-fifty when one knows about himself that he is full of sins and transgression? At the same time, one is compelled to confess, "We are guilty, we have betrayed," and "For the sin."

The thing is that our sages are letting us understand the order of the work. There is no issue of a court and judgment above, here. Only when one comes before the court above are his transgressions and merits sentenced.

Rather, here our sages are teaching us that one should always begin the work and choose the good and loathe the bad. This is so because choice is pertinent *precisely* in something that is fifty-fifty, for then he has the power to choose. But when one of the sides already has the majority, he can no longer decide because man follows the majority and then it is irrelevant to speak of choice.

This brings up the question, "How can he deceive himself and say that he is fifty-fifty when in fact he knows that he is full of sins?" However, we should know that the matter of choice that one is given is permanent and always existing, as in, "He who is greater than his friend, his inclination is greater than him." According to this rule, if one has many sins, then he has a small inclination, which is not greater than the good inclination, but is precisely fifty-fifty, so he will be able to decide.

And since the transgressions come through the evil inclination and the *Mitzvot* [good deeds/commandments] come through the good inclination, as RASHI interpreted, "You have created righteous through the good inclination; You have created wicked through the evil inclination," hence our sages said, "One should always consider oneself half sinful half righteous." In other words, regarding the choice, it is always, and if the transgressions are from ... then the evil inclination diminishes. Thus, he is fifty-fifty.

Similarly, if he performs a single *Mitzva* and has already sentenced to the side of merit, he is promptly given great evil inclination, as it is written, "He who is greater than his friend, his inclination is greater." Thus, now he has fifty-fifty, so he will be able to sentence to the side of merit.

Therefore, on *Rosh Hashanah*, one begins one's work anew. Additionally, the days of the ten penitential days are called "days of forgiving and atonement of sins," so a man will have every

Letter No. 34

opportunity to join in the work of the Creator once more, even though he's been so remote from the work.

And the essence of the work is prayer, since only by prayer can one exit the public domain and enter the domain of the Single one. This is so because when it comes to prayers, great and small are equal. Moreover, one who feels one's lowness can offer a more genuine prayer from the bottom of the heart, for he knows about himself that he cannot deliver himself from the strait on his own. Then, he can say that actually, those who were created with special talents and qualities of subtlety can do something on their own, whereas those without the special gifts and good qualities need heaven's mercy. Thus, only this person can offer an honest prayer.

However, one should be careful not to escape the campaign, since it is the conduct of the inclination that where one can offer a true prayer, it brings him sparks of despair and provides him with evidence, conclusions, and inferences that his prayer will be useless. Finally, a person becomes incapable of believing in "For You hear the prayer of every mouth." Our sages said, "The Creator longs for the prayer of righteous." This is so because a prayer is the primary tool for the inspiration of Divinity because it is considered a prayer for the poor.

And prayer applies even to the greatest of the greatest. Without it, one cannot achieve a state of "standing" in the work. This is the meaning of, "For the poor shall never cease from the land." We should understand why the Creator promised us this—that it is necessary to always have the poor. Wouldn't it be better if there was no such thing in Israel?

However, in the above interpretation, "poor" means a place for prayer, and if there is no place of deficiency, there is no place for prayer. Thus, is there no place for prayer once one is rewarded with greatness? In that regard, the Creator promises us, "The poor shall never cease," meaning there will always be a place where it is possible to find a need so that one can rise to a higher degree.

This is the meaning of, "Poverty befits Israel like a red strap for a white horse." This means that even if he is already a Jew in utter greatness, still, poverty is befitting, for it is a place of deficiency so that he will be able to offer a prayer.

This is the issue presented in the Gemarah (*Berachot* 9b): "Rabbi Ela said to Ulla, 'When you go up there, give my greeting to my brother, Rabbi Berona, in the presence of the whole group, for he is a great man and rejoices in *Mitzvot* [commandments/good deeds]. Once he succeeded in joining redemption with prayer, and a smile did not leave his lips the whole day.'" In other words, his being a great man is when he is already in a state of redemption, redeemed from all the deficiencies, with nothing more to do. In that state, he has work finding some fault in himself so as to pray for it. And when he was "Joining redemption with prayer," he promptly found a place for prayer and had endless joy, as it is written, "For the poor shall never cease from the land."

It follows from all the above that the most important thing is the prayer. Be strong in prayer and believe in, "You hear the prayer of every mouth."

May we be inscribed in the book of life.

Your friend, Baruch Shalom HaLevi

Son of Baal HaSulam

Letter No. 35

Eve of *Yom Kippur* [Day of Atonement], October 4, 1957

Regarding your question, "Why we were left so alone in the war?" our sages said, "All who weep and mourn over a worthy person," etc. (*Shabbat* 105b). What is the meaning of weeping and mourning?

It is known that there are two kinds of weeping: There is weeping of grief and there is weeping of joy. When the heart fills with overexcitement, whether the excitement comes from good things or bad things, this excitement manifests outwards. It is like a glass of water—when it fills up, it overflows. It is likewise with tears, which are a surplus that pours out. This is why there are tears of joy, and, of course, the opposite.

However, tears with no reason are impossible, although there are artificial tears, meaning one who wants to show another that he is impressed with something, this too is cause for tears. However, this is considered artificial.

Therefore, when a worthy person dies and we feel the lack, the feeling and sorrow accumulate in the heart, it manifests in tears. Naturally, when a person feels a certain measure of lack, that lack is called a "prayer," and through prayer we extend the loss once more. But when we do not pay attention and accept the situation, we grow farther each time until we forget.

It is known that the dead are forgotten from the heart, since death is called "despair." This is why there is a complaint about the deceased who was connected to that person—and that connection required that person's attention—that the righteous has perished but no one notices.

Therefore, in order to avoid slandering a person who was connected to the deceased righteous, the deceased righteous makes a correction by taking back from him what he gave to him. At that time, that person becomes very bad, since those who already had will to receive for spirituality, when they lose the spirituality, corporeal things begin to fill up the measure of pleasure of spirituality. Hence, they fall far lower, meaning into greater measures of lowly lusts and passion for honor.

This is why he explained after the event that happened to us they forgot the essence and took to themselves a path of dispute...

In any case, I knew what the outcome would be beforehand. There are people who can conceal their thoughts, and there are people who haven't that strength, and their thoughts appear outwards, meaning they do improper things and show to all that they have not, nor had before any connection with the righteous.

So why are you surprised now? It was determined right after *Yom Kippur* [Day of Atonement] of 1954, and since then it has been nothing but a succession of development of their thoughts and actions.

Now you will have a better understanding of the necessity to believe in the words of our sages, who obligated man to say, "The world was created for me." But how do you take this greatness—that one should have excessive pride? Yet, if the foundation is entirely of faith, we can believe this, too. If a person is working for himself, then there are such arguments. But if a person wants, at the very least, for his desire to be for the Creator, he can believe this, too, since we need faith every step of the way.

"The righteous are greater in their death than in their life." That is, we must increase the faith when they die more than when they are alive, since the whole basis of the way of the righteous is in faith. Only in this way does knowing appear, and only one who has been rewarded with walking in the path of faith will have the wisdom and the might.

"Anyone who is idle with the eulogy of a sage should be buried in his life" (*Shabbat* 105b). This means that where deficiency is not felt, idleness is felt. Since he does not feel the loss and is not impressed enough to awaken a eulogy in his heart, then even though he is still alive, before the vitality he had received from the sage has departed from him, still, he should be buried in his life.

As the dead can be corrected only through burial, this man should be buried because death is certain to come, meaning that life will depart him. This is why our sages tell us that he should be buried right now...

Baruch Shalom HaLevi
Son of Baal HaSulam

Letter No. 36

Eve of *Sukkot*, October 9, 1957, Manchester

To the friends in the Holy Land, may they live forever,

This week, I received two letters from... and regarding his question... I will answer privately.

In general, our sages said, "Anyone who is idle with the eulogy of a sage should be buried in his life" (*Shabbat* 105). We should ask, "Why does he deserve such a harsh punishment?" We should know that idleness always stems from absence of deficiency. Only there is there idleness. But where there is a deficiency, there are always movements in order to seek advice how to satisfy the lack. This is why specifically one who does not feel any lack in the departure of the sage, it is apparent in the eulogy of the sage—when he is idle in the eulogy of the sage.

The question is, "Why does he not feel the lack in the departure of the sage?" It must be said that during the sage's life he also did not receive anything from the sage, so he does not feel any lack upon the sage's departure.

This is why he should be buried in his life, meaning during the sage's life. It is not necessarily now that he is not alright, as he is idle in his eulogy. Rather, back then he was already not alright. This is why "buried in his life" means during the life of the sage.

However, there is a cure to all this. Conversely, "One who degrades a wise disciple, there is no cure to his plight" (*Shabbat* 119). In other words, if he does not settle for being idle with the eulogy of a sage, but says that he is standing on the same degree with the sage, in connection, there is no greater degradation to a wise disciple than this, and our sages said, "There is no cure to his plight." Instead, he keeps falling lower and lower until he shows to everyone his true form, meaning that his Torah becomes to him a potion of death.

My general answer is that the festival of *Sukkot* explains all the questions, even the hardest and worst, for it is known that *Sukkah* is the "shadow of faith," and with respect to the judgment, its shade must be bigger than its sun.

It is also known that the sun implies knowing, and the moon implies faith. It is as our sages said, "Israel count by the moon, and the nations of the world count by the sun." That is, each time we see the sun, and that it is more than the shade, we must cover more so that the shade will be more than the sun.

And if one is rewarded and does not add shade on his own, there is mercy on him from above and the sun is covered for him. But then a person becomes angry because he understands otherwise. According to the person's reason, if he has sun, he wishes to have more sun, but "My thoughts are not your thoughts," and he is given more shade.

And if a person overcomes the shade, he is given "a sun," and then he must add shade. If he does not add, he is given shade from above, and so forth until he is rewarded with eternal *Dvekut* [adhesion].

However, we must exert excessively to receive the shade and say it is a holy shade, that all this shade came from above and not from the *Sitra Achra*, that it was given so he would be able to assume faith. At that time it is called "shadow of faith" and it is holy, as in, "The ways of the Lord are straight, the righteous walk in them and the wicked," etc.

This is the meaning of making the thatch from the waste of barn and winery. Baal HaSulam explained that *Goren* [barn] comes from the words *Ger Anochi* [I am a foreigner], and *Yekev* [winery] from the words, *Nokev Shem Hashem* [puncturing the name of the Lord]. To interpret the words of Baal HaSulam, the thatch is the shadow of faith, called "faith above reason." This is opposite to reason, for reason brings him into waste, to barn, and to winery.

That is, from the perspective of reason, the way the corporeal eyes see it, there is room for waste of born and winery. This in itself makes a shadow, and he sits under it. That is, he makes for himself a seat out of all those lowest and worst things, and through the waste observes the *Mitzva* [commandment] of *Sukkah*.

Most importantly, he derives joy from this *Mitzva* because faith above reason is called "joy of *Mitzva*." It follows that all the quandaries and questions that exist in reality are corrected in the *Sukkah*, for without them it is impossible to make a thatch.

And one must be a good guest in this regard and say, "All that the landlord has done, he has done only for me." That is, one must say with the mouth that everything that is happening in the world—that there are people who suffer and are mistreated—is only so that I can receive the good, meaning to keep faith. Even though I see the bad in people, it is in order to be able to assume the burden of the kingdom of heaven.

Moreover, it is to say that others will suffer pain only so I can receive. In truth, it is hard to say this. But if a person works specifically in order to bestow contentment upon his maker, then he himself is completely inconsequential. Instead, everything is only for the Creator. At that time, if the person does not stand in the middle, then everyone can say that when he says, "The landlord has troubled himself only for me," meaning so that I could continue with the work of faith, is only for the Creator and not for himself.

When a person is concerned with pleasures, it is difficult to deceive oneself and say that the whole world was created only for him. But when a person is concerned with the sake of the

Letter No. 36

Creator, it is not so difficult to believe, since the self is completely inconsequential.

It follows from all the above that the thatch, called "shade," is made specifically from the waste of barn and winery. This is the meaning of what we say in the prayer inside the *Sukkah*, "And to take refuge from current and torrent." It means that faith saves a person from all the harm doers, since harm doers are alien thoughts and alien views, and faith is built specifically on waste. Only in this way is there refuge from current and torrent; otherwise one flows with the currents of the world.

The torrent is something that sustains the earth, since people who are still are nourished only by reason, and only reason sustains them. Where reason does not reach, they cannot hold out, and this reason keeps these people still.

But one who wishes to be as the vegetative must not accept this reason as support, since that torrent is unsuitable for one who wishes to walk on the path of truth. And if a person fails and takes support from that reason, he will immediately suffer a descent and a fall to the bottom of hell.

However, the still can keep them and do not suffer any falls. This is why they always seek reason, to support their work. In order not to fail in this reason, which is called "torrent," there is power in the above-mentioned thatch, as we say, "to take refuge from current and torrent." This settles the questions, and may we be rewarded with the shadow of faith.

In order to understand the matter more clearly, I will copy for you an article from a letter of Baal HaSulam for you to delve in and nourish your souls. These are his words: "And by the way, I will clarify for you the meaning of the charity for the poor, which is so praised in *The Zohar*, the *Tikkunim*, and by our sages: There is an organ in man with which it is forbidden to work. Even if the smallest of the small desires to work with it still exists in man, that organ remains afflicted and stricken by the Creator. It is called 'poor,' for its entire sustenance and provision are by others working for it and pitying it.

"This is the meaning of the words, 'Anyone who sustains a single soul from Israel, it is as though he sustains an entire world.' Since the organ depends on others, it has no more than its own sustenance. And still, the Creator regards it as though he sustained an entire world, that this itself is the entire blessing of the world and everything in it, multiplied and completed solely by the force of that poor soul, which is sustained by the work of other organs.

"This is the meaning of 'And He took him outside and said, 'Now look toward the heavens …' and he believed in the Lord and reckoned it to him as righteousness.' That is, by taking it outside, there was some desire to work with this organ; this is why He forbade him the work. This is why it was said, 'Now look toward the heavens.' At the same time, he was given the promise of the blessing of the seed.

"These are tantamount to two opposites in the same subjects, since all his seed, which is to be blessed, necessarily comes from this organ. Thus, when he is not working, how will he find a seed?

"This is the meaning of 'And he believed in the Lord,' meaning that he accepted those two receptions as they were, both the complete prohibition on the work, and the promise of the blessing of the seed. And how did he receive them? This is why he concludes, 'And [he] reckoned it to him as righteousness,' meaning as the form of charity [*Tzedakah* means both "charity" and "righteousness"] for a poor [person] who is sustained by the work of others.

"This is the meaning of the two sayings of our sages: One (person) thought that the Creator would treat him with righteousness, meaning keep and sustain him without work, and one thought that Abraham would act with righteousness toward the Creator. Both are the words of the loving God, for prior to the correction, that organ is in heaven, and the charity is counted for the lower one. At the end of his correction it is achievable, and then the *Tzedakah* is counted for the upper one. Know and sanctify for it is true." Thus far his words.

I ask that each of you will write to me the meaning of the above words of Baal HaSulam, for it is a wonderful article.

Letter No. 36

And now let us arrange the work of the winter, which is the time of working during the long nights. Thus far I have been speaking from the perspective of the left, called "the left rejects." This requires a lot of work and toil to overcome all the obstacles and all the alien views and thoughts. However, we should also engage in the right, as our sages said, "Make your Torah [teaching] permanent and your work temporary." Torah is regarded as right, which is wholeness. A person should regard himself perfect with virtues and noble qualities. He should adapt the works in Torah and *Mitzva* as is suitable for a whole person as much as one can.

However, one must not regret it if one is unable to complete one's will. That is, if a person wishes to do plentiful good deeds and study of Torah, but cannot, he should not regret it but be happy while working in the right. He should be content with whatever he can do, and praise and thank His name for being able to do a small service to the King. Even a minute a day or a minute in two days should be to him like finding a great treasure.

And even if it is a simple deed, meaning without vitality, he should still try to be happy and derive vitality from being allowed to serve the King. This is how he should be during the study, meaning whole. This is regarded as Torah, which is right, as it is written, "On His right was a fiery law." For every opportunity, one must praise the Creator.

I heard from Baal HaSulam that with the praise and gratitude one gives to the Creator for nearing the Creator, one draws the light of His holiness below. A person should feel whole, and then he is regarded as blessed, and the blessed clings to the blessed. But when a person regards himself as cursed, the cursed does not cling to the cursed, as our sages said.

Therefore, you must regard yourselves as whole while performing Torah and *Mitzvot* [commandments]. At that time you must not find any flaw in you, as it is written, "Anyone in whom there is a flaw shall not approach." This is called "Torah," meaning wholeness.

But only Torah is also not good, as our sages said, "He who engages only in Torah, it is as though he has no God," as it is said, "And many days to Israel without a true God" (*Avoda Zara* 17).

"Days" is regarded as wholeness, meaning Torah. "Many" means that he engages only in Torah, and then he is "without a true God." It is so because in the left, specifically this work guides on the path of truth. This is the meaning of "It is good to study Torah together with conducts, for toiling in both mitigates iniquity," and "Any Torah without work is eventually annulled and induces iniquity."

You might ask, "Why does Torah alone not only not mitigate, but also induce iniquity?" The reason is that if we do not walk on the path of truth, we remain as, "If they are not rewarded, a potion of death." And that work, discerned as the kingdom of heaven, only this discernment is regarded as work and labor. This is why our sages said that specifically toiling in both mitigates iniquity. But "Do little work and plentiful study; make your Torah permanent and your work temporary," because most of the day, a person must walk on the right, and a little bit of the day in the work of purity in mind and heart.

I will end my letter with hope that we will be rewarded with eternal *Dvekut* with His name.

Baruch Shalom
Son of Baal HaSulam

Letter No. 37

October 25, 1957

...As for separating love of friends from the work of the Creator, I do not understand it at all because it was never the custom with Baal HaSulam to connect those two together.

On the contrary, it was always forbidden to speak words of Torah or of states of greatness and smallness among the friends. Our way has always been, "Walk humbly." It was barely permitted to speak of matters of work among the friends, as said in several of Baal HaSulam's essays in that regard.

Rather, the devotion of the friends was that of ordinary people, where each one cares only about his friend's corporeality, not about his spirituality. Drawing closer among the friends was actually through meals and drinking of wine, not through words of Torah.

Therefore, I am not sure what innovations you are trying to make. Perhaps until now you believed that for love of friends there shouldn't be discussions or engagements in matters of work, and now you know for sure that this is the *only* way it should be, meaning by walking humbly.

The way is as one who goes to his friend's occasion. He doesn't think of himself—whether or not he is in a good mood—but must take part in his friend's joy. He must not frown, but show a happy face. It is the same here: bonding among the friends should be such that each wishes to delight his friend, and precisely with corporeal things, since precisely here is the matter of "Buy yourself a friend."

"Make for yourself a rav" is a different story. That is, sometimes among the friends, one wishes to execute, "Make for yourself a rav" toward another. However, this is specifically among friends who have great care and strict rigor, and not everyone is suitable for it. But this is no longer considered "love of friends," meaning what love of friends requires, since there is no connection to the work, as you wrote to me.

Baruch Shalom HaLevi
Son of Baal HaSulam

Letter No. 38

January 1958

Who Is the Self?

We should explain who is the person that we say must be a servant of the Creator, and in return for which he will receive reward. After all, man consists of 248 organs and the soul of life, which sustains the entire body. The question is, "Who is the operator, the mind, the heart, or the soul of life that sustains them? And what is the self, which was promised to receive a good reward in the future through good deeds?"

The verse says, "And God created the man in His own image." The term creation applies specifically to something new, meaning a reality existence from absence, where the Creator has created something new that did not exist before He has created it. Our sages interpreted that this reality is called "desire to receive pleasure." This is a lack and emptiness that must now be filled. There was no lack before He has created it, as before this creation there was only wholeness because it cannot be said that the Creator contains a lack. Therefore, this is the only thing that is new, meaning the will to receive.

Creation of the Will to Receive

The need to create the will to receive is because they interpreted that the purpose of creation was to do good to His creations. The Creator wishes to impart His goodness in order to delight the creatures, and consequently, creation must contain be a *Kli* [vessel] for reception of pleasure. It is impossible to receive pleasure if there is no need and lack for it, for then we do not feel any pleasure.

This is similar to a person treating his friend to a good meal, but he has no appetite and therefore cannot enjoy the meal, for only the craving for the food determines the measure of pleasure in the meal. For this reason, in order for the creatures to enjoy His gifts, He has imprinted in the creatures a nature of always wanting to receive pleasure.

This discernment that exists in a person, namely the desire to receive pleasure, is the whole of man which the Creator has created. Everything we speak of with regard to man is nothing more than the desire to receive. It was said about him that he must engage in Torah and *Mitzvot* [commandments], and in the future he will be granted eternal pleasure. That is, the desire to receive pleasure will be rewarded, at the end of its work, with receiving all the pleasure that the Creator contemplated giving to it.

The desire to receive was given organs to serve it, and through which it is to receive pleasure. That is, they bring it pleasure. These are the hands, legs, sight, hearing, and so forth. They are all servants, meaning that they all serve man. In other words, the will to receive is regarded as the master, and all the organs are its servants. It also has a butler, appointed over his servants, monitoring and making sure that they all work only toward the desired purpose of bringing pleasure, for it is the wish of the landlord, called the "will to receive."

Should one of the servants be missing, the pleasure associated with that servant will be missing, too. Thus, if a person is deaf, he cannot enjoy the sound of singing. If he is anosmic [lacking the sense of smell], he cannot enjoy the fragrance of perfumes. And should he lack the intellect, which is appointed over all the servants, like the manager of the business watching over all the servants, the whole business will go awry and could inflict losses.

This is like a business owner who has many employees but a poor manager. Instead of profiting, he might lose. But the owner remains even when he has no manager, as though the manager is sick and cannot run the business, but the owner of the business is still alive.

It is likewise here. If a person has no intellect, called "servant," but the owner is present, meaning that the desire to receive pleasure is not lost because of it, and the aspiration to enjoy remains—but lacks the ability to scrutinize—then he might sell a big pleasure in return for a small one. For example, if this mindless one is craving a sweet, and the shopkeeper tells him, "Give me ten pounds and I'll give you the sweet," if he is mindless, he might give him ten pounds for the sweet because he cannot evaluate the price of the sweet he wants.

Similarly, he could cause harm, break tools, and tear clothes because he thinks it will give him some sort of pleasure. Do not be surprised that there can be pleasure in harming. It is said about Aristotle, the great philosopher, that he burned a big and expensive house because he wanted to commemorate his name, meaning that his name would remain for posterity. He thought that because the mansion was a valuable thing, his name would be remembered because everyone would remember the big mansion that Aristotle burnt.

Thus, we see that people find pleasure in harming, too. Also, any deed that a mindless person does must give him pleasure, and that pleasure compels him to do some things even though they are bad, since he cannot weigh if it is worthwhile to cause great harm in return for a small pleasure.

It follows from all the above that the essence of man is the will to receive pleasure, and nothing else. That is, the mind, too, is not man's body, but as was said above.

Concerning Work

The will to receive, which is man's essence, is opposite from the Creator, namely that the Creator is the giver. In order to have equivalence of form, meaning that man's actions will also be only to bestow—or the pleasures he will receive from the Creator will not be whole because he will experience shame in them, since one who receives a gift from another is ashamed to look at his face and feels torment upon the reception of the pleasure—for this reason we were given the Torah and *Mitzvot*, by which we acquire a new power of wanting to bestow contentment upon the Creator. At that time he will be fit to receive all the pleasures from the Creator without any shame because he will not receive all those pleasures because he wants to enjoy, but because he is doing the Creator's will by accepting the pleasure, as the purpose of creation was for the creatures to receive pleasure in the world. Indeed, the whole work is about achieving this degree of wanting to receive pleasure only for the purpose of a *Mitzva* [commandment/good deed].

I repeated the words that I said verbally so that you can remember them, for these are the very basics.

From your friend who wishes you and your family all the best,

Baruch Shalom HaLevi Ashlag

Letter No. 38b

Who is the self that we say is the servant of the Creator, and who is the recipient of the reward that was promised, where by good deeds he will be rewarded with the good future?

All those things were said only about man, the apex of creation, as it is written, "And God created the man in His own image." Creation means something new, which is existence from absence. This is the desire to receive pleasure, meaning the creation of a deficiency that always craves to satisfy the lack with pleasure.

In order for the sensation of pleasure to be utterly complete, he was given work in Torah and *Mitzvot* [commandments], by which he is to be perfected and become fit to receive the pleasure without any deficiency. That is, one who receives pleasure from another feels torment along with the reception of the pleasure due to the shame, called "bread of shame." By being perfected with virtues he will have the ability to receive pleasure without the feeling of shame.

It follows that man is called "desire to receive pleasure," and the desire to receive pleasure was given hands and legs to serve it, as well as the most esteemed servant, called "intellect." All those servants bring him pleasure, and if one of the servants is missing, the pleasure associated with that servant is missing.

If he is lacking the most esteemed servant, meaning the intellect, he still feels pleasure and pain, except that he might swap, and instead of receiving great pleasure, he might receive minute pleasures. That is, he cannot judge with his intellect which is more worthwhile in terms of quantity and quality, and might therefore cause harm and break tools.

Even an insane person intends to receive pleasure through his actions, or he would not do this bad thing, but there is a reason that causes him to do this foul thing. Everything that he thinks might bring him pleasure, he does immediately, and does not have the mental capacity to weigh with his intellect if this is a real reason or an imaginary one.

And do not wonder how one can derive pleasure from breaking or spoiling. It is said about the philosopher, Aristotle, that he burned a big and expensive house because he wanted to commemorate his name, meaning that his name would remain forever because everyone would remember his name through this act. That is, everyone would remember that Aristotle burned the big mansion.

It follows that although he did a bad thing, he had a reason. That is, he felt pleasure in doing the bad thing that he did by commemorating his name. Likewise, anyone who is insane lacks the power of critique, but the essence of man still exists.

Also, there is pleasure in avoiding pain, since this is already a calculation for the future, meaning that he is acting now in order to avoid suffering later. This already belongs to the intellect, meaning that the intellect reminds him that this is something bad. And since his intellect is already flawed, he cannot put thoughts together and therefore feels only the present and not the past or the future. It turns out that the mind is only man's servant, like the rest of the servants, but the essence of man is the lack that craves to receive pleasure, meaning that he feels complete wholeness in the pleasure.

The will to receive exists in all the animals, but only man was given the ability to feel another. That is, he can share with his friend and sympathize with his friend, meaning derive pleasure from his friend's pleasure, as well as suffer when his friend suffers.

It follows that man was given an additional place to receive pleasure—outside his own body. Animals are impressed only by themselves, and not by others, but the speaking has been given the ability to feel another, too (with the exception of certain animals that were given this sensation by nature, but they feel it specifically toward the same species).

In addition to the speaking, a person from Israel was given a power—the sensation of Godliness. It is in this respect that it was said, "You are called man." It is an additional power to the speaking, meaning that he can regret the exile of the *Shechina* [Divinity] and rejoice with the glory of heaven that appears in the world. It therefore follows that a person from Israel was given another place to receive pleasure, additional to the speaking. This is the main pleasure for which the world was created—to receive the pleasure of the sensation of Godliness.

All the pleasures that exist in the world come from the Creator, since the Creator illuminates in all those things, but why are these pleasures called "corporeal pleasures"? It is because a person can enjoy them without having to include the Creator in them. That is, even if one does not feel Godliness, when he does not believe in the Creator, he can still enjoy all those things.

But tasting the flavor of Torah and *Mitzvot* is impossible without assuming the burden of faith. To the extent that the light of faith shines for him, to that extent the pleasure in Torah and *Mitzvot* grows for him. This is why we call the pleasure in Torah and *Mitzvot* "spiritual pleasure."

One can feel corporeal pleasure even when one has no relation to Torah and *Mitzvot*, since a person cannot live without vitality, for every person must taste the taste of pleasure, since the nature of creation is a desire to receive pleasure, for the thought of creation, called "His desire to do good to His creations," imprinted in the creatures the need to enjoy. When one sees no pleasure in the present or in the future, he must commit suicide because his coming into this world was only in order to receive pleasure.

And since man was given the work of choice, to reject the bad and choose Torah and *Mitzvot*—for only at the time of choice is it possible to nurture good qualities that can receive the true good—there was given a time of concealment during the work. That is, one does not feel the taste of pleasure in Torah and *Mitzvot*, since only during concealment is there choice.

In the meantime, until one is rewarded with the flavor of vitality of spirituality, he takes all his vitality only from corporeal things, whose pleasure is limited. But this is only a transition until he comes to taste spiritual flavor, so he must feel only the flavor of corporeal things. But even in those corporeal things it is possible to accustom oneself to receive pleasure for the Creator.

The will to receive is called "man's body." This is why it does not undergo any changes, but rather remains in that state of always wanting to receive pleasure.

Clothing: Anything that undergoes change is not the essence of the object, for an object does not undergo any change. Hence, all those things from which one derives pleasure are regarded as garments. For example, today he is wearing this garment and tomorrow another garment. There are clothes with which one works in the kitchen, and there are clothes with which one serves the king.

Any pleasure is regarded as light, and there is no light without a *Kli* [vessel], which is a spiritual thing, and any spiritual thing must be clothed in some corporeal clothing, but only through clothing can one receive the pleasure that is found within it. Therefore, we were given many garments in which there are pleasures, such as eating, drinking, royal apparel or simply respect that one is given, or delight from intellectual things or from Torah and *Mitzvot*. Every person has different attires, and no person is like another. However, there is one thing where all are the same—everyone wants pleasure.

Changing attires: The changes in a person—who sometimes wants to enjoy honor, and sometimes only lust, and sometimes Torah and *Mitzvot*—come from many reasons. Sometimes it is hereditary, meaning that the forefathers had chosen to enjoy certain pleasures, and it passes from generation to generation. This is the meaning of ancestry, where the good qualities pass from the father of the family to the following generations.

Also, we undergo changes through books and authors—where a person is impressed by the environment. As the tree sucks from what is around it, which is why the thorns and other bad things around the tree are always cut off, man, too, is the tree of the field—sucking from its environment. This is why he is impressed by authors. That is, he has good friends and he accustoms himself to enjoy the things that the friends say are good or are bad. Or, there is the environment of books, meaning what he learns and reads in books, and the books state which is a good thing and which is a bad thing, and then the person follows their advice.

Letter No. 39

March 6, 1958, Manchester

Hello and all the best to my friend,

I received ten pounds for Purim, which is half a shekel. Ten gerah [a coin that was used in Israel in ancient times. Twenty shekels are one gerah] is a shekel, and half of it is ten. It is written in holy *Zohar* that half a shekel is called ten, which is a stone with which to weigh the contribution to the Lord (*Ki Tissa*, item 4).

We should interpret the words of the holy *Zohar*. Half a shekel means that when a person begins to weigh how to return to the Creator, when he knows that he has many iniquities and transgressions, the holy *Zohar* says about this that the person should know that he is always regarded as half and half. That is, he is half merits and half faults, and he can always choose to sentence to a scale of merit. It is as our sages said, "One should always see oneself as half guilty and half not guilty. If he has performed one *Mitzva* [good deed/commandment], he is happy for he has sentenced himself and the entire world to a scale of merit," etc.

We should interpret the reason as our sages said, "He who is greater than his friend, his desire is greater than him." It is so because if he is not given a greater evil inclination, he will not have the choice, since if the good is more than the bad then he does not have choice, as choosing is precisely when both are equal and the person decides.

By that you will understand what our sages said, "In the future [end of correction], the Creator brings the evil inclination and slaughters it before the righteous and before the wicked. To the righteous, it seems like a high mountain. To the wicked, it seems like a hairsbreadth." We should understand who is right, meaning what is the measure of the evil inclination.

However, as I have explained, the wicked have few merits, so their evil inclination is not so big, but only as a hairsbreadth. This is so because in order for it to be half and half, when there is little good there must be little bad. But the righteous have many merits so their evil inclination must be big, as well. Therefore, in the righteous, the evil inclination is a high mountain.

By that you will understand people's questions about the verse, "Come unto Pharaoh for I have hardened his heart." Does it mean that the Creator denied him the choice by hardening his heart? According to what I have explained, it is the opposite. By the Creator hardening his heart he can make a choice once more, for when Pharaoh said, "The Lord is the righteous, and I and my people are the wicked," it means that he has already sentenced to a scale of merit and he is entirely good and has nothing more to do. For this reason, in accord with his good, the Creator had to increase the evil inclination, as our sages said, "All who is greater than his friend, his desire is greater than him." Therefore, when Creator hardened his heart, he could make a choice once more.

May the Lord grant us two portions—healing and salvation.

From your friend who wishes you and your family all the best,

Baruch Shalom HaLevi Ashlag

Letter No. 40

31ˢᵗ day of the Omer Count, May 6, 1958, Manchester

To the students, may they live,

I received a telegram from ... that we won. Let us hope that we will win the war on the inclination, too—that here, too, we will succeed and achieve the goal of bringing contentment to the Maker.

It is about time that we started moving forward toward our sacred goal like mighty strong men. It is known that the paved road that leads to the goal is love of friends, by which one shifts to love of the Creator. And in the matter of love, it is through "Buy yourself a friend." In other words, through actions, one buys one's friend's heart. And even if he sees that his friend's heart is like a stone, it is no excuse. If he feels that he is suitable for being his friend in the work, then he must buy him through deeds.

Each gift (and a gift is determined as such when he knows that his friend will enjoy it, whether in words, in thought, or in action. However, each gift must be out in the open, so that his friend will know about it, and with thoughts, one does not know that his friend was thinking of him. Hence, words are required, too, meaning he should tell him that he is thinking of him and cares about him. And that, too, should be about what his friend loves, meaning what his friend likes. One who doesn't like sweets, but pickles, cannot treat his friend to pickles, but specifically to sweets, since this is what his

Letter No. 40

friend likes. And from that, we should understand that something could be unimportant to one, but more important than anything to another.) that he gives to his friend is like a bullet that makes a hollow in the stone. And although the first bullet only scratches the stone, when the second bullet hits the same place, it already makes a notch, and the third one makes a hole.

And through the bullets that he shoots repeatedly, the hole becomes a hollow in his friend's heart of stone, where all the presents gather. And each gift becomes a spark of love until all the sparks of love accumulate in the hollow of the stony heart and become a flame.

The difference between a spark and a flame is that where there is love, there is open disclosure, meaning a disclosure to all the peoples that the fire of love is burning in him. And the fire of love burns all the transgressions one meets along the way.

And should you ask, "What can one do if he feels that he has a heart of stone toward his friend?" Forgive me for writing, "Each and every one feels that he has a heart of stone," I mean except for the friends who feel and know that they have no objection that their friend will love them and will give them presents (not necessarily in action, but at least in good words and special attention only to him). I am referring only to those who feel that they have very cold hearts in regard to loving their friends, or those who had a heart of flesh but the coldness from the friends affected them, as well, and their hearts have frozen still.

The advice is very simple: The nature of fire is that when rubbing stones against each other, a fire starts. This is a great rule, since "From *Lo Lishma* [not for Her sake] one comes to *Lishma* [for Her sake]." And this is so particularly when the act is *Lishma*, meaning imparting a gift to one's friend, and the aim is *Lo Lishma*.

This is so because one gives a gift only to one that we know and recognize as someone we love. It follows that the aim of the gift is like gratitude for the love that his friend gives him. However, if one gives a gift to a stranger, meaning he doesn't feel that his friend is close to his heart, then he has nothing to be grateful for. It follows that the aim is *Lo Lishma*, meaning ... the intention that should be.

Ostensibly, it could be said that this is called "charity," since he pities his friend when he sees that there is no one who is speaking to him and greets him, and this is why he does that to him. Indeed, there is a prayer for it—that the Creator will help him by making him feel the love of his friend and make his friend close to his heart. Thus, through the deeds, he is rewarded with the aim, as well.

But while at the time of doing the giver of the gift intended that the gift to his friends would only be as charity (even if he is giving his time for his friend, since it is sometimes more important to a person than his money, as it is said, "One cares for his lack of money but not for his lack of time." However, regarding time, each has his own value, since there are people who make one pound an hour, and there is more or less. And likewise with their spirituality—how much spirituality they make in an hour, etc.), then one is testifying about himself that he isn't aiming for love of friends, meaning that through the action, the love between them will increase.

And only when both of them intend for a gift and not for charity, through the wearing out of the hearts, even of the strongest ones, each will bring out warmth from the walls of his heart, and the warmth will ignite the sparks of love until a clothing of love will form. Then, both of them will be covered under one blanket, meaning a single love will surround and envelop the two of them, as it is known that *Dvekut* [adhesion] unites two into one.

And when one begins to feel the love of his friend, joy and pleasure immediately begin to awaken in him, for the rule is that a novelty entertains. His friend's love for him is a new thing for him because he always knew that he was the only one who cared for his own well being. But the minute he discovers that his friend cares for him, it evokes within him immeasurable joy, and he can no longer care for himself, since man can toil only where he feels pleasure.

Letter No. 40

And since he is beginning to feel pleasure in caring for his friend, he naturally cannot think of himself.

We see that in nature, there is love until the yearning becomes unbearable. And if you wish to ask, "How can it be that through love, a person will develop a desire to revoke his own existence?" there is only one answer to that: "Love deviates from the right path." In other words, it is irrational and is considered not right.

Only then, when there is such a love, each and every one walks in a world that is all good and feels that the Creator has blessed his share. Then the "blessed adheres to the blessed" and he is rewarded with *Dvekut* with Him forever.

And through the love, one is willing to annul his entire reality. It is known that as a whole, man divides into two parts: reality and the existence of reality. Reality means that a person feels himself as a deficiency, a desire to receive pleasure. The existence of reality is the delight and pleasure that he receives, by which the body is nourished and can persist. Otherwise, he will have to destroy himself and become absent from the world. This is the meaning of, "Which God has created," meaning the reality, "To do," referring to the existence of reality.

The existence of reality divides into three parts:

1) Necessity, without which reality will be cancelled. In other words, he must eat at least a piece of dry bread and a cup of water a day, and sleep for a few hours on a bench, with his clothes on, and not even at home, but outside, on the street or in a field. During the rains, to avoid getting wet and cold, he should go inside some cave to sleep. His clothes, too, can be rags, and this is enough for him because he wants only the existence of reality and nothing more.

2) Being ordinary, important bourgeois—having a home and furniture, household appliances, respectable clothes, etc.

3) Having a desire to be like the well-to-do who have many houses and servants, fine-looking furniture, and fine-looking paraphernalia. And although he cannot obtain what he wants, his eyes and heart

aspire to it and his only hope is to lead a life of luxury, and he toils and labors only to achieve the level of the well-to-do.

And there is a fourth discernment within all those three above-mentioned discernments: If he has already made enough for the day, then he no longer cares about tomorrow. Rather, he regards each day as all the years of his life, like seventy years. And as man's nature is to care for his necessities for all his seventy years, but not for the time past his demise, each day is regarded by him as his whole life and he thinks that he will not live longer than that.

And if he is revived the next day, it is as if he has been reincarnated and must mend what he corrupted in the first incarnation. That is, if he borrowed money from someone, he has become indebted. So tomorrow—in the next life—he pays him, and it is considered a merit. In the next life, he primarily mends all the debts that he caused others or that others have caused him. And the day after tomorrow is considered a third incarnation, and so on.

And now we will explain the above-mentioned matter, that through love, man is willing to make concessions. Sometimes, when a person has love for the Creator, he is willing to relinquish the third discernment, meaning the life of luxuries, since he wants to dedicate time and energy to give some gifts to the Creator by which to buy the love of the Creator (as mentioned above regarding love of friends). In other words, although he still doesn't have love for the Creator, it shines for him as surrounding light that it is worthwhile to acquire the love of the Creator.

Sometimes a person feels that to buy the love of the Creator, he is willing, if necessary, to concede the second discernment, too, meaning the life of important bourgeois, and to live on necessity alone.

Sometimes one feels the greatness of the love of the Creator to an extent that if need be, he would agree to relinquish even the first part—the basic needs of life—even though by that, his own existence would be cancelled if he did not give the body the nourishment it needs.

And sometimes a person is willing to give up his very existence; he wants to give his body so that through it, the name of the Creator will be sanctified in the masses, if he had a chance to carry it out. It is as Baal HaSulam said, "One should follow the quality of Rabbi Akiva who said, 'My whole life, I regretted this verse, 'With all your soul.' When would I come to keep it?'"

Now we can understand the words of our sages, "'And you shall love ... with all your heart,' with both your inclinations. And, 'With all your soul' means 'even if He takes your soul.' 'And with all your might' means 'with all your possessions.'" As we said above, the first degree of love is the existence of reality, meaning the nourishment of the body by property and possessions, means relinquishing the three above-mentioned discernments in the existence of reality. The second degree is, "With all your soul," meaning conceding one's very existence.

And we can keep that through the good inclination, meaning by coercion, when one lets the body understand that there is more delight and pleasure in delighting and giving to the Creator than in delighting and giving to oneself. However, without delight and pleasure, one cannot do anything. When one afflicts himself, we must say that in return he receives some kind of pleasure, or that he feels or hopes to feel the pleasure during the act, since suffering cleanses, so afterwards he will be rewarded with a wonderful pleasure in return for the suffering. In other words, either he will obtain pleasure in this world or he will take pleasure in believing that he will receive pleasure in the next world. Put differently, either he has pleasure in the form of inner light or in the form of surrounding light—from the future.

However, one should not think that one can do anything without pleasure. In fact, (one should know that) there are many discernments in *Lishma*, meaning in bestowal: "bestowing in order to bestow" means receiving pleasure from giving to the Creator. "Bestowing in order to receive" means that he gives to the Creator and by that will receive something else, whatever it may be—this world, the next world, attainments or high degrees.

However, one should be bestowing in order to bestow, meaning derive wondrous pleasure from giving to the Creator, as it truly is for those who are rewarded with it. One should plead to the Creator from the bottom of his heart to give him this feeling of loving the Creator because of His greatness.

And if he is still not rewarded, he should believe and compel his body that this is a wonderful pleasure and of great importance, and to love the Creator because of His greatness and sublimity. But one should know one thing: without pleasure, one cannot do anything to the fullest.

Let us return to the above-mentioned, "'With all your heart,' with both your inclinations," meaning that one should be complete in the love for the Creator; that is, that the evil inclination, too, will agree to bestow upon Him.

I will be brief due to the approaching Shabbat. I think that ... will be able to get answers to two letters that I received from him, and which I truly enjoyed. I am surprised that ... who was used to writing me letters, it's been a while since I received a letter from him. Please let me know if he is well and healthy. Also, many thanks to ... for his letters, which I receive from time to time from him, and to ... for the telegram. I suppose ... doesn't have my address.

Your friend,

Baruch Shalom, son of Baal HaSulam, the Rav Ashlag

Letter No. 41

May 23, 1958, Manchester

Hello and all the best to my dear friend,

Today I received your letter together with 18; may you taste the flavor of the pleasantness of the brightness and sweetness of the one who lives [also written as 18] forever. We should aspire for everything, for aspiring for good things is called a "prayer," which is a deficiency, when one feels that he lacks this thing and the Creator will grant him. That is, a person should await the time when he feels in his heart all the good things that the Creator has promised us upon the reception of the Torah, as it is written, "And now if you indeed obey My voice ... and you shall be unto Me a virtue from among all the nations ... and you will be unto Me a kingdom of priests and a holy nation."

We see that normally, one who has a lot of property and many possessions is high spirited. But we, the chosen people, as it is written, "You have chosen us from among all the nations," so each one from the people of Israel should have been always happy and elated. However, as long as one was not rewarded with feeling in the heart all those good things, a person is not impressed by uttering, "You have chosen us."

This is so because receiving the Torah refers primarily to the internality of the Torah, which is clothed in externality. The internality of the Torah is called "the names of the Creator." This means that the general name of the Creator is "Good Who Does

Good." Since the Creator gives many pleasures that are included in doing good to His creations, the Torah is names of pleasures, where each pleasure has a different name. That is, the general name, Good Who Does Good, spreads over several details, and this internality dresses in the outer Torah.

Man should crave to be rewarded with the internality of the Torah, for then we feel all the good things that the Creator has promised us, so when we say, "You have chosen us," it means that we already feel all the good possessions with which we have been granted, and for which we are called a "kingdom of priests and a holy nation."

This is the meaning of, "And the whole of the people were seeing the voices." When the voice of the Creator is heard in the heart, that feeling is as sufficient as actual seeing "for man shall not see Me and live." However, by seeing the voices, meaning by the voice of the Creator spreading into the heart, not into the ear—for the ear is external and only the heart is the man—hence, the voice of the Creator must be felt in the heart. This is when it is called "seeing the voices," and then each one lives in a world that is utterly good, and the heart feels the "You have chosen us" because it tastes the brightness of the upper pleasantness and the sweet savor of the light of the Creator spreads throughout his heart. This is when we see, "Happy are you in this world and happy are you in the next world."

Due to the sanctity of the Sabbath and the festival I cannot elaborate now. May the Lord help us be granted the complete reception of the Torah.

From your friend who wishes you and your family the very best,

Baruch Shalom HaLevi Ashlag

Son of Baal HaSulam

Letter No. 42

Hello and all the best to my friend,

I wrote you a letter before Passover, but since the address was incorrect, the letter returned. Now, before the festival of Shavuot, which is the time of the giving of our Torah, I shall write you a few lines...

The preparation for the Torah, as it pertains to us, is the matter of fear, as it is written, "And the people encamped, as one man with one heart." This means that they all had one goal, which is to benefit the Creator. It follows...

We should understand how they could be as one man with one heart, since we know what our sages said, "As their faces are not similar to one another, their views are not similar to one another," so how could they be as one man with one heart?

Answer: If we are saying that each one cares for himself, it is impossible to be as one man, since they are not similar to one another. However, if they all annul their selves and worry only about the benefit of the Creator, they have no individual views, since the individuals have all been canceled and have entered the single authority.

This is the meaning of what is written, "The view of landlords is opposite from the view of Torah." It is so because the view of Torah is cancelling the authority, as our sages said, "'If a man dies in a tent,' the Torah exists only in one who puts himself to death," meaning he puts himself to death, namely his self-gratification, and does everything only for the Creator.

This is called "preparation for reception of the Torah," since it is written that it is forbidden to teach idol-worshippers the Torah, as it is written, "He shall not do so to any nation, and they do not know the ordinances" ...

Letter No. 43

December 10, 1958, Jaffa-Tel-Aviv

To my friends in Gateshead, may they live long,

I am sending my Hanukah greetings: May we feel the light of Hanukah in our hearts, by which our eyes will open and our hearts will rejoice.

I shall write what I said concerning Hanukah: It is known that the candles cannot burn until three conditions are met 1) the candle, which is the vessel in which the oil is placed; 2) the oil; 3) the wick [a woven cord (in a candle or oil lamp) that draws fuel up into the flame]. When those three are brought together we can enjoy their light.

We should interpret the three above discernments in the work and ethics. The *Kli* [vessel] where the oil and wick are placed is the body, called a "candle."

In the labor in Torah and *Mitzvot*, one feels contrast in His providence, concerning things that are not revealed to him, namely that the guidance of the world is in benevolence. According to man's view, the Creator should have guided the world differently, meaning that His goodness would be revealed to all. Thus, it contradicts man's reason. This is called a *Petillah* [wick], from the word *Petaltol* [winding] and from the word *Pesulah* [flawed], since it is flawed to think such thoughts.

The clarity and awakening that bring one to crave Torah and work, and to feel the sweetness and pleasantness in Torah and work, are called "oil."

If one of them is missing, it is impossible to enjoy their light. Likewise, when the body consists of labor and clarity, one is rewarded with attaining the light of the Creator, which emerges specifically through the two of them. And just as there is nothing to illuminate once the oil and wick have burned out, and it becomes dark, once the labor and clarity are over he has no light and it becomes dark for him once more.

If he wishes to obtain more light, he must try to find more labor, called "wick," and more clarity, called "oil," since the light has nothing through which to seep and hold. The reason for this is that there is a rule: "The reward is according to the effort."

The clarity, called "oil," comes mainly through faith, which is one's prevailing over the evil inclination that brings one to exertions and contradictions to the external intellect. This is called "tests" in the work of the Creator.

After prevailing over it, one is rewarded with receiving the light of the Creator that illuminates to man's soul, and then there is no more room for contradictions. This is called the "light of Hanukah." That is, he is rewarded with open providence, that His guidance is benevolent to His creations.

By that we can interpret what our sages said about the Hanukah candle, "It is commanded from sundown until all feet have vanished from the market" (Shabbat, 21). By this they implied the above-mentioned manner.

The "sun" refers to the shining light. *Regel* [foot] comes from the word *Meraglim* [spies], when he spies after His guidance. It is as was written about the spies, "See what the land is like ... is it good or bad?" This means testing if the upper guidance in the world is benevolent.

"Market" implies public domain. It is so because specifically in the public domain are there spies. But when a person is rewarded with entrance to the single authority, meaning that there is no other force in the world but the Creator, for "He alone does and will do all the deeds," then there is no more room for spies.

This is why they implied that we must draw the light of Hanukah so it illuminates the open providence as benevolent, "from sundown until all feet have vanished from the market," meaning from the time when he was still in darkness until all the spies are gone from the public domain, when there is no more room for spies and they have all vanished from the world.

In this way we should interpret what we say in the song, "Mighty Rock of My Salvation": "Greeks have gathered around me ... and have broken the walls of my towers and defiled all the oils." *Homat* [walls of] has the letters of *Hotam* [seal] and *Tehum* [area/zone]. "My towers" is the tower full of good abundance (*Midrash Rabah*, Chapter 8). The "wall" concerns keeping foreigners from entering the city and robbing its good.

It is likewise here—in order to avoid entrance of foreign thoughts and uninvited desires, we must make a wall by which we keep from the outer ones. This wall is called "faith," for only by faith can one be saved from all the above. This is called "zone," for thus far the outer ones can approach, but when they see that the person did not go outside the wall they return to their place.

This is so because faith is specifically above reason, and the domination of the *Sitra Achra* is specifically within the reason of the outer mind. Thus, it has no connection or contact with the person.

The *Klipa* of Greece was for the people of Israel to enjoy specifically through the external intellect, which is the damned philosophy. This contradicts faith, which is called a "wall." To the extent that they succeeded in admitting philosophy into Israel, to that extent it is regarded that they have breached the wall.

This is the meaning of "broken the walls of my towers," namely the wall around the tower full of good abundance, by which we are rewarded with open providence, that the Creator leads the world benevolently.

Through the above-mentioned breach they have "defiled all the oils," meaning that they were denied all the vitality and clarity they were granted through faith, for *Tuma'a* [impurity] comes from *Timtum* [dumbness] and *Situm* [blocking]. Finally, a miracle happened and the Creator helped them, and they were rewarded with the revealed light once more, called "light of the face."

And regarding what my friend is asking, these are his words concerning the *Shofar* [horn blown in special festivals]: The Creator ascends from the quality of judgment to the quality of mercy. In several places it is implied that the indication is to the quality of judgment, such as "At the time of ostracizing, blow the *Shofar*," etc.

The interpretation of *Yaarot Hadvash* [*The Honeycombs*—title of a book], that just as the *Shofar* awakens judgment, when a person sentences himself to a scale of sin, it means that he is telling the Creator that he wishes to take his punishment as long as he gets rid of the sin and is cleansed. By that man's body evokes mercy. Certainly, we must not doubt the words of the *Yaarot Hadvash*.

See in *The Zohar, Emor* (Say, p 99): "On judgment day, Israel need a *Shofar* and not a trumpet [other kind of horn] because a trumpet implies, wherever it is [meaning the quality of judgment, and see there in the *Sulam* [Ladder commentary]] and we need not awaken judgment." This means that the *Shofar* is the quality of mercy.

We should interpret that he brings the matter of ostracizing because the blowing of the *Shofar* is due to fact that when ostracizing, the ostracized one is under the power of the quality of judgment. In order to prevent the quality of judgment from governing him, we must awaken mercy on him, which is akin to associating the quality of judgment with mercy, and with a *Shofar*, which has the power to evoke mercy.

It is likewise with the verse, "Blow the *Shofar* in Zion," which is to warn the people to repent. Since we see that there is the quality of judgment, we must blow the *Shofar* to awaken the quality of mercy, for the *Shofar* can evoke mercy and give strength to the people to repent.

It is like a person standing on a mountain and watching. He sees from afar that an army is coming to fight with the city-people and rob its bounty, so he blows the *Shofar* so the people will assemble and go out to fight and save the city. It follows that the *Shofar* is the quality of judgment, as implied in the words of the holy *Zohar*.

And concerning the second matter that you wrote me, regarding the love of the Creator, these are your words: "Concerning the love of the Creator, it is as with anyone who loves his friend—he wants to cling to him (be with him). Similarly, with love of the Creator there should be a desire to be with the Creator and feel the pleasure of His nearness until he does not wish to part from Him.

"RASHAR Hirsh interprets that the love of the Creator is the desire in the heart to give gifts, to cajole one's maker. As with any love of people, the lower wishes to give to the loved one. Likewise, the love of the Creator is called a desire deep in the heart to give and to bring contentment to one's maker," thus far his words.

I would add to this that both are true, but we should distinguish between them in terms of time, for we should always distinguish between reality and the persistence of reality. After all, we see that when a baby is born, we see a complete reality—that the baby is alive and nothing is missing in it.

At the same time, if the newborn does not receive its necessary nourishment, that reality is certain to be cancelled, for without nourishment the baby will die. Thus, in order for reality to persist, we need nourishments by which the newborn will grow. Also, if it receives spoiled or insufficient nourishment it will be very weak.

Likewise, the love of the Creator requires both these things:

The first is the purpose, regarded as "reality," which is the love, the unification and *Dvekut* [adhesion] when one wants to be annulled before Him and has no other concern in life except to focus one's mind and heart solely on Him day and night. He has no greater torment in the world than the suffering of being separated from this connection, as it is written, "If a man gives his entire fortune for love he will be despised."

The second is the persistence of reality, so the love will not be cancelled, as well as for the love to grow and proliferate. This requires nourishment, meaning to provide food, which are called *Mitzvot* [commandments] and good deeds. To the extent that one engages in good deeds, the love between him and his maker grows. At that time the Creator, too, gives gifts, as lovers do. The gifts of the Creator are called "the revelation of the secrets of Torah," called *Maase Merkava* and *Maase Beresheet*.

It follows that both interpretations are true. Subsequently, one is rewarded with a higher degree, called "unconditional love."

The Creator will help us attain the love of the Creator.

From your friend who wishes you all the best in corporeality and spirituality.

Letter No. 44

December 10, 1958, Tel-Aviv

Hello and all the best to my dear friend,

I miss hearing from you and from your family, as well as how you sustain yourself, since prior to my departure you told me you needed success ... so I would like to know your situation.

And let me conclude with words of Torah. In the song, "Mighty Rock of My Salvation," it is written, "Greeks have gathered around me ... and have broken the walls of my towers." We should interpret that the *Klipa* [shell/peel] of Greece was that they wanted to cancel Shabbat and circumcision. Shabbat and circumcision are called "token," and the token of the covenant is called "the *Mitzva* [commandment] of faith." This is why they wanted to cancel specifically those two *Mitzvot* [plural of *Mitzva*], for by cancelling faith in the whole of Israel, all the *Mitzvot* in the Torah are cancelled by themselves.

Faith is an iron wall, meaning meticulous guard that no stranger will enter the holiness, for to the extent that one has faith, to that extent he is keeping Torah and *Mitzvot*. By keeping Torah and *Mitzvot*, we are rewarded with receiving the light that is hidden in it and feel the goodness, pleasantness, and vitality, as it is written, "for they are our lives and the length of our days."

This is the meaning of "broken the walls of my towers," meaning created a breach in the wall, called "faith." Through the *Mitzva* of faith, we are rewarded with "a tower full of good abundance," which is sweetness and the savor of the upper pleasantness that is found in the Torah. A miracle happened and the Creator helped them, and they defeated the *Klipa* of Greece, and by that were once again rewarded with the great light. This is called the "Hanukah candle," meaning the lights one receives by keeping the faith.

May we all be awarded His light together soon.

From your friend who is pleading on your behalf and on your family's behalf

Baruch Shalom HaLevi Ashlag

Son of Baal HaSulam

Letter No. 45

January 22, 1959, Tel-Aviv

Hello and all the best to my dear friend,

I hereby reply to the letter you sent on the 25th of November. You asked two questions regarding the primordial serpent: 1) Why was it punished, for we find nowhere that it was warned not to incite? 2) What is the punishment, "On your belly you will walk," with regard to the evil inclination?

It is written in *Lips of the Wise* about the verse (Genesis, 3:14), that the serpent was punished only because a mishap occurred through it, for it was not commanded not to incite. This means that the punishment is not that it deserves to be denied its power because it sinned, but for a different reason: so that others will not fail through it. It therefore follows that it was not punished because it was not commanded not to incite.

In regard to "On your belly you will walk," we should interpret that there are three degrees in holiness, called *Nefesh*, *Ruach*, *Neshama*. *Nefesh* comes from the word, *Nefisha* [rest/pause], when the vitality is so small that one cannot move at all. *Ruach* is already a measure where there is ability to move toward correction of the qualities, called *Hesed*, the right hand, and *Gevura*, the left hand, meaning he can use his hands with vitality of holiness.

Neshama means that he already has the intellect and mind of holiness, meaning that he has already been awarded the reason of holiness. This is regarded as having a *Neshama*.

The order of reception of spiritual light is as it is in corporeality. We see that when a baby is born, its vitality is so small that it cannot move by itself, but others must assist it. All it can do is lay down. Laying means that the head is not higher in virtue than the body, but rather the head is at the same level as the feet. This is called *Nefesh* in spirituality.

When the baby grows, by receiving more strength, its vitality is sufficient for it to be able to sit. Sitting indicates that it can move its hands, and by that the head grows. This is discerned as distinguishing between the level of the head from that of the body.

When he grows more, meaning when he has already obtained intellect in his head, his vitality is so great that it spreads to its legs, as well. At that time there is a big difference between the level of the body and that of the legs.

It follows that there are three degrees. However, this is so specifically in the speaking—that the head is on top, the body is lower, and the legs are the lower still—since he has intellect and thought, and in that he is higher than the animate degree. But in animals, the head and the body are on the same level, indicating that their heads are not more important than their bodies. Hence, we discern only two degrees in them, which are *Nefesh* or *Ruach*.

When they use their legs, it shows that they have great strength, which is that their body is higher than the legs. But when they have no legs it means that their vitality is very small, they were not given the vitality power of two degrees, but that the head and legs are equal.

By that we can interpret, "On your belly you will walk." That is, the *Ruach* was taken away from it, its mobility, and with that power it could incite Eve into eating from the tree of knowledge. When its legs were taken away from it and it walks on its body, called "belly," it means that its vitality is very small. This is called *Nefesh*, immobility, lacking sufficient vitality to move. By this it will not be able to harm the world so much.

Nefesh is called "female light" receiving what she is given. She cannot receive vitality on her own, but only what she receives through the bad deeds of others, and from this comes her vitality. Therefore, when a person commits transgressions and imparts upon her vitality, she has the power to make one sin.

This is the meaning of "On your belly you will walk," meaning that now it has nothing more than *Nefesh* of *Klipa* [shell]. This is why it cannot do much harm to man. But when it is given power, it grows stronger.

This is the meaning of "transgression induces transgression," since its power has increased. Therefore, now that a person has become stronger in Torah and *Mitzvot* [commandments], it is possible to defeat it and attain the real perfection.

Letter No. 46

January 25, 1959, Tel-Aviv

Hello and all the best to my friend, whom I love as my own soul,

I am writing to you what I said yesterday, on the 24th of January.

The Gemarah says about *Rosh Hashanah* [beginning of the year] for the trees: "What is the reason that (it is) on the first of *Shevat*? Rabbi Elazar said, 'Rabbi Oshaaia said, 'because the majority of the year's rains have fallen.''" And RASHI (interprets), "It is the time of rain, and the resin flows in the trees, and from now on the fruits are ripe." The *Tosfot* write that the above reason also corresponds to Beit Hillel, who concur that the fifteenth of *Shevat* is *Rosh Hashanah*. It is said in the Gemarah, "One who comes out on a *Nissan* day and sees blooming trees says, 'Blessed is He who did not deny His world of anything and created in it good creations and good trees with which to delight people.'"

We should understand, 1) what it means that "He did not deny His world." If one sees that the trees are blooming, what proof is this that nothing is missing? 2) What is "and created in it good creations"? What proof is this that the creations are good? 3) What is the connection between man and tree, which makes them interdependent? 4) Why is the passing of the majority of the year's rains a sign for *Rosh Hashanah*?

We should interpret this in ethics. It is known that *Rosh Hashanah* [beginning of the year] is a time of judgment, when the world is sentenced favorably or unfavorably. *Rosh* [head/beginning] means "root," and the branches emerge from the root. The branches always extend according to the essence of the root. Thus, a root of figs will not produce branches of dates, and so forth. As the root and beginning that a person establishes for himself in the beginning, so he continues his procession of life. Also, the judgment that a person is judged in the beginning of the year means that the person judges himself, and he is the arbiter and executor, for man is the arbiter, the litigant, and the knowledgeable one, and witness. It is as our sages said, "There is judgment below, there is no judgment above."

Rains are called "vitality" and "pleasure." Man enjoys the fruits that the tree bears. Man's main work is during the winter, on the long nights of *Tevet*. From *Tishrey*, which is the general *Rosh Hashanah*, to the month of *Tevet*, the majority of the year's rains have fallen, meaning that a person has already received vitality and pleasure from his Torah and work (since the rain comes from above, implying the abundance that comes from above, passes through the tree, and dresses in the fruit). At that time a person judges himself, if he should continue with Torah and *Mitzvot* [commandments/ good deeds] through the rest of the year, or to the contrary, that it is better to focus his mind on corporeal matters.

By that we can interpret the above-mentioned words of RASHI: "because the majority of the year's rains have fallen, and the resin flows in the trees, and from now on the fruits are ripe." That is, if the majority of nights in Torah and work have passed and the resin flows in the trees—for the tree implies man (as it is written, "for man is the tree of the field")—and he sees that a fire burns in his heart, as it is written, "Her flames are flames of fire, the flame of the Lord," then he decides to pursue this throughout the year. This is the meaning of "and from now on the fruits are ripe." In other words, from now on he will be rewarded with abundant fruits. This is why the fifteen of *Shevat* is the beginning of the year, since then he inspects himself and sees if it is worthwhile to continue with Torah and *Mitzvot* or not.

Now we will understand all the above. Since people are as trees, "One who comes out on a *Nissan* day and sees blooming trees," meaning that the trees have already begun to demonstrate their power, that they wish to impart fruits in man's favor, this is the meaning of "good trees." "Good" means "giving," as it is written, "My heart is overflowing with a good thing," and interprets what is good: "I say, 'My work is for the King.'" That is, he wishes to do all his work for the king, and this is regarded as wanting only to bestow and not to satisfy his heart's desires.

Therefore, when he sees that the trees are blooming, meaning that the trees are bearing fruits, he says, "and created in it good creations," for there must be good people in the world who are also giving, or the trees would not be giving their fruits. It is as our sages said, "The whole world is nourished by merit of my son, Hanina," meaning thanks to the righteous, since while there are people in the world who engage in bestowal, by that merit the trees bear their fruits, as well.

This is the meaning of "who did not deny His world of anything." That is, although by nature there are dishonorable qualities in us, the Creator has prepared for us engagement in Torah and *Mitzvot*, whereby engaging for the sake of the Creator we will be rewarded with all the delight and pleasure that the Creator has prepared for us.

I will end my letter with words of blessing: "May the Creator help us all to be rewarded with complete redemption soon in our days, Amen."

From your friend who wishes you all the best in corporeality and spirituality

Baruch Shalom HaLevi Ashlag

Letter No. 47

March 11, 1959, Tel-Aviv

Hello and all the best to my friend,

I will hereby write you the entire talk that I gave on Shabbat, portion *Shekalim* [March 7, 1959]. "On the first of *Adar* we speak of the *Shekalim*." We should understand the meaning of *Shekalim* [plural of Shekel], which is one of the things that Moses found perplexing. RASHI interprets the verse, "This ... will give." He showed him what seemed like a coin of fire weighing half a shekel and told him: "This ... will give." We should understand why Moses found it perplexing.

We should interpret this in ethics: Half a shekel is called a "fissure per head." It is written in the holy *Zohar* (*Nasso, Idra Raba*, item 20): "Each *Galgalta* [head/skull] brings a reward of whiteness to *Atik Yomin*... To accept it, he split the head downward. Thus it was calculated." Baal HaSulam interpreted that *Galgalta* means beginning, as the head begin with the skull. "Whiteness" means "white," which is faith and *Dvekut* [adhesion] "Fissure" means splitting and breaking.

To interpret his words we should precede with the meaning of the Torah being written with "black fire over white fire." We should interpret that to be rewarded with the light of Torah we need two states: a state of "black" and a state of "white." Black means a time when the faith and *Dvekut* [adhesion] in the Creator do not shine. This comes to a person by having a nature that burns as fire, and wishes to satisfy the lust of the will to receive only for oneself, and one cannot do anything ... will not see in advance that by this he will later receive delight and pleasure.

At that time, when a person begins to look at the whole world and wishes to believe that the Creator leads the world with benevolent guidance, he falls into foreign thoughts, and these thoughts cause him a fissure and a breakage in the work that he took upon himself—to believe above reason. This fissure creates in him darkness because then the faith departs from him and he lacks the *Dvekut* with Him. This is called "a fissure in the skull, half a shekel," meaning a state of darkness.

This is what Moses found perplexing: Why do we need this darkness, since it would better if there were always a state of open providence, where the light of faith would illuminate clearly? And why is it necessary to fissure the skull, which is splitting and breaking, in order to keep "Take the head ... of the children of Israel"? This is what Moses found perplexing.

The Creator replied to Moses: "This ... will give," meaning the nature of fire, which is what the will to receive compels them; this they will give as a donation to the Creator.

The necessity to overcome that black state obligates His help, as our sages said, "He who comes to purify is aided." The holy *Zohar* interprets that he is aided by the Creator giving him a holy soul so he can overcome his situation. Subsequently, He can help him by giving him a higher degree. And he must always extend "white," which is the upper whiteness, as explained in the book *Tree of Life*, Gate *Akudim* (Chapter 1), and this whiteness is called "white."

This is the meaning of "black fire over white fire." This is also the meaning of "Each *Galgalta* [skull/head]," meaning each beginning, namely that one must always make new choices, causing him to draw each time the upper whiteness, which is a new *Neshama* and degree, by having to overcome his state, which is called "black fire." When the help comes from above, there is "white fire," until a person is rewarded with the complete purpose for which he was created.

May the Creator help us be rewarded with the revelation of the light of Torah and the coming of the Redeemer soon in our days, Amen. Your friend who sends you regards and wishes you all the best,

Baruch Shalom HaLevi Ashlag

Letter No. 48

April 13, 1959, Tel-Aviv

Hello and all the best to my friend,

I read the book you wrote me about and enjoyed it because it is just as you said.

Concerning the approaching Passover, it is written, "The Torah spoke in relation to four sons," etc., "and the one who does not know how to ask, to him you shall open." We should interpret the word, "ask," from the words, "asking about the rains," which means prayer. That is, one who does not know how to pray, the reason is that he does not have a deficiency, for prayer pertains specifically to a place of deficiency. Then, "to him you shall open," meaning that a place of deficiency shall open to him, he will have what to pray for, and the Creator will be able to bestow upon him the light of Torah. This is why the Torah spoke specifically in relation to him, for one who has no deficiency, it means that he has no *Kli* [vessel] in which to receive, so it is impossible to give him.

"The Torah spoke" means that it teaches us how to qualify ourselves to be rewarded with the light of the Creator, which is all that is valuable that was given to us, as it is written, "For it is your wisdom and intelligence before the eyes of the nations ... for what great nation has a God near to it as the Lord our God whenever we call upon Him?" This means that the Creator is close to us in that

He wishes to bestow upon us all of His goodness. All that is lacking is the call, the deficiency, for only where there is a lack there is room for asking, which is the prayer, namely the *Kli* for reception of the abundance. This is the meaning of "and the one who does not know how to ask, to him you shall open," open a place of deficiency.

When he has the lack and he asks and requests the Creator to satisfy it, it is said, "He who has one hundred wants two hundred." It follows that by satisfying the lack that one has for spirituality, a greater lack appears. That is, afterwards he obtains bigger *Kelim* [vessels], and through these *Kelim* he receives bigger lights because he can already call upon the Creator, as our sages said, "Open for me one cleft in repentance, as the tip of a needle, and I will open for you gates for wagons and carts to enter." That is, a person should keep the "to him you shall open" even if it is only as the tip of a needle.

There are two meanings to it:

1. It is as small as the tip of a needle. This means that if there is a deficiency to spirituality, even if the deficiency is small, it is already possible to call upon the Creator to help him satisfy the lack. When the Creator satisfies the lack, then "He who has one hundred wants two hundred" anyway, and this is why the light itself creates the *Kli*, meaning the place of deficiency until the Creator promises him that He—the light itself—will open to him gates through which wagons and carts enter.

2. Another meaning in the words, "as a tip of a needle," is that the small lack will sting and pain him like the tip of a needle that pricks with. One who has a lack but does not feel it, this still does not help him. But if his lack pains him then he asks and requests of the Creator to satisfy his lack.

May the Creator satisfy our lack favorably in corporeality and spirituality, and may we have a happy and kosher festival.

From your friend who wishes you and your family the very best,

Baruch Shalom HaLevi Ashlag

Letter No. 49

September 14 [1959], Bnei Brak

Hello and all the best to my friend,

It has been a while since I received a letter from you ... there is nothing new with me and let us hope that the Creator will help us with every good thing.

We should understand the *Midrash* [interpretation] about the verse we say during the Eighteen Prayer of *Rosh Hashanah*: "And the Lord of Hosts will be high in judgment, and the holy God is sanctified in almsgiving." It is written, "The Creator said to Israel: 'My sons, I am pleading you, by your observing the judgment, I ascend.' How so? It is said, 'The Lord of Hosts will be high in judgment.' By your elevating Me with judgment, I give alms and instill My sanctity among you.' How so? Because it is said, 'And the holy God is sanctified in almsgiving.'"

We should understand the following: 1) Is ... below, that He must be elevated? 2) Is judgment a real thing, that we can lift something with judgment? 3) If the Creator wishes to give alms, why does He need judgment? Can He not give alms and instill holiness without judgment?

We should interpret this according to the ethics of the work of the Creator. Man consists of two elements: evil inclination and good inclination. In order to avoid the bread of shame, man was given the work in Torah and *Mitzvot* [commandments] whereby choosing the good and loathing the bad, one is rewarded with receiving His gifts without any shame.

It therefore follows that man is the judge and must sentence and determine who is right. That is, the evil inclination claims, "It is all mine," that the whole body belongs to it and man should be concerned with and work only in favor of the evil inclination. Likewise, the good inclination argues, "It is all mine," that the whole body belongs to it and man should be concerned with and work only for the sake of the good inclination.

When a person wishes to carry out the sentence and choose the good, the question is, "Why does he need to choose the good and say that the good inclination is correct?" It cannot be said that it is in order to receive reward in the next world, since it was said, "Be not as slaves who are serving the Rav in order to receive reward." Rather, one should choose the good because of the greatness of the Creator. As the holy *Zohar* writes, we must serve the Creator "because He is great and ruling, fills all the worlds, and encompasses all the worlds." That is, the primary element in his work is the greatness of the Creator.

It follows that when a person sentences, he must engage in the greatness of the Creator. Thus, the Creator is elevated by the judgment. Then, once a person has chosen the good—not for a reward—the Creator can give him all His gifts and there will not be any shame. At that time the Creator instills His holiness, meaning lets him feel the holiness.

All these gifts are regarded as almsgiving that the Creator has given because a person does not work for a reward. Therefore, now the gifts of the Creator are called "almsgiving."

May the Creator help us merit feeling the sanctity, and the words of the above *Midrash* will come true in us. I bless you with good writing and signing.

From your friend who wishes you and your family all the best,

Baruch Shalom HaLevi Ashlag

Letter No. 50

December 22, 1959, Bnei Brak

Hello and all the best to my friend,

The interpreters asked about the verse, "And Jacob was very frightened and distressed." But the Creator had promised him in the spectacle of the ladder to keep him wherever he went, as it is written, "And I will be with you and keep you wherever you go." If this is so, why did he have to pray, "Save me please from the hand of my brother, from the hand of Esau"?

The holy *Zohar* (*Vayishlah* [Jacob sent], item 70) interprets the words of the angels to Jacob: "And [he] also walks toward you and four hundred men are with him." It asks, "Why did they tell him so?" It replies, "Because the Creator always wants the prayers of the righteous and crowns Himself with their prayers." That is, the Creator craves the prayer of the righteous.

Baal HaSulam interpreted why the Creator does not give abundance to the creatures without prayer, but wants them to ask of Him and then He will give them, since it is known that the cow wants to nurse more than the calf wants to suckle. However, there is a rule that there is no light without a *Kli* [vessel]. A *Kli* means desire, for there is no coercion in spirituality because it is impossible to enjoy something we do not want, as the sensation of pleasure depends primarily on the measure of desire and craving for it. This is why the Creator gives only when the creatures have desire and craving.

The desire is fashioned specifically by prayer, for by feeling a lack, one begins to pray. By this the prayer grows and intensifies until it reaches the necessary measure to receive the upper bestowal. This is why the Creator longs for the prayer of the righteous, since only by that they can receive His abundance.

It is known that we discern two things in His abundance: 1) Surrounding Light, 2) Inner Light. Surrounding Light is what the person will receive in the future, and which he is currently unfit to receive this giving. Inner Light is what a person receives in the present, meaning that the abundance enters him inside.

According to what we said above, that for each thing we must first pray so as to have a *Kli* to receive the giving, it follows that even after the Creator promised him in the spectacle of the ladder, it is regarded as Surrounding Light. But when he met Esau and needed salvation in the present, he had to pray and show the desire, which is regarded as the *Kli* for salvation, since it is impossible to receive without a *Kli*. This is called "Inner Light," since the promise is called "Surrounding Light," but when we come to keep our promise in actual fact, we need a prayer, and this is called "Inner Light," for Surrounding Light is awakening from above, and Inner Light is awakening from below.

With blessings of Torah and friendship,

Baruch Shalom HaLevi Ashlag

Letter No. 51

March 27, 1960, Bnei Brak

Hello and all the best to my friend,

I hereby confirm that I received your congratulation telegram for my daughter's wedding, along with the triple blessing. May your household always know joy, merriment, happiness, and contentment.

I am writing to you what I said on Shabbat, portion of the (new) month. RASHI says about the verse, "This month shall be for you the beginning of the months." These are his words. "Moses was perplexed regarding the beginning of the moon, to what extent should she be seen and be worthy of sanctifying? He showed him with the finger the moon in the sky and said to him: 'This see and sanctify.'" RASHI also interprets the verse, "In the beginning (God) created, and these are his words: "Rabbi Yitzhak said, 'He should have begun the Torah from "This month shall be for you," which is the first commandment that Israel were commanded. What is the reason it began with 'In the beginning'? it is because He told His works to His people to give them the inheritance of the nations. Thus, should the nations say to Israel, 'You are robbers, you have conquered the lands of seven nations,' they will reply, 'The whole earth belongs to the Creator; He created it and gave it to whom He pleases. Upon His wish he gave it to them, and upon His wish He took it from them and gave it to us.'"

We should understand, 1) why Moses found this more perplexing than other things? 2) had the Torah not begun with "In the beginning," could it be said that it was not the Creator who created the world?

We should interpret this according to the ethics. The earth is called a "body." The Creator created the body and gave it to the nations of the world, meaning to the evil inclination, for as soon as one is born, the evil inclination enters him, as it is written, "For the inclination of a man's heart is evil from his youth." Hence, the evil inclination, which is the nations, say that the body belongs to them, meaning that they must govern it and do with it whatever they want.

Therefore, after thirteen years, when the good inclination comes and wishes to enter the body and govern it, and wishes to throw out the evil inclination, the evil inclination claims, "You are robbers," for the good inclination is called Israel. It follows that the nations say that they want to steal the bodies, which belong to them, for they are arguing, "The Creator has given to us all the bodies, and after only thirteen years you, Israelis, meaning the good inclination, want to rob us of this body."

Here comes the reply that the Torah begins with "In the beginning," for Israel are called *Resheet* [beginning]. That is, the Creator created the world only for Israel, and the fact that He had let the nations govern the body first is only so as to give room for choice and to be able to enjoy all of His bounty without any shame.

This is the meaning of what RASHI says, "and gave it to whom He pleases," meaning to Israel. This is the beginning of the intention, to give the people of Israel the full dominion over the body, as the goal is that the evil inclination will control the body. This is the meaning of "Upon His wish he gave it to them," meaning that His giving to the evil inclination in the beginning was according to His will so that this way the people of Israel would have room to work on choice. "...and upon His wish He took it from them," meaning that it was all according to one desire, and the Creator did not change His mind. Thus, it cannot be said that in the beginning He gave power to the nations and then regretted it and gave it to Israel. Rather, it was all according to one desire, meaning one thought and intention. This is the precision that RASHI makes, "Upon His wish he gave it to them, and upon His wish He took it," etc.

It follows that in order to have choice, he first gave the command to the evil inclination. This is why the world is in concealment, for concealing the face gives room for choice.

Also, it is known that the moon implies *Shechina* [Divinity], meaning faith, and one must constantly renew the faith. This is what bewildered Moses, since in its inception, the moon is in utter *Katnut* [smallness], meaning that it is the time of concealment. And then the Creator said to him: "This see and sanctify," that the greatest holiness is precisely when a person can sanctify himself even during the greatest concealment, and then ... with exile from Egypt.

From your friend who wishes you and your family all the best,

Baruch Shalom HaLevi Ashlag

Letter No. 52

April 30, 1960 [48th day of the Omer Count], Vienna

To the friends, may they live forever

The festival of Shavuot—the time of the giving of our Torah—is approaching. It is known that Shavuot is regarded as *Malchut* in the worlds and the heart in man. It is as Baal HaSulam interpreted about *Mekadesh Shevi'i* [seventh sanctifier] that *Shevi'i* comes from the words *Shebi-Hu* [who is in me].

He means that the Creator is clothed in the heart, and the time when we can interpret that the Torah dresses in the soul. This is why it is called Shavuot and "the giving of the Torah," meaning that at that time the Torah dresses in the hearts of each and every one from the whole of Israel. During the count from Passover to Shavuot it is the purification of the *Kelim* [vessels], which is purification in heart and mind. When the *Kelim* have been perfected, we are rewarded with the Torah.

Therefore, before Passover, the preparation of purifying the *Kelim* was with faith, called *Mitzva* [commandment/good deed]. Through the exodus from Egypt they were rewarded with faith, as in "I am the Lord your God who took you out from the land of Egypt." After Passover begins the work on purification as preparation for reception of the Torah. When the Torah dresses in the soul it is called "Shavuot, the time of the giving of our Torah."

We need heaven's mercy, to be given the strength to come out of Egypt and be awarded faith, since we go through many states before we are rewarded with faith. Sometimes, a person has no need for pure faith because he thinks that it is better to go by the usual ways, as it seems to him, since all the Hassidim and practical people do as they were taught, meaning the usual way. He wishes that in this way he will have the complete desire to keep Torah and *Mitzvot* [plural of *Mitzva*], since he sees that in this, too, he is declining and sometimes has no time to think about it. That is, he engages in Torah and *Mitzvot* without any introspections, that in the Torah and *Mitzvot* he is doing, it is not worthwhile to introspect.

The calculations that a person does are in order to gain something. In that state he is in a state where it is preferable to reflect on his corporeal needs, since his vitality is specifically in corporeality.

However, we must remember the rule that Baal HaSulam said, that the punishments are mainly on the time when a person engages in Torah and *Mitzvot*. Concerning the time when he is in a state where his vitality is only corporeality, his sentence is as the sentence of a beast. Only when engaging in Torah and *Mitzvot* without being careful to keep it pure, this is called "idolatry."

Therefore, when a person agrees to do something in Torah and *Mitzvot*, it is preferable to work for the Creator, since the work begins primarily in the mind, but with the heart it is a completely different work. At that time his work is regarded as exiting the beast and becoming a man, and it was said about it, "You are called 'man,'" and then begins man's work in the mind, when beginning to weigh on a scale which is more worthwhile, knowledge or faith. At that time he becomes angry that the Creator is not rewarding him with faith.

By that we can interpret the words of the Gemarah, "Rabbi Yehuda said, 'Rabbi Shmuel said in the name of Rabbi Meir: 'While I was learning with Rabbi Akiva, I would put the ink into the inkwell. When I came to Rabbi Ishmael, he said to me, 'My son, be careful with your work, for your work is the work of heaven. If you omit one letter or add one letter, you are destroying the entire world.' I said to him, 'I have one thing, and it is called ink, which I put into the inkwell.' He replied, 'But do you put ink into the inkwell? The Torah said, 'write, and erase,' writing that can erase. What did he tell him and what did he reply to him? This is what he said to him: 'Not only am I not mistaken to think I know about omitting or adding, I am not even afraid that a fly will come ,land on the *Dalet* [Hebrew letter, ד], and turn it into a *Reish* [a similar looking letter, ר]' (*Iruvin* 13a).'"

We should interpret the scribe. When a person engages in the work of the Creator he is called a "scribe," as in "Write them on the tablet of your heart." Omitting or adding means that either he is lacking right or adding left, meaning two times "nest" [also 150 in *Gematria*], as our sages said, "We can purify the pest with 150 reasons [also flavors]." This is why there are two times: impure nest and pure nest. Also, ink is called "blackness," since the labor is regarded as darkness.

We should understand that if Rabbi Ishmael told him, "Be careful with omitting and adding," what is the reason that Rabbi Meir told him that he was putting ink into the inkwell?

We should interpret that when Rabbi Meir told him that he was a scribe, meaning engaging in the work with purity, he told him, "Be careful with omitting and adding," meaning that he will not have too little faith and too much knowledge. To that he replied to him that he was putting the ink in the inkwell. That is, during the labor, called "blackness," he throws his (hands) there, as in, impure nest and pure nest, so he always has room for faith because to him the nests are equal.

He asked, "But do you put ink into the inkwell?" Can you place a pure nest from a place of darkness? It should be writing that you can erase. That is, during the labor, which is the time of reception of faith, it is precisely when we can erase the writing. And yet, he did not erase, for in that state, when he determines and takes upon himself the faith, it is regarded as "completed writing," which is a *Kli* fit for holding the light of the Creator.

The Gemarah asks about this: "What did he tell him and what did he reply to him?" (RASHI interprets that he warned him about omitting and adding, and replied to him that he has ink. RASHI interpreted that "ink" means writing that cannot be erased because its writing is visible).

The Gemarah answers that he replied to him that he was careful with omitting and adding, and also even that a fly might come and land on the tip of the *Dalet* and erase it, turning it into a *Reish*. A fly means a foreign thought that erases the *Dalet* and turns it into a *Reish* (see the beginning of "Introduction of the Book of Zohar," item 200).

That is, at the time of *Mitzva*, when he should be careful with omitting or adding, meaning that he will not want faith to be less important than knowledge, which means that he lacks the importance of faith, and too much means that he gives excessive importance to knowledge.

During the writing of the ink of the Torah, it is considered that he is careful with the tip of the *Dalet*, which is "doing mercy." If he has a fly, meaning an impure thought, then he does not want to do mercy, and then he is regarded as completely destitute. By that he always puts the ink, meaning that he is always careful to keep them equal, and then he is certain to be steadfast in his state, since when he sees that he is always at a crossroads, he is naturally under keeping, and by that achieves the full completeness.

May the Creator grant us with full completeness and with coming out to the light of Torah in purity.

Baruch Shalom HaLevi Ashlag

Son of Baal HaSulam

Letter No. 53

December 19, 1960 (Hanukah), Bnei Brak

To my friend,

I long very much to hear how things are going for you and especially your family. I have no news and we are trusting in the Creator to hear good news. I will conclude my letter with words of Torah.

Our sages said, "What is Hanukah? Our sage taught," etc. We see that Hanukah has the letters of *Hanu* [parked/paused] *Koh* [here/thus far], meaning that on the 25th of *Kislev* [third Hebrew month] they had a pause in the war, as pausing happens specifically in the middle of the work. The pause in the middle is in order to muster strength in order to be able to continue the work.

We need to understand what they still had to do once they have completed the first war, and what they still needed to do until they could say that they have finished the war.

We find that during the Second Temple, the Greeks inflicted decrees on Israel and did not let them engage in Torah and *Mitzvot* [commandments]. It therefore follows that the whole miracle was that after the war they were able to engage in Torah and *Mitzvot*, and this is regarded as the miracle being only on spirituality.

But on Purim, the miracle was over the bodies, meaning over corporality. This is why on Hanukah we are to commemorate the miracle with praise and gratitude and not with feast and joy. But regarding Purim, it is written, "feasting and rejoicing," meaning things that relate to the body, too, since then the miracle was on the bodies, called corporeality.

We need to understand all this in relation to the work of the Creator. Our sages said, "With all your heart—with both your inclinations, the good inclination and the bad inclination." We need to understand how we can serve the Creator with the evil inclination. First we need to understand the meaning of the evil inclination. It is known, and we already said that the evil inclination is the will to receive for oneself. That is, wanting to please oneself causes one to make all the sins. This means that wanting to transgress is only because he wants to receive pleasure for himself, so he steals and robs and lies, and does not want to take upon himself the burden of the kingdom of heaven because "a slave is happy when left alone."

But the good inclination is wanting to please others: either wanting to please people or to please the Creator. This is the meaning of the commandments between man and man and between man and the Creator.

The Creator created the world in order to do good to His creations. For this reason, a desire to receive pleasure—to enjoy, to please themselves and not give to others—was installed in the creatures. Hence, when one has to work in order to please others, it is very difficult for him because it is against nature.

The Torah's obligation that we should work in order to bestow is only a correction, to avoid the bread of shame, for one who receives a gift from his friend is ashamed to receive, but the Creator wants wholeness in the pleasures that He wishes to impart us. For this reason, He has given us work and labor, so that each will receive according to his work. Then, if one achieves a degree where he can receive all the pleasures while his intention is only to bestow contentment upon his maker, there will be wholeness in the pleasures.

For this reason, we have two works: 1) the work of the good inclination, when one does not want to receive any pleasure for oneself, but all of one's actions are only to bestow, and this is why he prays and engages in *Mitzvot*. This is called a "soul," "spirituality." This is the degree that they were awarded on Hanukah, meaning that the Greeks did not let them engage in Torah and *Mitzvot*, and they had a pause from this work.

2) However, the war was not over yet. Now they have the work of receiving all the pleasures that the Creator wanted the creatures to receive, so now they have to work on achieving a degree where we can receive all the pleasures while their intention is only to give by that contentment to the Creator. At that time, when receiving all the pleasures, it is regarded as serving the Creator with the evil inclination, meaning that he is performing a *Mitzva* by receiving the pleasures with the body.

Therefore, when they succeed and can receive everything that the Creator wants to give, the miracle is called "redemption of the bodies," when the miracle was on the body, which is the will to receive.

This is why it is written about Purim, "feasting and rejoicing," which imply that the miracle belongs to the body, meaning to corporeality. For this reason, on Purim they observed and received, which is already regarded as the end of the work. But on Hanukah, it was only a pause in the war and we must carry on. This is why on Hanukah the intimation is *Hanu-Koh* [paused here].

May the Creator open our eyes and award us complete redemption soon in our days, Amen.

Baruch Shalom HaLevi Ashlag

Son of Baal HaSulam

Letter No. 54

March 18, 1961, Bnei Brak

Hello and all the best to my friend,

I am informing you that I received the five folios [sheets of paper] in your book and thoroughly enjoyed it.

This week, I said a commentary about a question presented in *The Zohar* (*Tazria*, item 9): "Rabbi Aba said, 'We learned that the Creator sentenced that drop, which would be a male and which would be a female, and you said, 'A woman who inseminates first delivers a boy.'" Rabbi Yosi said, 'Of course the Creator distinguished between a drop of a male and a drop of a female, and because He distinguished it, he sentenced it to be a male or a female.'"

Baal HaSulam interprets this in the *Sulam* [Ladder] commentary: "We learned that a woman who inseminates first delivers a boy. Rabbi Aha said, 'We learned that the Creator sentences the drop to be either a male or a female, and you say, 'A woman who inseminates first delivers a boy.' This means that we do not need the sentencing of the Creator.' Rabbi Yosi said, 'Of course the Creator distinguishes between a drop of a male or a drop of a female, and because He distinguished it, He sentences whether it will be a male or a female.'"

He interprets that "there are three partners in a person, the Creator, his father, and his mother. His father gives the whiteness in him; his mother the redness in him, and the Creator gives the soul. If the drop is that of a male, the Creator gives the soul of a male. If it is a female, the Creator gives the soul of a female. It follows that the woman inseminating first, still did not make the drop eventually become a male if the Creator did not install in it the soul of a male. This distinguishing that the Creator distinguishes in the drop, that it is fit for a soul of a male or a female, is regarded as the Creator's sentence, for had He not distinguished it and did not send a soul of a male, the drop would not eventually become a male."

To understand it by way of ethics we can interpret that each birth can be only by male and female. It is so because the male is the power of bestowal in a person, and the female is the power of reception in a person, meaning one's wish to delight himself, where his only concern is his own pleasure. Through these two forces, we have the work of choice—to choose the good, meaning for the Creator, and loathe the bad, which is to satisfy his lusts.

Concerning insemination, it is as though we place a seed in the ground and it does not bear fruit. Only when the seed that was placed in the ground has decayed and become annulled, it yields fruits. Therefore, in ethics, sowing means something that is cancelled.

By that we will understand all the above said. A woman inseminating first means that "first" means the thought. That is, if the first thought is to annul the power of receiving pleasure only for oneself, then she naturally "delivers a male." That is, from the cancelling of the force of reception emerges the force of bestowal, for then his wish is to bestow contentment upon the Creator.

And if the man inseminates first, meaning that his initial thought is to annul his power of bestowal, then she naturally delivers a female, for then the act that the thought begets is to receive, to satisfy only his wishes.

This is the meaning of the Creator distinguishing the drop, meaning the thought—if the intention is for the Creator or for self-gratification. If it is a male, namely that he has cancelled his power of

Letter No. 54

reception, which is the meaning of "A woman who inseminates first delivers a male," then the Creator sentences the drop to be a male.

The thing is that only the Creator can discern and know the truth, if his intention was for the Creator, and then the Creator gives him the soul of a male, as our sages said, "He who learns Torah *Lishma* [for Her sake], etc., the secrets of Torah are revealed to him," meaning that the Creator reveals to him the secrets of Torah. If he is a female, meaning that he has cancelled his power of bestowal, which is called a "male," she delivers a female. That is, the act that he begets is only for his own pleasure, and then the Creator does not give him the assistance from above. Rather, it is as our sages said, "He who comes to defile, it opens for him."

It follows that by the Creator distinguishing and sentencing, this is what really happens, for only the Creator knows the truth, since he can deceive himself and think that his intention is only for the Creator. But when the Creator brings him closer and gives him the attainment of the soul of Torah, he knows that he was born a male, that the act he is doing is for the Creator, and then he is rewarded with the revelation of the secrets of Torah and becomes an ever flowing fountain. At that time, he achieves the true completeness.

I will end my letter with wishes of a happy and kosher festival.

From your friend, who wishes you and your family all the best,

Baruch Shalom HaLevi Ashlag

Letter No. 55

January 19, 1962, Eve of *Rosh Hashanah* to the Trees, Bnei Brak

Hello and all the best to my friend,

I thank you for the invitation to the wedding that I received. Yet, I regret not being able to participate in your joy from up close, but I will participate from afar, for joy is a spiritual matter, and in spirituality space has no influence at all. Only in corporeality does space set apart or bring close, but in spirituality I can partake in your joy even when far away, for it is only nearing of the hearts that we need. So blessings to the groom and bride, and may there be a generation of upright and established forever.

And by the way, I am writing to you what I said regarding the fifteenth of *Shevat*. Our sages said, "Rabbi Yohanan said, 'Why is it is written, 'For man is the tree of the field?' Is man the tree of the field? But because it is written that you will eat from it but do not cut it, and it is written, 'This you will destroy and cut down,' how so? If he is a decent wise disciple, eat from it but do not cut it. If not, 'This you will destroy and cut down.'"

We should understand the connection between a decent wise disciple and the tree of the field. The verse says, "You shall not destroy its tree by swinging an axe against it; for you may eat from it ... Only the trees which you know are not fruit trees you shall

Letter No. 55

destroy and cut down." It follows that the verse speaks of a tree, so what does it prove about man?

The holy *Zohar* says, "'Another god is sterile and does not bear fruit.' That is, one who is not working for the Creator does not see fruits in one's work. What are the fruits? It is written in the Midrash: 'These are the generations of Noah.' It is as it is written, 'A fruit of a righteous, a tree of life.' What are the fruits of the righteous? *Mitzvot* [commandments] and good deeds." Thus far its words.

In the Gemarah, before the words of Rabbi Yohanan, it is said there: "Tania, Rabbi Banaa says, 'Anyone who engages in Torah *Lishma* [for Her sake], his Torah becomes for him a potion of life, as it is said, 'She is a tree of life to they who hold her,' and it is said, 'It shall be a healing to your flesh,' etc. Anyone who engages in Torah *Lo Lishma* [not for Her sake], it becomes to him a potion of death, as it is said, 'Let my lesson decapitate as rain.' There is no decapitation but killing, as it was said, 'And they decapitated the heifer there by the stream.'" We should understand the proximity of the matters.

However, we should interpret this by ethics. Rabbi Yohanan asks, "Is man the tree of the field?" That is, what similarity is there between man and the tree of the field? What do we learn by the comparison in text between man and the tree of the field? He brings evidence to that from the verse, "Do not eat of it and do not cut it down," etc., referring to a wise disciple. If he is decent, meaning learning *Lishma*, which means that he is learning things that will lead him to yielding fruits, it means that this learning will make him bear fruit, meaning *Mitzvot* and good deeds. He will learn this because by that he will be rewarded with the potion of life. This is the meaning of, "You may eat from it but do not cut it down." If not, if you see that the learning you are learning does not bring you to do *Mitzvot* and good deeds, called fruits, then know that it belongs to the *Sitra Achra* [other side] and not to the *Kedusha* [holiness].

This is the reason for the custom to eat fruits on the fifteenth of *Shevat*, to imply that we are going by the way of holiness, and we have fruits.

From your friend, who wishes you and your family all the best,

Baruch Shalom HaLevi Ashlag

Letter No. 56

June 6, 1962, Antwerp

To...

Because I am moving about, the letters do not reach me by order. Only last week I received the first letters from Israel. I already wrote four letters to Jerusalem, to those who wrote me, and they are...

And regarding the words that you want to elaborate on, I am repeating the entire excerpt: Our sages said, "Rabbah bar Rav Huna said, 'Any person in whom there is Torah but no fear of heaven is like a treasurer who was given the inner keys but was not given the outer keys; how will he enter?'" RASHI interpreted that fear of heaven is like the outer doors through which to enter the inner ones. Thus, if he is fearing heaven, he becomes anxious to keep and to do. If not, he does not fear for his Torah. "Rabbi Yanai declares, '"Woe unto he who has no house but built a gate for the house"' (*Shabbat*, 31).

We should ask:

1. Rabbah bar Rav Huna likens fear of heaven to externality, and Torah to internality when he says, "But was not given the outer keys; how will he enter?" That is, if he has no fear of heaven, how will he enter the internality? Rav Yanai

likens the fear of heaven to internality, for he said that fear of heaven is like a house, and the Torah only to a gate, and a gate is externality. It follows that he thinks that the Torah is externality.

2. What did Rav Yanai add to Rabbah bar Rav Huna, and said, "Woe," and gave the example of of Rabbi Yanai.

It is known that the purpose of creation is to do good to His creations. In order to be able to receive the good that has been prepared for us, we need qualification, which is equivalence of form. This means that our intention should be only to bestow and not receive for ourselves. After we are rewarded with the light clothed in the inner Torah (when we attain the hidden light clothed in the inner Torah, it is called "the Torah and Israel and the Creator are one"). Our sages said about this, "There is no good but the Torah," of which it was said, "Who are nicer than gold," etc., meaning that the sweet tasting light of life is clothed in the inner Torah.

It is known that "A man is born the foal of a wild ass," for "the inclination of a man's heart is evil from his youth," and as our sages said, "I wish they had left Me and kept My Torah [law], since the light in it reforms him" (Jerusalem (Talmud), *Hagiga*).

I have already interpreted this article for it is difficult to understand the connection between leaving the Creator and keeping the Torah. How can there be Torah without the Creator, of which it was said, "left Me"? The answer is written next to it: "because the light in it reforms him."

This means that when a person wants to bring himself closer to the Creator, the Creator tells him that as long as he is immersed in evil lusts, the Creator cannot bring him closer, for then a person is still in the quality of falsehood, and the verse, "He who speaks falsehood will not be established before My eyes." When a person is proud, the Creator says, "He and I cannot dwell in the same abode," and so forth.

Rather, by keeping the Torah, whose light reforms him, he will come out from the evil qualities, called "reception," and will be able

Letter No. 56

to engage in bestowal, which is the meaning of reforming him, as it is written, "My heart overflows with a good thing; I say, 'My work is for the King'" (Psalms 45).

In other words, everything he does is only in order to bestow upon the king, and only afterwards does the Creator bring him closer. That person is rewarded with permanent faith (as it is written in the *Sulam* [Ladder commentary], in the "Introduction of the Book of Zohar").

Therefore, for a person to obtain fear of heaven and the ability to do good deeds, he has no other choice—as explained in the words of the Jerusalem (Talmud)—but to "keep My Torah [law]." That is, through the Torah, whose light reforms him. Then, when he has been reformed, meaning when he has obtained fear of heaven through the Torah, he will be rewarded with the inner Torah, meaning the light of Torah that is clothed in the outer Torah.

It is as our sages said, "In the light that was created on the first day, Adam saw from the end of the world to its end. The Creator looked at the works of the generation of the flood and the generation of Babylon, and saw that their works were flawed. He stood and concealed it. Where did He conceal it? In the Torah.

By that we can interpret the words of Rabbah bar Rav Huna, who likens the fear of heaven to the outer keys, and the Torah to inner ones. He is referring to a person who wishes to be rewarded with the internality of the Torah, where all the life and good, and pleasure is found. Before he tries to acquire fear of heaven, he lacks the proper qualification to be fit for reception of the hidden light, as it is written, "And will deny the wicked their light" [see the beginning of *Mesilat Yesharim* [Path of the Upright]. But before a person has corrected his bad deeds and has acquired fear of heaven he is unfit to receive the good.

It turns out that fear of heaven is called "externality," meaning that through fear of heaven he will be able to receive the inner Torah. This is why in his view, one who wishes to receive the internality of the Torah before he has fear of heaven, it is as though he has the inner keys but was not given the outer keys; how will he enter? Since he does not have fear of heaven, he is unfit to receive the delight and pleasure.

This is what Rabbi Yanai was excited about and declared, "Woe unto he who has no house but built a gate for the house." That is, the words of Rabbah bar Rav Huna mean that one who wishes to be awarded the internality of the Torah must first acquire fear of heaven, which is external to the internality of the Torah.

It follows that the main thing that one needs to acquire is fear of heaven, for then the fear of heaven will be like a room where you can place objects and fine-looking furniture and precious artifacts. But if he has no room in which to put things, he cannot be given anything. For Rabbi Yanai, the fear of heaven will be the house where he puts the internality of the Torah.

Therefore, he saw that the main thing on which one needs to exert in the world is fear of heaven, that this is the receptacle for the upper pleasures, and saw that people are learning Torah their whole lives but their intention is not to acquire fear of heaven through it, since the study of Torah should be as the above-mentioned Jerusalem way, in the words, "I wish they left Me and kept My Torah, for the light in it reforms him," meaning that through the Torah they will be awarded being good.

That is, through the light in the Torah—even if he is still learning *Lo Lishma* [not for Her sake], since he was still not rewarded with fear of heaven, so how can he study *Lishma* before he has been rewarded with faith, which is fear of heaven? But through the light in the Torah that is *Lo Lishma*—he is later rewarded with the fear of heaven. This is considered that it "reforms him."

It follows that the Torah *Lo Lishma* is the gate through which to enter fear of heaven, called "house" (a receptacle for the good in the internality of the Torah). This is why he adds to the words of Rabbah bar Rav Huna and says, "Woe unto one who has no house," meaning who still has no fear of heaven, "but built a gate for the house," since normally, one who contemplates building a house can build a door for the house that he will have. But if he is not contemplating building a house, why would he make for himself a door?

This is why Rav Yanai declares, "When a person is concerned with fear of heaven, which is a house, it is worthwhile for him to learn Torah, since the Torah will bring him the light, and through the light he will be rewarded with fear of heaven, called a "house," in which to place the internality of the Torah.

But if he is not concerned with being rewarded with fear of heaven because he has no need for fear of heaven, why should he trouble himself with spending his life in Torah, for it is only a door to enter the house called "fear of heaven"?

If he does not intend to acquire fear of heaven, it turns out that he is troubling himself for nothing, pointlessly, since the whole point of Torah that in *Lo Lishma* is that it is only a door through which to enter fear of heaven. Then, when one has fear of heaven, it can be said that he is learning Torah *Lishma*. But when he has no fear of heaven, when he has no faith, the question is for whom he is learning.

But when a person wants to acquire fear of heaven and the evil within him does not give him the strength to be able to believe in the Creator, our sages advise us that from *Lo Lishma* he will come to *Lishma*. That is, he will be rewarded with fear of heaven and faith in the Creator, and he will know for whom he is learning. This is called a "house."

One who learns Torah *Lishma*, meaning that he has fear of heaven, is awarded many things. As Rabbi Meir said [*Avot*], he becomes as a flowing fountain and the secrets of Torah are revealed to him, for the secrets of Torah are the delight and pleasure, and it is the purpose of creation that he will receive delight and pleasure.

It follows from all the above that a door is called Torah *Lo Lishma*, which means he still hasn't fear of heaven. A house is called "fear of heaven," since once he has received the light of Torah, which is in *Lo Lishma*, he is rewarded with *Lishma*, meaning with faith in the Creator, and then he will do everything for the Creator. Subsequently, he is rewarded with the inner Torah, which is the delight and pleasure, called "secrets of Torah," as it is written in the Mishnah, *Avot*.

I think that I have clarified this thoroughly, and if you have any comments on this, write me and I will know what to correct.

I began the letter but only today [May 31] I finished it. This week I received your letter from the 23rd of May; I am grateful for the details you wrote me, do continue.

Baruch Shalom HaLevi Ashlag
Son of Baal HaSulam

Letter No. 57

June 7, 1962, Eve of Shavuot, Antwerp

Hello and all the best to...

I have no news to write; I move about from place to place and from country to country until we return to the land of Israel. We should hope that when we return, we will merit tasting the good taste of the land of Israel and there will be no need for exile anymore. Exile comes only when one does not cautiously keep the value of the land, and the land is not appreciated as it should be. As a result, the land throws that person out, as it is written, "And the land shall vomit out."

Although the reception of the Torah was specifically in the desert, the intention was that we would keep it in Israel. Therefore, if we accept, during the reception of Torah, that we will keep it in Israel, then we are rewarded with entering the land and keeping the Torah. However, without Torah it is impossible to enter the land, for only the light in the Torah reforms one.

This is the meaning of "Everyone admits on the eighth of the assembly that you are needed, too." It is known that there is the "Torah [teaching/law] of the Creator," and there is "His Torah." On the eighth of the assembly, which is the reception of the Torah, it should be for you (in plural form), meaning that it will be His Torah. Otherwise it is not the reception of the Torah, but is rather called the "Torah of the Creator." Through the Torah of the Creator we are rewarded with the light of Torah, by which we are rewarded with entering the land of Israel, and subsequently with His Torah, which is the Torah that comes after the land of Israel.

But then, at the time of reception of the Torah by Moses, they were immediately awarded freedom, as our sages said, "Do not pronounce it, *Harut* [carved] but *Herut* [freedom]." At that time they were not enslaved to enter the corporeal land of Israel and were immediately rewarded with the spiritual land of Israel.

However, this was for the time being. Later, our sages said that the two crowns that Israel were given when they preceded "we will do" to "we will hear" were taken away from them.

At that time the work began anew—in order to enter the land of Israel and be awarded the light of Torah, and then the actual Torah, called the "names of the Creator."

May the Creator grant us understanding of the great merit of the land of Israel, and to know how to appreciate it so it will not vomit us out. It is written in *The Zohar* (*Tazria* [Inseminate], item 6) about the verse, "Who can find a virtuous woman, for her sell (price) is far above pearls?" The holy *Zohar* asks, "It should have said, 'Her price is far above pearls,' so why does it say, 'her sell'?" It replies that one who does not know how to keep it and appreciate it, she sells that person to the *Klipot* [shells]. This is why it is written, "sell."

Therefore, let us hope that from this day on we will know how to walk on the straight path and be awarded the reception of the Torah.

With blessings of a happy festival,

Baruch Shalom HaLevi Ashlag

Letter No. 58

June 7, 1962, Eve of Shavuot, Antwerp

To my friend...

Concerning your question, "One transgresses only if a spirit of folly has entered him," which means that without the spirit of folly he would not transgress, so why did the spirit of folly enter him? After all, he has not committed any transgression yet. And also, who is causing the entrance of this spirit of folly? And if it already entered, why is this his fault? After all, he has no choice in the matter because the spirit of folly caused it.

Our sages said, "The eye sees and the heart covets." That is, the eye causes the sin. Seeing means both seeing something forbidden with the eyes, or seeing with the mind, meaning a foreign thought.

Our sages also said, "Delight that comes to a person involuntarily ... not permitted and unintended, the whole world agrees it is permitted" (*Pesachim* 25b).

It is known that one cannot control the eye and the mind. Therefore, seeing does not constitute a sin. Rather, afterward, when the heart covets, then the sin takes place. And since he saw the sin, he must promptly repent for seeing, so it does not make him covet. At that point he still has the choice because he still did not sin.

If he did not awaken right away to repent for the coercion, which is called "seeing," then the coercion is the cause of the coveting, which is called a "mistake." But if he did not repent for the mistake, meaning for coveting, he comes into sinning.

The spirit of folly enters a person promptly after seeing if he did not repent for seeing. At that time the spirit of folly enters him for the purpose of correction. This is so because when he does not know how to keep himself—to repent for the thought—he blemishes the glory of heaven. This is called "knowing his master and intending to rebel against him," since the thought must lead to coveting.

At that time it is a great correction that he does not feel the greatness of the Creator and the spirit of wisdom that was in him departs from him, for then he does not place such a blemish on the greatness of the Creator, since then he does not feel the greatness of the Creator because a spirit of folly has entered him.

This is the meaning of, "One transgresses only if a spirit of folly has entered him." It teaches us that one should know that all the calculations that he does during the sin, although he thinks his calculations are full of wisdom, our sages told us that one should know that everything, meaning all the calculations, is done by the spirit of folly.

This is so because now this is the operator, and not the spirit of wisdom, for it has already departed from him, even though he is a wise disciple and does good deeds. It was said about this: "The righteousness of the righteous will not be remembered on the day of his wickedness."

Therefore, at that time he mustn't be smart, but take upon himself the kingdom of heaven above reason. That is, he should annul his view and thought completely, and then, when he repents, he will be able to make some calculations with regard to the *Mitzvot* [commandments] and the transgressions.

It was said about that (*Avot* 4), "Be careful with a minor *Mitzva* [commandment] as with a serious one, for you do not know the reward of the *Mitzvot* [plural of commandment]." This means that

Letter No. 58

one should be mindful and perform the *Mitzva* when it is minor in his eyes, from the words "shame" and "contempt" (in Hebrew the word *Kalah* [minor/light] sounds similar to the word *Kalon* [disgrace]), although the *Mitzva* is in a state of sin, like a minor, unimportant thing, so why should I do them now? In any case, my actions have no importance above.

It is one thing when the *Mitzva* is for him in a state of "serious," meaning that while having fear of heaven, he felt the graveness of the transgression and the seriousness of the *Mitzva*. That is, he felt the benefit and honor, and understood that it was worthwhile to engage in Torah and *Mitzvot*. But now that the *Mitzvot* are minor in his eyes, it is not worthwhile to be so cautious.

It was said about this that a person does not know which state gives contentment above. That is, if we say, "The reward is according to the effort," it means that when he regards Torah and *Mitzvot* as degradable and contemptible, he has greater labor to observe them. For this reason, it is possible that there is more contentment above from this state. Therefore, one must be cautious and keep them.

May the Creator help us keep Torah and *Mitzvot* abundantly.

Baruch Shalom HaLevi Ashlag

Letter No. 59

June 8, 1962, Shavuot, Antwerp

To my friend...

Concerning your question about our sages' words, "A stubborn and rebellious son was not, nor is destined to be. Rather, demand and receive reward" (*Sanhedrin*, p 1). The Torah is longer than the earth, so why was it given things only on "demand and receive reward," and not on real things?

You also asked about the reward. Actually, one should serve the rav not in order to receive reward, meaning *Lishma* [for Her sake].

We should also understand that it is known that the purpose of creation is to do good to His creations, namely that the creatures will receive delight and pleasure. And the reason why the creatures must engage in Torah and *Mitzvot* [commandments] without reward is that it is only a correction on the part of the creatures, since the creatures cannot taste reception of pleasure without shame. The holy *Zohar* calls it, "One who eats that which is not his, is afraid to look at his face."

That is, we feel deficiency upon reception of pleasure, so we were given the remedy of Torah and *Mitzvot*, by which one becomes fit to receive all the pleasures that the Creator has contemplated in our favor, and there will not be the flaw of shame because it is only for the Creator. It therefore follows that the interpretation is a correction by which we can receive the reward and it will not be for ourselves, but for the Creator. Otherwise it is impossible to receive reward, namely pleasures, for pleasure is called "reward."

And concerning "was not, nor is destined to be," it is explained that there are things one can attain during the six thousand years. Since it is possible to attain the secret, those things were given to us in corporeality as things to do. This applies to the world of actions.

However, there are things that can be attain only in the seventh millennium. Therefore, although they are implied in the corporeal act of *Mitzva* [commandment], such as a stubborn and rebellious son, they are not practiced during the six thousand years. Therefore, this is not to become an actual work, but rather "demand and receive reward," for only the demanding applies to the six thousand years, but the reward, meaning the upper attainment, will be in the seventh millennium. This is called "was not," in the beginning of the six thousand years, "nor is destined to be," at the end of the six thousand years. Rather, it will appear at the beginning of the seventh millennium.

By way of ethics, we should interpret that sometimes one comes to a state of such lowliness that he does not taste any taste in Torah and prayer. Although he is learning, he knows and feels the truth about himself—that the real cause he is continuing to learn Torah is not because of fear of heaven, but because of habit, and especially because of what people might say. Meaning when the environment he is in sees that he is slacking in the study of Torah they will consider him an empty vessel without fear of heaven, and will not respect him as much as they respected him before. Therefore, when he leaves the study of Torah he will suffer from his environment and his family will despise him.

It is likewise in prayer; he prays only out of habit, but without any obligation due to fear of heaven. He is continuing with it also due to the same cause as with the study of Torah. But most importantly, he sees no purpose in his life and he cannot carry on in such a state much longer.

To this there is a correction called "minister of forgetfulness." He forgets the goal, meaning the reason that necessitates his continuing engagement in Torah and prayer. When he forgets the reason that compels him he continues with Torah and *Mitzvot* only out of habit. If he has an opportunity to come out of that environment he does it right away.

In such a state we need great mercy in order to be able to hang on until the wrath—meaning the lowliness—is over. And since torments cleanse man's iniquities, through suffering he is pitied from above and is given an illumination of fear of heaven, and he returns to life. Thus the situation returns to being as it was prior to his fall into the state of lowliness.

That above-mentioned time of lowliness is called "was not, nor is destined to be," meaning it was not in the purpose of creation nor is it destined to be. Such a thing is called a "pit stop," since there is a state of *Kedusha* [holiness] and a state of *Tuma'a* [impurity].

He can hope to repent from a state of *Tuma'a*, but the above-mentioned state is called a state of "death." That is, everything he does is lifeless and regarded as dead. It was not in the goal nor is it destined to be. In that case, why is this needed? However, demand and receive reward, meaning that in that state one must demand the Creator, as our sages said, "Zion; no one requires it, meaning that a demand is required." That is, such a state is given to a person in order to have room for demand, that he will intently demand of the Creator to bring him closer to *Kedusha*.

But when a person makes *Mitzvot*, he feels about himself that the Creator will bring him closer. But precisely at that time, called "pit stop," is the place for demand with prayer and request.

May the Creator open our eyes in His Torah [law]

Baruch Shalom HaLevi Ashlag
Son of Baal HaSulam

P.S.

Concerning the *Omer* count (a count of seven weeks beginning on Passover eve and ending in Shavuot), it is known that man's primary work is to connect himself to the Creator.

Omer comes from the word (n Hebrew) "gathering sheaves." RASHI interpreted, "as it is translated, gathering sheaves, collecting." It means that by becoming mute and not opening the mouth with complaints against the Creator, but rather, for that person 'Everything that the Merciful One does, He does for the best' (*Berachot* 9), and says that he, meaning his thought and desire, will be only for the Creator, then he is gathering.

That is, by connecting all of one's thoughts and desires with a tight connection of having only one goal—to bring contentment to the maker—a person is regarded as "gathering."

The interpreters say that the *Omer* count comes from the words, "and under His feet there appeared to be sapphire brick, as pure as the bodies of the sky." This means that by a person connecting himself to the Creator, he is rewarded with the revelation of the light of the Creator appearing on him. It follows that by a person gathering, tying all the desires in one knot, meaning to one purpose—for the Creator—then that *Omer* shines. This is the meaning of the *Omer* [gathering] count, where a person shines with the light of the Creator.

And since a Jew consists of seven qualities, which must be corrected into being for the Creator, and there is a rule that each quality comprises the others, then we have seven times seven, thus forty-nine days. This is why we count forty-nine days to the days of the reception of the Torah.

Omer comes from the word *Seorim* [barley/measures]. This means that it comes from measures, by measuring in the heart the greatness of the Creator, as the holy *Zohar* interprets the verse, "Her husband is known at the gates." The holy *Zohar* says, "Each according to what he assumes in his heart," to that extent the light of the Creator is on that person.

This is called "faith." When a person is rewarded with faith in the Creator, it is regarded as a "beast." This is the meaning of the *Omer* being of barley, which is animal food, meaning that he has not yet been rewarded with the view of Torah. But on Shavuot, when rewarded with the reception of the Torah, one receives the view of Torah. For this reason, we offer the offering of wheat, which is food for man, who is the speaking. But before one is rewarded with Torah, which is the speaking, it is regarded as an offering of barley, which is animal food. At that time it is called "gathering sheaves," regarded as being mute, which is only animate, and not speaking, for only by the Torah are they rewarded with being "speaking."

Letter No. 60

June 11, 1962, Antwerp

To my friend,

I received what you wrote, and in these lines you open your heart, what is missing and what is abundant. May you succeed in the new place. "Arise and go up" means that the place causes. That is, sometimes a person rises by sitting, meaning by "sit and do not do," as our sages said, "Sat and did not commit a transgression; it is as though he performed a *Mitzva* [good deed/correction]." Also, sometimes he ascends in degree by rising and doing.

It follows that "Arise and go up" refers to his ascent by rising and doing. This means that the "do" is more important than "do not do," as our sages said, "Do repels do not do," since man's way is to love rest, and in "do," when he must get up he has more labor, so it is more important.

In ethics, "do not do" is more important, as explained in the holy *Zohar*. But in the revealed, regarded as the externality of the Torah, where we begin with externality, and then, when we keep the externality, we begin delve into the internality, the order of the work is that "do" is greater.

This is so because initially, man chooses only rest. Hence, where he should arise and not be in "sit and do not do," it is more difficult for him. And in all the places where there is more labor, it is more important. But once he is used to the work, he considers only the profits.

"Do not do" indicates that the pleasure appearing by Torah and *Mitzvot*, and there is the matter that a great reward and pleasure appears, which is forbidden to receive before the end of correction, as our sages said, "The pig is destined to return to the Torah" …

And let us return to our issue. We must know that man's main purpose in this world is to be rewarded with the sweet pleasantness and savor of the Torah. Only when one feels the sweetness of the Torah can he see that he is the happiest man in the world.

But when he looks at the rest of the people, it evokes in him pity at how they are spending their lives in torment, and never feel any flavor in life that will be worth suffering the torments they are suffering in the world in return for the pleasure they are receiving for the toil.

And even they cannot explain why they agree to live under such conditions. But the real reason is that "You live against your will," and this is why they want to live, and "All that a man has he will give for his life." And even though according to the calculation that he will do it is better to give up living, still, the "You live against your will," does not let him think this, but rather man wants to exist.

However, we need to understand why the Creator would do such a thing—that man's vitality will be only because of recognition and not because of pleasure. Indeed, it is done only for man's correction. That is, on the one hand he sees that it is not worthwhile to live for corporeality, meaning that corporeal pleasure will not suffice for him, for the labor that one must pay for this. And for this reason there is room for one to introspect and place all his ambitions in the Torah. If he is satisfied in corporeality, he will never conclude that it is better to move from corporeal needs to spiritual needs. Were it not for the matter of "You live against your will," every person would immediately commit suicide, so as to not suffer torments. It

Letter No. 60

turns out that "You live against your will" helps him only so as to not escape from the torments.

Suffering cleanses one's iniquities. That is, the suffering causes him to place all his passions only in Torah and *Mitzva* [commandment], by which he is rewarded with the vitality of the Torah. We say about this, "for they are our lives and the length of our days." That is, we want long lives not because "You live against your will," but because "They are our lives," which is really life, and this is why we want such days to prolong.

And since now you have made the "Arise and go up," meaning went into a new place, "And you have not a thing that has no place" (*Avot* 4:3), you should try to always be as in "Arise and go up," and not be idle but rise higher and higher and be rewarded with the pleasantness of the brightness of the light of Torah.

From your friend, Baruch Shalom HaLevi,

Son of Baal HaSulam

Letter No. 61

June 11, 1962, Antwerp

To my friend,

I was belated replying to the letters I received from the friends since the mail I receive is not working properly because I move from place to place, so by the time the letters reach me I am already elsewhere, in another country. I received your letter only last week. Because it was before the festival of Shavuot I had no time to reply. I also received a letter from... last week, and I replied to him very briefly.

Regarding your request for an explanation about the article, "Anyone who is happier with his *Daat* [knowledge] than with his *Hochma* [wisdom], it is a good sign for him," we need to understand the meaning of the signs. It is known that one should always know and test whether he is going on the path of truth, which is the direct way to the goal for which man was created. Therefore, we were given signs to as to know the truth.

In Kabbalah, *Daat* [knowledge] is the middle line, but now I do not wish to interpret this. In ethics, *Daat* means faith in the Creator. This is so because *Daat* is referred to in all the books as "*Dvekut* [adhesion] with the Creator," and *Dvekut* is specifically through faith.

Letter No. 61

This is the meaning of "Anyone who is happier with his *Daat* than with his *Hochma*." This means that the *Hochma* he has obtained does not diminish his faith. This is called being happy with his *Daat*. But if the *Hochma* one has obtained cancels the faith, meaning the *Daat*, then he is not happier with his *Daat* than with his *Hochma* because his *Hochma* wants to cancel his *Daat*, and this is a good sign that he is walking on the path of truth.

We should also understand what our sages said, "One who settles with his wine has of his master's *Daat* [knowledge]," "enters wine, out comes secret."

The holy *Zohar* interprets the verse, "Eat friends, drink and be drunken, O beloved." It interprets that the drinking refers to *Hochma*. Accordingly, we should say "One who settles with his wine," meaning through the *Hochma* that he has obtained he remains settled with faith and has of the *Daat* of his master. This shows that he has *Dvekut* with the Creator, regarded as having of his master's *Daat*.

In this way we should interpret, "Anyone who is happier with his *Daat* [knowledge] than with his inclination, it is a good sign for him. And one who is not happier with his *Daat* than with his inclination, it is a bad sign for him." Since it is the inclination's way to interfere, a man is not satisfied with the inclination. Rather, specifically when the inclination is exhausted, then one is happy. It follows that he can advance in the work of the Creator precisely when he does not feel such great pleasures in corporeal things.

That is, one can engage in Torah and *Mitzvot* precisely where he cannot gain great pleasures. At that time he is willing to dedicate his time and effort for high needs. But when the inclination lets him understand that he will receive great pleasures in corporeality, one cannot subdue one's inclination because one can work where there are great profits, and small profits are rejected before great profits. It follows that the work is like trading.

All this is so if a person has taken upon himself the work for a reward. At that time the inclination may argue that it can profit more in corporeality. It follows that he is displeased because the inclination is in control. This is a bad sign for him, meaning it is a sign that he is not walking on the path of truth.

But if the reason for his engagement in Torah and *Mitzvot* is to be "as an ox to the burden and as a donkey to the load," meaning established on faith above reason, and because of "He said, and His will was done" (I am not elaborating on this because I have spoken many times about this), the inclination has no basis to argue that he should stop his work. He answers everything that the inclination argues with "Now you have given me room to work above mind and reason." That is, had the inclination not argued with intellectual arguments, he would have had nothing with which to go against his intellect. It follows that he is happier with his *Daat* than with his inclination, and this is a good sign for him, a sign he is walking on the path of truth.

May the Creator help us walk on the path of truth.

Baruch Shalom HaLevi

Son of Baal HaSulam

Letter No. 62

June 26, 1962, Antwerp

Hello and all the best to my friend,

I received your letter, and regarding your question concerning *Lishma* [for Her sake] and *Lo Lishma* [not for Her sake], I will give you a simple rule: *Lishma* means that the intention while performing a *Mitzva* [good deed/correction] is that we must intend to bestow contentment upon the Maker. The Creator has let us do things so we will be able to give something to Him through this actions, namely by wanting to please Him.

And why do we want to give Him contentment? It is because it is a great privilege for us that we are serving the King. That is, all of our pleasure is that we are serving the Rav (great one), and this is our reward. This means that it comes to show if we want a reward for the service or the service itself is the reward.

Sometimes we see that a wealthy person will walk some place with a great and wise person, and the wealthy man carries the package of the wise one and does not let anyone else carry the package, but says that he deserves the privilege of carrying the sage's package, and none other.

Sometimes, if the package is difficult to carry due to the weight of the load, and another wealthy person accompanies the sage, as well, he wants to swap with him, meaning he wants to carry the package, too, but he does not agree because it is a great privilege for the wealthy man to serve the sage.

Also, the pleasure of the wealthy mean depends on the wisdom of the rav, since the wiser the rav, compared to his contemporaries, the more the wealthy man enjoys serving him.

In order to pay the porter the sum that the rav should have given, say two dollars, when he departs from the wealthy man, the rav gives the wealthy man three dollars and tells him: "Here, this is for your effort."

He also tells him: "I would have given a simple porter only two dollars, but because you are rich and distinguished, I am adding to it and giving you three dollars." What an insult this would be to the rich man if he were to reward him for the service? The greatness of his reward is only that he served the rav, not the reward for the service.

It is likewise in spirituality. Man's intention should be only the service, since by that he shows his value and importance of serving the King. But when he is asking for reward for the service, he shows that he has no importance for the King, but his aim is only the reward.

But most importantly, it matters not whom he serves, but how much he will receive for the service, like a porter, whose only focus is the reward and does not care whose package he is carrying. His focus is only on how much he will gain. This is the whole difference between serving the King for a reward or serving him not in order to receive reward.

But in order to have strength to work, for a person to be able to engage in Torah and *Mitzvot* [commandments], one must examine the greatness and sublimity of the Creator. It is so because to the exact extent of the greatness of the King it is easier for him to serve the King, since he feels that He is the King of Kings. At that time the joy and pleasure should be boundless.

By that we should depict that he can say that the King let only him stand and serve him, since He did not give that strength to others. And what do they do? Their intention is not to serve the king but to serve some master, for the master to pay for the Master's packages, which they carry all day long.

They do not mind who is the master. What is important for them is who pays a higher salary; this is the master they are serving and for whom they work.

By that you will understand what you asked, that when one feels vitality in Torah and work, namely that the Creator is bringing him closer and letting him serve him, and a person feels delight, then it should be said who is obligating the Torah and work—it must be the Creator because He is the one who is giving him the pleasure in Torah and work, and not that his intention is that through engagement in Torah and work he will obtain corporeal rewards, meaning honor or money. Still, this is considered *Lo Lishma*. Why?

The reason is that pleasure is what compels him to engage in Torah and work. And since man contains the desire to receive pleasure, when he feels pleasure in Torah and work, the will to receive pleasure commits a person engage in Torah and work. Thus, who is the obligator? That is, what is the reason he engages in it? It must be the pleasure, which is called "reward."

This is regarded as serving the King in order to receive reward—where the intention is on the reward, which is the pleasure. At that time it does not matter who is giving him the pleasure. Rather, what matters is that the pleasure is so great that a person surrenders before it.

This is as our sages said about the rule, "This is different because his inclination overpowers him." It follows that he is coerced (*Ketubot* 51:53-54). This means that she no longer has a choice because when the pleasure comes in greater measures than one is used to receiving, a person (no) longer has the strength to overcome. This is regarded as having no choice.

It follows that we should always divide between *Lishma* and *Lo Lishma*. That is, if the pleasure comes by receiving a great pleasure while engaging in Torah and work then his reason is the pleasure, and it does not matter to him who is giving the pleasure. But if the pleasure comes from serving the King, this is called *Lishma* because here it depends whom he is serving. According to the greatness of the King, so is the measure of pleasure.

It follows that his reason is the King, and the pleasure is only the result of serving the King. If he is serving a small King, he has little pleasure. If he is serving a great King, he is great pleasure.

Therefore, if the king is what determines and the cause for the work, it is called *Lishma*, although he is enjoying serving the King, and although he is annulled by the King's greatness and has no room for choice, but everything is for the King. It follows that this is called *Lishma*, when the intention is to serve the King, and not the reward. That is if he feels pleasure while serving the King, but the pleasure is not the cause, but rather the greatness of the King is the cause.

But if he craves the pleasure that comes to him by engagement in Torah and work, it means that the pleasure is the reason and the cause. This is called *Lo Lishma*, but for the purpose of pleasure.

It follows that man's primary work is to examine the greatness of the Creator. That is, one should delve in books that speak of the greatness of the Creator, and while delving, one should depict to oneself to what extent our sages, the Tanaaim and Amoraim, felt the greatness of the Creator.

One should pray to the Creator to shine so he may feel His greatness, so he can subdue his heart and annul before the Creator, and not follow the currents of the world, which is pursuing only the satisfaction of beastly lusts, but that the Creator will open his eyes so he may engage all his life in Torah and work, and "In all your ways, know Him." That is, even when engaging in corporeal matters, it will be for the purpose of *Kedusha* [holiness], as well.

But from *Lo Lishma*, we come to *Lishma*. That is, *Lishma* is already a high degree, and one must begin from *Lo Lishma*. In other words, one should be fully aware that pleasure is found primarily in Torah and work, and not in corporeality.

Although at the moment he feels more pleasure in corporeal things, more than he feels in spiritual things, it is because he lacks the qualification in Torah and work, which also depends on faith in the Creator. At that time, through Torah and faith in the Creator, one feels the light in the Torah, and that light reforms him.

May the Creator open our eyes and delight our hearts, and we will be rewarded with raising the importance of Torah.

Your friend, Baruch Shalom HaLevi Ashlag

Son of Baal HaSulam

Letter No. 63

July 26, 1962, Gateshead, England

To...

I received your letter from the 23rd of July, as well as a letter from... from the 20th of July. And since this week I came to England, I will begin to reply to each and everyone of the letters.

Regarding the gathering of the fellows on the eve of Shabbat, it is very important, and I do not understand why the orthodox cannot gather without the fellows. I think they are already grownups, and do not need the support of the fellows to be the foundation without which they cannot get together. They can sit by themselves, while you fellows sit by yourselves. Therefore, I believe that none should be postponed because of the other.

And regarding... he should take upon himself the burden of persistence, and not think so much about such serious problems. But most importantly, I see that he is afraid of the truth, that he might, God forbid, see some truth and will have to surrender before it. Tell him, "Buy truth and do not sell." Selling means revealing outwards, meaning that one who wants to buy truth not for himself but in order to have something to sell to others, such a man should fear that he may have nothing to sell.

But one who has no interest in life other than to live in the world of falsehood in a truthful way does not care. If he can walk on the path of truth when he sees the truth, then he has nothing to regret. And if it is hard for him to walk on the path of truth, it is still worthwhile for him because he has contact with the truth, and he sits and waits for a time of good will when he can take upon himself to walk by its way.

But fearing that he might, God forbid, see the truth? I have never heard of a person being afraid of that. Although it is written, "Happy is he who is always afraid," but there are many interpretations to this.

I have no time to elaborate now, but in the coming letters I will write in greater detail.

Baruch Shalom HaLevi Ashlag
Son of Baal HaSulam

Letter No. 64

August 20, 1962, London

To...

In response to your letter from June 8, 1961, Jerusalem, I would like to make a few comments about your letter:

1. You write that if the Torah were given in the land (of Israel), the nations of the world would say that Israel received the Torah out of gratitude for the Creator giving them a land flowing with milk and honey, and so they were compelled to receive it.

We should understand, for we see that all the nations have big and abundant lands, yet they have no need to be compelled to receive the Torah, so why is only the people of Israel obliged to receive the Torah if He has given them a land?

2. You write that every nation creates the law on its own land, which is called a "homeland."

That, too, I don't understand, since it is known that any sedentary society, wherever it may be, creates rules in order to sustain the society. Otherwise it cannot exist. As we see that there are large groups that come to Israel from overseas, even if they are together for only a month, they already have judges and officers and special rules. It is all the more so with the people Israel, who were in the desert for forty years and were such a big crowd, so why wouldn't they need laws?

3. We should also understand the connection between laws that politicians fabricated in favor of the people, where the laws are only in favor of worldliness and have no connection to spirituality, to the law from heaven, where the intention is mainly the spirituality of it.

4. You interpret the question about how when the Creator said, "I am the Lord your God," the nations of the world said that He was seeking His own glory, but when He said, "Honor your father," etc., they admitted to the first commandments, and the reason is that they saw that He diminished His glory by saying, "Honor your father."

The explanation is insufficient. After all, we see that it is the order with every king that every soldier must honor his commander when he sees him. If not, the soldier is punished for dishonoring his superiors.

Moreover, we see that sometimes, if the soldiers do not obey their commanders there is a punishment of imprisonment, and the commander can even punish a soldier by death if he disobeys his commanders, since he is diminishing the king's glory. So why was it said that if the Creator gave a commandment to honor the father and mother it diminishes His glory, and say that for this reason the nations of the world admitted to the first commandments?

Also, if they admitted to the first commandments, why did they stay idol worshippers and did not assume the Torah and *Mitzvot* [commandments]?

5. You write that the nations of the world thought that as long as the children are with the parents and are dependent on them, they must respect them, and in the desert, the children were dependent on the Creator, who provided for their needs, so they immediately understood that they must respect only the Creator and not the parents. But when they saw that the Creator said, "Honor your father

and your mother," that even here they must honor the father and mother, they regarded it as exceptional and admitted to the first commandments.

This, too, requires explanation, since even in the desert, the parents tended to their children, as it is written, "Every man as much as he eats; sheaves per head according to the number of your souls." RASHI interpreted that you should take according to the number of people that each has in his tent, take sheaves per head.

Also, the manna, the bread from the sky, needed tending, as it is written, "Bake what you will bake and boil what you will boil, and all that is left over put aside to be kept until morning."

Thus, even then the children were dependent on their parents, and the only difference is that the parents did not have to toil in buying groceries for their children as they do now, when they have to toil in order to get the groceries. So what did they see in the Creator's commandment to honor the parents in the desert?

We can give a simple reason, that this is why the Torah was given in the desert, since as soon as we come out from the governance of Egypt, we must promptly receive the Torah, and must not walk even one moment without the Torah. Therefore, the preparation for the reception of the Torah began as soon as they went out of Egypt.

Even in Egypt the Creator promised them that He would give the Torah, as it is written, "When you take out the people from Egypt, you will worship the God on this mountain." It is so because exodus from Egypt without the Torah is incomplete, since the Torah is the most important thing. This is why the Torah was given in the desert.

While the body is enslaved to the *Klipa* [shell/peel] of Egypt, it has no choice. But as soon as it is liberated, the rule, "And you shall speak of them and not of idle matters," immediately applies to it, for then it can be attributed the iniquity of cancellation of Torah, as it is written, "when you sit in your house and when you walk by the way."

Letter No. 64

And concerning the nations of the world admitting to the first commandments, we should interpret this in intimation: The holy *Zohar* refers to father and mother as *Hochma* and *Bina*. The ways of Torah are clarified by three discernments, called *HBD*. *Hochma* is as in "Who is wise? He who sees the future," and "if you call out for intelligence [*Bina*]," for the Torah is clarified through *Hochma* [wisdom] and *Bina* [intelligence]. There is also the *Daat* [knowledge] that connects, for *Daat* means *Dvekut* [adhesion] and connection, as in "and the man knew Eve, his wife."

We should know that the basis of Judaism is faith, which means above the intellect, when a person believes in the Creator without any understanding or sophistication. It is only acceptance in the heart, as in "And you will know this day and reply to your heart that the Lord is the God."

Once we are rewarded with faith, called *Daat*, which our sages regard as learning *Lishma* [for Her sake], then "He is rewarded with many things, the secrets of Torah are revealed to him, and he becomes as a flowing spring." That is, once a person has been rewarded with faith, he is rewarded with the Torah, called *Hochma* and *Bina*.

Afterward, once he has been rewarded with the Torah, he must extend faith once more because a person must serve the Creator not in order to receive reward. Once he has been awarded the Torah he can say that now he sees that it is worthwhile to serve the Creator because he has the Torah, which is as it is written, "The precepts of the Lord are right, rejoicing the heart." It follows that he is blemishing the faith, which is above the intellect, where he does not see for himself any existence, and only works in faith to annul reality. This is the meaning of "with all your heart, with all your soul, and with all your might." That is, he wants nothing for himself and his only desire is to annul his existence completely.

Therefore, once rewarded with the Torah, a person must renew the faith, which is called *Daat* [knowledge] and *Dvekut* above the intellect, and then he has *HBD*.

Accordingly, there are two times of faith: The first order is "faith first, and Torah next." At that time the order is *Daat* above and *Hochma* and *Bina* below. In the words of the holy *Zohar* (*Beresheet* Vol. 1, item 212), it is called *Segolta de Taamim*.

There are two kinds of *Segol* [Hebrew punctuation mark]:

1) *Segol de Taamim*, whose shape is that the deciding line is above [⋯]. At that time the deciding line that is above is called *Keter*, and the two lines—right and left—are named *Hochma* and *Bina*, for the Torah includes within it *Hochma* and *Bina*. *Hochma* is called "the secrets of Torah," which a person receives, and *Bina* is called what the person attains by *Hochma*. That is, after one has scrutinized the *Hochma* he has received and understands in it as much as he understands. This is called *Bina*.

2) There is another form of *Segol de Nekudot*, whose shape is such that the deciding line is below [⋯]. This means that once he has attained the Torah, he must renew the faith once more. This is called "*Daat* that connects the two discernments," *Hochma* and *Bina*. If he does not return to search for faith above intellect once more, the Torah he had attained before departs from him because a person falls into saying that now he has support for his work, since he says that it is worthwhile to serve the Creator because he already has a basis on which to apply his work, so he no longer needs to serve the Creator above the intellect. It follows that now he is serving the Creator in order to receive reward.

Therefore, faith prior to attaining the Torah is called *Keter*, which decides between *Hochma* and *Bina*, and faith that comes after attaining the Torah is called *Daat*. This is called *Daat de Kedusha* [holiness], since only then can he keep the Torah from departing from him.

By that we can interpret the above words: "When He said, 'I,' etc., idol worshippers said that He was seeking His own glory." "I and you will not have" is called "faith above the intellect," which is annulment of man's existence, which is called "equivalence of form," as in "As He is merciful, so you are merciful," where one does not want to exist at all, but to be annulled before the Creator, since he is not receiving any reward for his work.

"But when He said, 'Honor your father and your mother,' etc., they admitted to the first commandments." That is, when they saw that the Creator commanded to respect *Hochma* and *Bina*, called "father and mother," which is regarded as the Torah and the attainment of the secrets of Torah, they saw that the Creator was giving them a good reward, and realized that faith is only a means for attaining the sublime and lofty things, which is the sweetness of the light of Torah.

It follows that He was not demanding for His own glory, which is called "annulment of reality," but that by that they will be able to come to a state of *Gadlut* [adulthood/greatness], which is a state of persistence of reality. At that time it is to the contrary—to the extent that a person attains the greatness and sweetness of the Torah, to that extent he can praise and glorify the King, since he sees and attains the greatness of the King, and they agreed that on the light of Torah, it is worthwhile to serve the Creator.

And yet, they remained idol worshippers and did not convert because they did not want to receive the *Daat de Kedusha* [knowledge of holiness]. That is, once they were awarded the revelation of the light of Torah, called *Hochma* and *Bina*, they must renew the faith once more in order not to say that the faith they had had before they attained the Torah was only a means, and the most important thing for them is the *Hochma* and *Bina*, which is the persistence of reality and the reception of pleasure.

By extending faith once more, the people of Israel show to all that they are not aiming for *Hochma* and *Bina*, meaning for the reward, but that their sole intention is for the Creator, and the most important thing for them is faith above intellect, which is called "*Daat* that connects a person to the Creator," and is regarded as *Dvekut*.

By that a person determines between the two lines, right and left, at which time there is the unification of man with the Creator and the Torah, which is called *HBD*. In the words of the holy *Zohar*: "The Torah and Israel and the Creator are one." This *Daat* they do not want to receive, and this is called *Daat de Kedusha*.

Therefore, although they admitted that the Creator's will is not His own glory, that He is not intending to receive reward, for they saw that His saying, "Honor your father and your mother," which are regarded as Torah and as reward, is only from the perspective of the Creator. But man must do the work of *Daat* and say once more that to him, the essence of his work is not in order to receive reward. To this the idol worshippers could not agree and they remained in their situation.

May the Creator open our eyes with His Torah and we will be rewarded with *Daat de Kedusha*.

Baruch Shalom HaLevi Ashlag
Son of Baal HaSulam

Letter No. 65

September 5, 1962

To the friends, may they live forever,

Now is the month of *Elul* [August/September] and it is customary that even ordinary people, meaning those with view of landlords, engage in matters of *Teshuva* [repentance], as well.

What is the difference between landlords and students of Torah? The difference is that a "landlord" is one who wants to feel that he is the landlord in the world, meaning that his presence in the world will grow, that he himself will be rewarded with a long life and many possessions, which is called the "persistence of reality."

"Students of Torah" are those who engage only in annulment of reality. He wants to be annulled before the Creator, and his only entitlement to exist in the world is because the Creator wants it. But he himself wants to be annulled. Also, he wants to bring all his possessions as an offering to the Creator, and the only reason he engages in obtaining possession is because it is the Creator's will.

This is the meaning of saying that the view of landlords is opposite from the view of Torah, since the view of Torah is annulment of reality, and the view of landlords is the persistence of reality. On the month of *Elul*, the landlords, too, understand that they must engage in annulment of reality.

Our sages said, "In a place where those who repented stand, complete righteous cannot stand." We should interpret this according to the Kabbalah.

It is known that there is a time of *Katnut* [infancy/smallness], called *Kelim de Keter* and *Hochma*, which are vessels of bestowal. When all we obtain are vessels of bestowal, and bestowal is called "annulment of reality," when he wants only to bestow upon the Creator and not to receive anything, it is called "complete righteous." That is, he has no desire for himself, but all his works are only about how to be annulled before the Creator. This is called a "time of *Katnut*," since all that shines in vessels of bestowal is *Ohr de Hassadim*, called *Nefesh Ruach*.

The time of *Gadlut* [adulthood/greatness] is when a person obtains the vessels of reception, which are *Kelim* of *Bina* and ZON that were below the *Parsa* during the *Katnut*. That is, they departed from the degree because of *Malchut*, which is the will to receive that is on them. In other words, the *Kelim de Bina* and ZON were placed under the governance of the will to receive so it was impossible to use them to receive in order to bestow. Hence, they departed from the degree.

During the time of *Gadlut*—when they improve their works—they return to the degree, for then they can engage in reception in order to bestow. At that time they use the *Kelim de Bina* and ZON, which are called "vessels of reception," since now they have returned to the degree.

This is called *Gadlut* because now the light of *Neshama* and *Haya* illuminates, and this is called the "persistence of reality," since now he engages in reception, except that it is in order to bestow.

It follows from the above that *Katnut* is called "complete righteous," which is the annulment of reality, being *Kelim* of *Keter* and *Hochma*, vessels of bestowal. But the *Kelim* of *Bina* and ZON, which are vessels of reception, are regarded as the persistence of reality, which is for obtainment of possessions, and his only wish is for the possessions to grow and multiply. However, they come and go, meaning that at the time of *Katnut* they are outside of the degree, and during the *Gadlut* they return to the degree, but the light that they draw is that of *Gadlut*.

Therefore, "where those who repented stand," meaning who have light of *Neshama* and *Haya* through their labor, "complete righteous cannot stand." Thus, one who is complete righteous, who engages only with vessels of bestowal, which are *Kelim* of *Keter* and *Hochma*, has only *Katnut*, which is *Nefesh* and *Ruach*, which is only *Ohr de Hassadim* and not *Ohr Hochma*.

And then he is a "landlord," as it is written, "A house shall be built with wisdom," since "house" means possession, which is the persistence of reality. This is done specifically through the light of *Hochma*, which is received specifically in vessels of reception, called *Bina* and *ZON*, which require *Hochma*. But vessels of *Keter* and *Hochma* are regarded as vessels of bestowal and are considered annulment of reality because he does not want to receive anything. But in the end, he is drawing only light of *Katnut*, called *Ohr Hassadim*.

It follows from all the above that a person should repent to at least become a "complete righteous." Later, when he reaches the degree of righteous, he should repent once more.

May the Creator help us to at least be complete righteous.

The main thing in the work is that there is no giving of half a thing from heaven. Otherwise, it could happen that if a person repented half way he would receive assistance from above for half the work. But since there is no giving of half a thing from heaven, a person must pray to the Creator to give him complete help. This means that during his prayer, a person sets what is in his heart in order, since prayer is work in the heart, so a person must decide that he wants the Creator to give him a desire to completely annul before Him, meaning not leave any desire under his own authority, but that all the desires in him will be only to give glory to the Creator.

Once he decides on complete annulment, he asks the Creator to help him execute it. This means that although in the mind and the desire he sees that the body disagrees with him annulling all his desires before the Creator instead of for his own sake, he should pray to the Creator to help him want to annul before Him with all the desires, leaving no desire for himself. This is called a "complete prayer," meaning that he wishes that the Creator will give him a complete desire without any compromises to himself, and he asks of the Creator to help him always be with his righteousness.

That is a complete righteous means that he has unwaveringly determined to always live in a desire of a righteous. This is the meaning of "complete righteous," meaning that this discernment is already completely resolved in him. "Incomplete" means that he still has work on whether or not to annul before Him with all the desires. It follows that the beginning of the work is to be a complete righteous, and then we arrive at the other work, called "those who repent," who restore the vessels of reception and returning them to holiness.

I would like to present evidence that there is no giving of half a thing from heaven. See what our sages said (*Yoma* 69b): "They said, 'Since it is a time of good will, let us ask for mercy on the inclination for transgression.' They asked for mercy and it was granted to them. He told them, 'Note, if you kill it, the world will be ruined.' They locked it up for three days and sought a one-day old egg throughout the whole of the land of Israel, but none was found. They said, 'What will we do? If we kill it, the world will be destroyed. If we ask for mercy on half,' there is no giving of half from heaven. They blinded its eyes with sand, and what helped was that a person does not lust for his kin," thus far their words.

This clearly proves that only wholeness is given from heaven. Baal HaSulam said why this is so: Since the Creator is whole, if He gives some abundance below, the man below must also receive wholeness. Otherwise, even if the Creator gives him, the person cannot receive because he does not have *Kelim* for wholeness.

Therefore, before a person qualifies himself to be fit to receive wholeness, he cannot see the length of the way that he has already traversed on his way toward the goal of wholeness, for only at the end of his work he will be able to see, but not midway, since he will not be able to receive His abundance before he has complete *Kelim* that are ready for it. This is why we must brace ourselves and say that we are already near the king's palace, for every penny joins into a great amount, and perhaps soon we will see that the gate is open before us and we will be rewarded with entering delighting with the king.

We should interpret the above words according to the Kabbalah. We know what is written in several places in the *Sulam* (Ladder commentary on *The Zohar*), that first we draw the right line, then the left, and then the middle line. And the role of the middle line is to make the left line illuminate only half a degree, called VAK *de Hochma*, and not to receive the GAR *de Hochma*.

There is always the question, "Why as soon as we draw the left line, we draw only half a degree, meaning VAK without GAR?" Also, "Why the necessity to draw a complete degree, and only then, through the middle line, we split the degree, where the GAR *de Hochma* are removed upward and the VAK *de Hochma* are extended downward?"

With the above words we will understand it, since there is no giving of half a thing from heaven. We will interpret this by order.

"They said, 'Since it is a time of good will, let us ask for mercy on the inclination for transgression.'" All the transgressions extend from the left line, meaning that they cancel the left line through the *Masach de Hirik*. This is called "They asked for mercy and it was granted to them. He told them," meaning the left line, "Note, if you kill it, the world will be ruined." That is, the intention of creation was to do good to His creations, referring to *Ohr Hochma*, since *Ohr Hassadim* is only the light of *Dvekut* [adhesion], namely the means by which we can remove the blemish of separation, but this is not the light of the purpose of creation.

"They locked it up for three days," meaning they did not use the left line, called *Ohr Hochma* and GAR, "and sought a one-day old egg throughout the whole of the land of Israel, but none was found."

Baal HaSulam explained that "egg" means small vitality, when it is known that there is an animal but it is still not revealed outside. The beginning of the appearance is called a "day old fledgling," meaning a new vitality of today and not of yesterday.

"Throughout the whole of the land of Israel" means those who are using the light of *Hassadim*, which is regarded as the "land of Israel," but no vitality, since vitality extends from *Ohr Hochma*, as he interprets in "Inner Reflection" of Part Two in *The Study of the Ten Sefirot* (items 46-47) regarding "Not Possible but Do Intending," that there must be *Hochma* and vitality. But once the left line has been completely removed, no vitality was found throughout the land of Israel.

"They said, 'What will we do? If we kill it, the world will be destroyed.'" That is, the purpose of creation will not be accomplished, and this is called the "destruction of the world." "Let us ask for mercy on half," meaning we will make such a correction that we draw *Hochma* for only half a degree, meaning to initially draw only half a left line. "There is no giving of half from heaven," since from above there always comes a whole thing.

"They blinded its eyes with sand," which means that after the correction of the *Masach de Hirik* we use the light of *Hochma* only as illumination of *Hochma*, called "female light." This is the meaning of "receiving and not giving downward." Blinding the eyes means that that the sight will not spread below, and this is called "They blinded its eyes with sand," as in "You set a boundary that they may not pass over." The boundary becomes the sand, since the minute they want to extend from above downward the holy immediately becomes secular [in Hebrew, *Hol* means both "secular" and "sand"].

"What helped was that a person does not lust for his kin." That is, we use only illumination from below upward, called "blind," for it does not look down. This will help a person not to lose the nearness, called *Dvekut*. But if we draw from above downward, it will lead to removal and separation. This is why the order must be that we must extend the light of *Hochma* in wholeness.

Letter No. 65

The intention is that they wanted to make a correction: Once they made the point of *Hirik* and cancelled the left line, they wanted to make a correction that they would not draw the left line at all, and there would not be room for the inclination for transgression. However, they saw that this will mean the ruin of the world, since "You have made them all with wisdom," where precisely through *Hochma* [wisdom], the world will exist, and this is the purpose of creation. They wanted to make a correction that only half a degree of *Hochma* would be drawn for fear that there will be people who will not be able to make the correction of the middle line and will fail with the left line.

However, "there is no giving of half a thing from heaven," so there must be the correction through three lines, as is written in the *Sulam* in several places.

Letter No. 66

March 27, 1963

Hello and all the best to my dear friend,

In *Psachim* (116b), "Begins with admonition and ends with praise." Why admonition? Rav said, "In the beginning, our fathers were idol worshippers," etc. And we also say in the *Haggadah* [Passover story], "In the beginning our fathers were idol worshippers, and now the Creator has brought us closer to His work."

To understand the matter, what we can learn from what they were before, we should interpret this in ethics. A person needs to know, when he engages in man's exodus from the exile in Egypt (and we see that all the *Mitzvot* [commandments] are dependent on this matter, because in every thing we say: "In memory of the exodus from Egypt," which means that it is impossible to keep a commandment to the fullest before a person comes out of the exile in Egypt. Although generally we have already come out of Egypt, but in person, each person must come out of this exile). It is impossible to come out of the exile in Egypt before entering the exile. Only then can it be said that we are coming out of the exile.

The author of the *Haggadah* tells us about this that we need to know that in the beginning our fathers were idol worshipper, meaning that they were in exile under the rule of idol worshippers, and only then the Creator brought our fathers closer. But if they did

Letter No. 66

not feel that they were placed under the rule of idol worshippers, it could not be said that the Creator had brought them closer. Only when a person is remote from the Creator can it be said that the Creator is bringing him closer, because the absence should always come before the presence, for the absence is the *Kli* [vessel] and the presence is the light that fills the absence and the darkness.

Therefore, we have to know that we have to prepare ourselves thoroughly, meaning that a person should check himself meticulously and carefully, to see his real condition, what his faith in the Creator is like, if he has complete faith, meaning, is it truthful or superficial, meaning only going by rote, which means that he does it only out of habit and not because of his own desire.

And also whether his qualities are in order. That is, is he in the form of, "All of your actions will be for the Creator," or God forbid to the contrary, meaning that everything he does is only with the intention to please himself? Our sages said about the verse, "And the grace of the nations is sin. All the good that they do, they do for themselves," and they cannot do anything for the Creator.

And if a person is placed under this rule, like the nations of the world, then he is in exile, and then he is regarded as an idol worshipper. And then there is room for prayer that the Creator will help him out of this exile. And then it can be said: Now, meaning once he is in exile and regarded as an idol worshipper, it can be said, "Now the Creator has brought us closer to His work," meaning, to work in the work of the Creator, and to not work for the governance of idol worshipping.

This is called the "exodus from Egypt," when all the works are for the Creator. For this reason we relate the commandments to the memory of the exodus from Egypt. Only then, once we have come out of the exile in Egypt, can we keep the commandments because of the Creator's commandment and not for other reasons. This is the meaning of what the Tanah says, "Beginning with admonition and ending with praise." This means that when a person wants to begin with the work of the Creator, he must begin with admonition, meaning, with how we are placed under the governance of idol worshippers. Then we can come to the degree of, "Now the Creator has brought us closer to His work." And this is "ending with praise."

The order of the work is in two ways, meaning in faith in the Creator, as well as in qualities, meaning that all of his work will be for the Creator. By that we should interpret what our sages said, "Our sages said, when Rabbi Elazar ben Parta and Rabbi Haninah ben Tardion were captured, Rabbi Elazar ben Parta said to Rabbi Haninah ben Tardion, "Happy are you for being caught for one thing. Woe to me for being caught for five things." Rabbi Haninah said to him, "Happy are you for being caught for five things and you are saved. Woe unto me, for being caught for one thing and I am not saved. You engaged in Torah and in charity, or doing mercy, etc., as Rav Hunah said, 'All who engage only in Torah is as one who has no God,' as it was said, 'and many days for Israel without a true God.' What is without a true God? All who engage only in Torah is as one who has no God.'"

It is difficult to understand this excerpt. We should interpret that the main thing that a person should do in the world is to make all his works be for the Creator. And since man was created with a quality of delighting only himself, to the point that it is impossible for him to do anything unless he sees that some good will come out of it for himself, then how can one work for the Creator?

But the Creator has given us commandments between man and man, by which man accustoms himself to work in favor of his neighbor. By that he comes to a higher degree, to having the ability to work for the Creator as well. Otherwise, even though a person engages in Torah and *Mitzvot*, he cannot engage for the Creator. It therefore follows that if he engages only in Torah, and not in doing good, he cannot work in order to bestow because he lacks the quality of love of others. It therefore follows that although he engages in Torah and *Mitzvot*, if it is not for the Creator, it is as one who has no God, for if he truly had the sensation of Godliness, he would certainly be engaging in order to bestow. But if he had engaged in doing good, then he would have the quality of love of others, by which he would also come to love the Creator, and would have the ability to observe Torah and Mitzvot for the Creator.

It turns out that a person should have the power and force to overcome his qualities, to turn them into being in favor of others, for by that he will later be rewarded with working with those qualities for the Creator.

Because once a person has already been corrected in his qualities so he can work in favor of others, he can work on the matter of faith in the Creator, for then he is fit to be rewarded with faith, for then he already has equivalence of form, called, "Cleave onto his attributes," as in, "As He is merciful, be you merciful."

And may the Creator help us come out of the exile and be rewarded with the complete redemption soon in our days, amen.

May you rise in the degrees of blessing and success and happiness, and happy and kosher festival.

From your friend who wishes you and your family all the best,

Baruch Shalom HaLevi Ashlag, son of Baal HaSulam

Letter No. 67

September 27, 1963 (Eve of *Yom Kippur*)

Hello and all the best to my dear friend,

I received your letter and may the Creator help you and your family be always healthy and well. And for the new year, may it be a year of blessings and success in all your works. I ask that you will write me more often since I long to hear how you and your family are doing.

On the *Selichot* [penitential prayers] that we say on the eve of *Rosh Hashanah* [Hebrew New Year's Eve], we say, "How will I open my mouth, and how will I raise my eyes? I have neither deeds nor merits." We also say, "And if You complement my measure according to my work, and I shall see that I am naked," and also, "Neither by mercy nor by deeds we come before You. We knock on Your doors as meager and destitute." That is, there is nothing good about us, yet afterwards we say, "You must not do such a thing: put the righteous to death together with the wicked, as though the righteous is as the wicked. You must not; You who judges the whole earth will not pass judgment."

We should understand how it is possible that while saying that there are no good deeds in us, we complain to the Creator and say, "You must not do such a thing: put the righteous to death together with the wicked." This brings up the question, "Who is the righteous?" (see RASHI's commentary on the portion, *Vayera*, regarding this verse).

It is known that man is a small world, meaning comprising all the nations of the world, which are generally referred to as the "evil inclination." This means that in each person there is every foul trait that exists in each and every nation. But he also consists of Israel, which is called the "good inclination."

When there are no good deeds in a person, it is because the evil inclination is controlling the body. At that time a person is called "wicked" (See in Baba Batra, 16a: "Raba said, 'Job sought to rid the whole world of the judgment. He said to Him: 'Master of the world, You have created righteous and created wicked, who is stopping You?' RASHI interprets there, 'You have created righteous through the good inclination and You have created wicked through the evil inclination. Hence, no one is saved from You, for who will stop [You]? The sinners are coerced.'" From this we see that the good inclination is called "righteous," and the evil inclination is called "wicked").

It therefore follows that when one has no good deeds, it is only because the wicked within one is leading, and the righteous within is trailing, meaning following the wicked without any permission to protest. This is regarded as the righteous being in exile, meaning that Israel in him is in exile, placed under the governance of the nations of the world, and has no authority of his own.

By this we can understand our complaint to the Creator: "You must not ... put the righteous to death together with the wicked," since the very life of the wicked is regarded as death. It is as our sages said, "The wicked, in their lives, are called 'dead,'" since the life they enjoy in this world prevents them from obtaining eternal life. Since the whole intention of creation, namely to do good to His creations, is unattainable while being far from the Creator, since "the cursed does not adhere to the blessed." Therefore, the wicked in their lives are called "dead." This is the meaning of the wicked being sentenced to death.

And while the righteous is under the governance of the wicked and has no power or might to overcome him, the righteous, too, is sentenced to death, since he cannot receive any goodness from the Creator, as the wicked within him interferes with adhering to the Creator. Thus, the righteous, too, is regarded as dead. This is the complaint to the Creator: "You must not ... put the righteous to death together with the wicked." That is, the righteous in us, the good inclination, cannot do a thing because the wicked do not let it draw spiritual life.

Therefore, when one sees that there are no good deeds within him, he knows that the reason is that the wicked in him is governing, and Israel, who is the righteous, called the "good inclination," is in exile. At that time we ask of the Creator and complain to Him that He has given us a good inclination that is powerless because it is in exile, and for this reason the righteous is sentenced to death, as well. This is the meaning of "You must not do such a thing."

However, the Creator will deliver us from the exile because what use is there in having a good inclination, called "righteous," that is completely powerless? It follows that the good inclination was given to us for nothing. This is our complaint: "Putting the righteous to death together with the wicked, as though the righteous is as the wicked." That is, it is as though both are doing the same thing. However, the Creator will have mercy on us and will deliver us from exile.

This pertains specifically to when we see that there are no good deeds in us, or that one knows that this is the only reason—that the righteous is in exile under the governance of the wicked.

This is why we ask of the Creator and mark a sign on *Rosh Hashanah* saying, "May we be the head and not the tail." That is, may the Israel in us be the head, and may the wicked be the tail, and then we will be rewarded with long life and the goodness in the intention of creation, which is to do good to His creations.

May we be awarded good writing and signing,

Baruch Shalom HaLevi Ashlag
Son of Baal HaSulam

Letter No. 68

December 18, 1963 (eighth day of Hanukkah)

Hello and all the best to my friend,

I am sending you and your family congratulations. May your family know contentment, peace, and health. As your family has grown, may all the works you are engaged in grow, as well, both in corporeality and in spirituality, and may you find in them success and blessings.

We see that our sages have determined to publicize the miracle regarding two miracles that occurred to the whole of Israel: Hanukkah and Purim. On Hanukkah, it is by lighting the candles, and on Purim, it is by reading the *Megillah* [Purim scroll]. We should understand why on Hanukkah we need to show the candles outwards, for all to see, and why the candles should be lit when everyone has left the market, which is in order for people outside to see, unlike Purim. We should also understand why on Hanukkah our sages asked, "What is Hanukkah," which was not so on Purim?

We should distinguish between a miracle that pertains to spirituality and a miracle that pertains to corporeality, and what is a miracle at all? It is known that something natural is not regarded as a miracle, but what is above nature, this is considered a miracle. Natural means something that man can do alone. This is called natural. But what man cannot do is already regarded as above nature.

For example, if someone is critically ill at a person's home, and all the doctors have given up and said that they cannot help that patient, then a believing person says to the Creator, "Dear Lord, now no one can help me but You," so he asks of the Creator, "Perform a miracle and heal this sick person." And when the sick is healed, it is called a "miracle from heaven."

By that we can understand the meaning of a miracle in spirituality. When a person is born, the evil inclination immediately connects to him, as it is written, "Sin crouches at the door," and the good inclination comes after thirteen years. Our sages said, "It is a caution for a courthouse not to hear the words of the litigant before the defendant's advocate comes," since they will justify the argument of the plaintiff. Accordingly, when the evil inclination comes to a person with its arguments, he is compelled to listen to it. Later, when the good inclination comes, its words are not heard. It follows that the good inclination is in exile, and the evil inclination has full control over the body. This is regarded as spirituality in exile, under the corporeality.

A person cannot come out of this exile, and only the Creator can deliver him, as our sages said, "Man's inclination overpowers him each day and seeks to put him to death. Were it not for the help of the Creator, he would not have prevailed over it." From this we see that only the Creator can help, and this is why it is called a "miracle."

On Hanukkah, we say, "The evil kingdom of Greece came over Your people, Israel, to make them forget Your teaching and move them from the laws of Your will." This means that the exile was only on spirituality, since the Greeks wanted to rule over the people of Israel with their philosophy.

This is the meaning of what we say, "Greeks have gathered around me ... and have broken the walls of my towers." The holy

Letter No. 68

ARI says that *Homat* [wall] comes from the word *Tehum* [area/zone], meaning that the people of Israel have a limit to what is permitted to think. That is, one must believe that the Creator leads the world with benevolent guidance, even though we do not understand it.

When a person has that boundary, he has a wall his enemies cannot penetrate. This is a keeping from foreign thoughts. This is why faith is called a "wall." The Greeks broke that wall, and a miracle occurred and the Creator helped them, as it was mentioned, "Were it not for the help of the Creator, he would not have prevailed over it."

It follows that the miracle of Hanukkah was a spiritual miracle, and in spirituality we must ask "What?" or we do not feel the miracle. This is why they said, "What is Hanukkah?" so that each one will ask about the miracle of spirituality, meaning so as to first know the meaning of spiritual exile, and then be able to be granted spiritual redemption.

And because of it we should divulge it publicly, to make everyone interested. Otherwise, we do not feel the exile or the redemption, since exile is a matter of feeling. For example, one who sees one's friend driving a car on Shabbat (orthodox Jews don't drive on Shabbat), and approaches him and asks him, "Listen friend, do you regret driving on Shabbat? After all, our sages said, 'The wicked are full of remorse.'" There is no doubt that he will laugh at him. So what does it mean that our sages said that the wicked are full of remorse?

Rather, we must say that one who feels that he is wicked regrets it. But one who does not feel it does not regret. Therefore, the person who is driving on Shabbat and does not regret it, certainly does not feel that he is wicked because he does not believe in the Creator, so he does regard himself as wicked for driving on Shabbat.

It follows that a person cannot be in spiritual exile if he does not feel it. This is why we should ask, "What is Hanukkah?" so that one will begin to reflect on himself. But on Purim, the redemption was on corporeality, so there is no need to ask "What?" since a corporeal exile is something everyone knows and feels, so when the miracle is publicized, everybody knows.

Therefore, on Hanukkah, we say, "These candles ... and we have no permission to use them," since the miracle was only on spirituality. But on Purim, it is written, "feasting and rejoicing," since the miracle was on the bodies.

May the Creator help us be granted redemption in spirituality and corporeality, Amen.

From your friend who wishes you and your family the best,

Baruch Shalom HaLevi Ashlag

Letter No. 69

February 17, 1964

Hello and all the best to my friend, the dearest of men,

Our sages said, "It is written, 'Do not reply to a fool according to his folly lest you will be like him.' It is also written, 'Reply to a fool according to his folly lest he will be wise in his own eyes.' This is not an issue: one concerns matters of Torah, and one concerns worldly matters." RASHI interpreted, "Concerning matters of Torah, it is permitted to answer him according to his folly" (*Shabbat*, 30b). We should understand the prohibition to reply concerning worldly matters; what is there to fear? It seems as though it should have been the opposite, that in spiritual matters we should fear because it is not good to argue with a fool, but why should it be forbidden to answer him in worldly matters?

We should also understand what our sages said about the verse, "Let me know Your ways." "He said to Him: 'Master of the world, why is there a righteous who is happy, and a righteous who is suffering, a wicked who is happy, and a wicked who is suffering?' He said to him: 'Moses, a righteous who is happy—a righteous, son of righteous; a righteous who is suffering—a righteous, son of wicked; a wicked who is happy—a wicked, son of righteous; a wicked who is suffering—a wicked, son of wicked'" (*Berachot*, 7a).

In its literal meaning, this is difficult to understand. We see that there are also wicked, son of wicked, who is happy, and a righteous, son of righteous, who is suffering.

However, we should interpret that this does not refer to matters of providence as they seem to us, for it is written about this: "My thoughts are not your thoughts, nor your ways My ways." Rather, saying, "Let me know Your ways" refers to the ways of the work of the Creator.

It is known that the purpose of creation is to do good to His creations. That is, as long as one has not achieved a state where he is happy in the world, he should know that he has not achieved the purpose for which man was created. Another rule that we should know is that in matters of work, father and son are cause and consequence. That is, the previous state causes the next state, where the first state is called "father," and the second state is called "son."

By this we will understand all the above-mentioned. An ordinary person, who does not engage in Torah and *Mitzvot* [commandments], if he sees a righteous man engaging in Torah and comes and asks the righteous, "What is this work for you?" there is no doubt he is coming to mock the righteous for engaging in Torah and *Mitzvot*. He certainly does not want the righteous to give him a real answer, which will obligate him to engage in the work of the Creator, too, for this is not his intention. Therefore, do not reply to him, for he himself does not want you to reply. This is called a "wicked."

One who is in such a state, meaning that the wicked in the world install such thoughts in his mind, do not reply to him. That is, one must not heed such thoughts. This is called "wicked, son of wicked." This is the meaning of "suffering," if such thoughts come into one's mind. "Do not reply" means that one must not answer such questions, as it is written, "lest you will be like him." This is why he is regarded as "suffering" because it is utterly bad and no good will come out of it.

But there is also one who engages in Torah and *Mitzvot*, and when he begins to engage only *Lishma* [for Her sake], and not with any intention for his own good, the question, "What is this work for you," comes to him, meaning what will you get out of working only for the Creator. That person—whose intention for it to be for the Creator is what caused him these thoughts—is "happy," since this is a sign that he truly wants to engage for the Creator, as this is why his body does not agree to walk with him on this path.

Therefore, that person craves for the righteous to answer him clearly, so he will know what to reply to his body and will have something with which to convince it. Therefore, "reply to him." This is regarded as being permitted to reply in matters of Torah, since he really does want an answer.

In such a state, one is called "wicked, son of righteous," since the argument of the wicked, "What is this work," comes to him from engaging in Torah and *Mitzvot*. It turns out that he is regarded as righteous, and the righteous deeds that he wants to be for the Creator engender in him the question, "What is this work?" This is why he is a "wicked, son of righteous." He is "happy" because it is a sign that he is walking on the path of truth.

This is the meaning of what our sages said, "Man's inclination overpowers him each day and seeks to put him to death. Were it not for the help of the Creator, he would not have prevailed over it." Only the Creator can help a person be able to intend for the sake of the Creator. When the Creator helps him, he becomes a righteous and is rewarded with permanent faith in the Creator. In the words of our sages, this is called, "One who learns Torah *Lishma* [for Her sake]," meaning that his only aim is the sake of the Creator.

However, this does not achieve the purpose of creation, as it is written, "If you are right, what will you give Him?" since the Creator has no need for us to work for Him, since the correction of working *Lishma* was given only to avoid the bread of shame. Therefore, on the one hand, that state is considered "righteous, son of wicked," since the previous state, before the Creator helped him, was wicked, but once the Creator has helped him he has become a righteous. This is why he is called "righteous, son of wicked." However, he is still "suffering" because he has still not achieved the purpose of his creation.

Subsequently, he comes to a state called "Torah," where the secrets of Torah are revealed to him and the whole world is worthwhile for him. The Torah is called a "gift," as our sages said about the verse, "From Matanah [Heb: gift] to Nahliel," since it is the gift of the Creator. That is, once a person has been awarded faith, he can be awarded the next state.

The next state is called "Torah." The difference between faith and Torah is that we know we have two matters in the ways of the Creator: 1) work, 2) Torah. The difference between Torah and work is that work means that a person does not enjoy what he is doing, and does it only to be rewarded. And since one needs to work not in order to be rewarded, his work is called *Tzedakah* [righteousness/charity]. This is why the first state, which is faith, is called "righteousness," as it is written, "And he believed in the Lord and He regarded it for him as righteousness."

Conversely, the Torah is called a "gift" because he enjoys it. Otherwise it is not regarded as a gift, for when one receives a gift from one's friend, he does not ask him for a reward for receiving the gift from him.

Thus, when one is rewarded with the Torah, it is considered that he has reached his purpose, and is therefore "happy." And because in the previous state he had faith, which is regarded as righteous, he is considered a righteous, son of righteous. This is the meaning of "righteous who is happy," as he has achieved the purpose of creation and already feels the benevolence to His creations. In that state he is called a "good guest," as our sages said, "What does a good guest say? 'All that the Landlord has toiled, He has toiled only for me.'"

May the Creator help us be granted with what we must, and with complete redemption.

From your friend who wishes you and your family all the best,

Baruch Shalom HaLevi Ashlag

Son of Baal HaSulam

Letter No. 70

November 20, 1964

To my friend, the dearest of men,

How have you been ... may the Creator help you in all that you wish for the best, and may you succeed wherever you go.

It is written in the holy *Zohar* (*Vayishlach*, 19-20): "'It is better to be ignoble and a slave to Him than respectable and breadless.' Ignoble means Jacob, who lowered his spirit before Esau so that afterwards, Esau would be his slave, etc. From the verse, 'It is better to be ignoble,' etc., this is Jacob, who lowered his spirit before Esau so that afterwards Esau would be his slave and he will rule over him and exist in him: 'Let peoples serve you, and nations bow down to you.'

"Come and see about '...Because Jacob knew that he was now needy of him, he became ignoble before him. By that, he was wiser and shrewder than on any deed he had ever done against Esau,' etc. Interpretation: 'Because Jacob knew that he was now needy of him, he became ignoble before him. By that, he was wiser and shrewder than on any deed he had ever done against Esau. And had Esau sensed this, he would have killed himself, so he would not come to that.'"

We should understand what wisdom is there in surrendering himself before Esau now, to the point that *The Zohar* says that had Esau known about this he would have killed himself.

We should interpret this according to Baal HaSulam, which is by way of ethics, namely that one should know how to handle oneself in the work of the Creator. We see that with Laban it was the opposite. With Esau we see that Jacob subjugated himself before him and gave him presents, but Esau did not want to receive and replied to Jacob, "I have plenty," until Jacob pleaded with him to accept his gifts. Conversely, with Laban we see that Laban told him the opposite: "The daughters are my daughters, the sons are my sons, and all that you see is mine."

We should know that there are two kinds of evil inclination, called "two kinds of *Klipot* [shells/peels]":

1) First there is the act. When a person wants to perform a *Mitzva* [good deed/commandment] or study a lesson, it comes and tells him: "You are not worthy of doing this; after all, what you are doing is not for the Creator; you are doing this only for me," meaning for the evil inclination.

"The daughters are my daughters" means all the understandings that you have in serving the Creator is what I have given you, and you have no view (knowledge) of Torah. "And all that you see is mine," meaning all that you see with regard to Torah and *Mitzvot* [commandments] is on my name, namely the evil inclination. Thus, why exert so hard in Torah and good deeds since it is not for the Creator anyway, and your work is not accepted before Him, so you will have no reward for this anyhow. Therefore, you need not do anything good.

At that time one must overcome and say to it: "What you are saying is incorrect. Rather, I am doing everything for the Creator, and everything I'm doing is accepted by the Creator and gives Him contentment. It is enough for you that I work for you, meaning my giving you to eat and drink, and so on. But with regard to serving the Creator, you have no permission to interfere with such matters.

2) Once he has done the good deeds, it is to the contrary, meaning that then he should say to his evil inclination (which is then called Esau, from the (Hebrew) word, *Asu* [done/deed], meaning after the

fact): "I am giving you everything. That is, everything I did was for you, which is regarded as *Lo Lishma* [not for Her sake]." This is regarded as giving him the gifts, which is the Torah and *Mitzvot* that he claims belong to Esau.

At that time Esau claims the contrary: "I have plenty, and I do not want your Torah and *Mitzvot*." That is, Esau tells him, "You did everything for the Creator, so you are therefore a great Jew, so you should be proud over all your friends who are not working for the Creator, while you are. He wants him to come into haughtiness.

But one who is in a state of Jacob argues otherwise: "The Torah and *Mitzvot* belong to you. Now I need to repent because I want to bring contentment to the Creator and I feel my lowliness, that I am still far from the truth, from being able to direct all my works to the Creator."

This is the difference between Laban and Esau.

May the Creator help us be saved from Laban and from Esau, and may we be granted complete redemption soon in our days, Amen.

From your friend who wishes you and your family all the best.

Baruch Shalom Ashlag
Son of Baal HaSulam

Letter No. 71

January 22, 1965

To my friend,

I do long to know how you are doing.

"Thus you shall say to the house of Jacob and tell the sons of Israel." RASHI interpreted "to the house of Jacob" to be the women—speak to them with a soft tongue. "And tell the sons of Israel"—punishments and precisions—he interpreted it to be to the men, words that are as hard as tendons [*Mechilta*].

It is said in *The Zohar* (Jethro, item 161): "Thus you shall say to the house of Jacob," meaning by saying, from the side of judgment. "And tell the sons of Israel," the sons of Israel means the men, who come from the side of *Rachamim* [mercy]."

It seems from the words of *The Zohar* that to the women it is in saying, which is from the side of judgment, since women are from the quality of judgment, and to the men, "tell," with the quality of mercy, for they come from mercy.

But the words of RASHI imply the opposite, that with the men you will speak words as hard as tendons, and to the women you should speak with a soft tongue.

We should interpret that they are saying the same thing, but first we need to understand what is judgment and what is mercy. Judgment is when two people go to court, one says, "It is all mine," and the other says, "It is all mine." That is, one who argues, "It is all mine," is regarded as judgment. Mercy means giving, which is as our sages said, "As He is merciful, so you are merciful." It follows from the above that the quality of judgment means one who is receiving, and mercy is one who is giving.

A female is one who is deficient, meaning receiving, and a male is one who is in a state of giving.

Accordingly, it follows that a female is judgment, meaning receiving. If one who is receiving is told to engage in bestowal, he cannot do it because it is against his nature. Therefore, when we want him to engage in work of the Creator, we must speak to him with a soft tongue, meaning with a language he understands, namely the langue of reception. This is so because one who is in a state of *Nukva* [female], which is judgment, agrees to work only in order to receive reward. This is called "with a soft tongue."

To the men, who are regarded as "giving," it is possible to speak with a tongue "as hard as tendons," for bestowal is difficult for the body to hear, since the body wants specifically to receive. And since he is regarded as a male, meaning has the power to overcome—that he overcome his qualities—we speak to him from the side of mercy, for mercy means bestowal.

By that we will understand the words of RASHI: "to the house of Jacob" is the women; speak to them with a soft tongue." That is, one who is in a state of female, who cannot prevail over the power of the body, and he is called "female," as in "He was as faint as a female," we must speak to him with a soft tongue, namely in order to receive reward. To this the body agrees.

To the men, it is with a harsh tongue, namely bestowal, with which it is difficult for the body to agree. However, he has the power to overcome, so we can speak to him with a tongue of mercy, which means bestowal.

May the Creator help us overcome the evil within us and may we be rewarded with the reception of the Torah.

From your friend who awaits hearing good news from you,

Baruch Shalom HaLevi Ashlag

Letter No. 72

April 26, 1965

Hello and all the best to my friend,

I ask that you will please write me often about how you and your family are doing, about your health and provision, for I become very worried if I don't hear from you.

Raban Gamliel would say, "Anyone who did not say these three things on Passover, did not fulfill his duty. These are: *Pesach* [Passover], *Matza* [unleavened bread], and *Maror* [bitter herb]." We should interpret what this means in ethics. It is known that the order of the work is that one should begin, and then comes help from above. It is as our sages said, "Man's inclination overcomes him everyday and seeks to put him to death, and were it not for the Creator's help, he would not have overcome it." This means that only when one wants to work he receives help from above.

However, there is a rule that one receives help only when he needs help, meaning when he sees that he cannot do it alone. Otherwise the request for help is not a genuine request because he knows that he can do it all alone, but he is lazy, and the lazy receive no help, as only those who long for the Creator receive help, as our sages said, "Be as fierce as a leopard, as light as an eagle, run like a gazelle, and as strong as a lion."

Therefore, the order is that the beginning is a state of *Matza*, from the words *Matza* and *Meriva* [quarrel], as it is written, "When they strove with the Lord," and as our sages said, "One should always vex the good inclination over the evil inclination, as it is said, 'Be angry, but do not sin.'" RASHI interprets, "Make war with the evil inclination.

When a person makes war with it each day, but sees that it has still not moved an inch, but on the contrary, it has grown worse, he begins to feel bitter. This is called *Maror* [bitter herb]. It is as the holy ARI wrote, that at the time of redemption, Israel stood at forty-nine gates of impurity, and then the Creator appeared to them and redeemed them.

This is truly hard to understand: How can it be said that before Moses and Aaron came to the people of Israel as messengers of the Creator, they were not so deep in gates of impurity, but only after Moses and Aaron came and they saw all the signs and tokens that were in Egypt did they fall so deep into the gates of impurity? The thing is that everything depends on the sensation. One cannot feel the true reality itself, as our sages said, "one does not see one's own faults," and "one learns Torah only where one's heart desires." Therefore, he cannot see the truth as it truly is. Rather, being able to see the truth is help from above.

Therefore, before Moses and Aaron came, they did not see the truth. But afterwards, when they saw all the signs, they were awarded seeing the truth as it is. That is, they saw that they were at the lowest degree, at the forty-nine gates of impurity.

And then they were rewarded with redemption. That is, after they felt the bitterness, they were able to make a real prayer over their situation. It follows that the *Maror*, too, is help from the Creator, meaning by Moses and Aaron, and the signs and tokens that the Creator had shown them.

And then they were rewarded with *Pesach* [Passover], meaning that the Creator passed over the houses of the children of Israel. This is the meaning of "skipping," called "skipping over the degrees."

Normally, one who learns some wisdom adds gradually. But here it was the opposite—each time they would descend lower into impurity, and only when they saw their real state they could ask of the Creator for real prayer, and then the Creator helped them.

This is the meaning of *Pesach*, *Matza*, *Maror*, which go together. Otherwise, it is impossible to be awarded redemption. The letters of *Golah* [exile] and *Geulah* [redemption] are the same (in Hebrew), and the only difference between them is the *Aleph*. This shows us that only when one feels the exile the *Aleph*, which is the Champion of the World, is revealed to him.

By that we will understand what our sages said: "What is *Maror*? *Hassah* [lettuce]. And why is it called *Hassah*? Because the merciful one *Has* [had mercy] on us."

This is difficult to understand, since we understand that an intimation that the Creator had spared us should have been with something sweet, and not with something bitter. But as said above, in order for one to receive help from the Creator, he must first feel the bitterness of the situation, and it is impossible to feel bitterness because "one does not see one's own fault." Only through help from the Creator can one see one's true state. This is why there is the intimation of *Maror*—that the merciful one had mercy on us and showed us our true state, which is bitter, and then we can be awarded salvation and redemption.

May the Creator send us the complete redemption soon.

From your friend who wishes you and your family peace, health, and much contentment, Amen.

Baruch Shalom Ashlag

Letter No. 73

December 14, 1965

Let me clarify a bit concerning your question, "What is decoration at the point of desire," which you said was difficult for you to understand.

To understand the meaning of decoration we must first understand to what things are referring, meaning what is perplexing to him and what he wants to explain.

We know that there are only two things in the world: Creator and creatures. This means that the Creator wants to bestow pleasures upon the creatures, as it is written, "His desire to do good to His creations." Out of that discernment, the first world that emerged is called "the world of *Ein Sof* [no end]," which means that since He desires to do good, He has created "existence from absence" a desire to receive the pleasure that He wants to give.

Of course, that desire was precisely the size suitable for reception of all the light, for otherwise, meaning if the *Kli* [vessel] is smaller than the light, the creature will not emerge whole, and the certainly Creator created something whole, meaning that He has created a desire to receive that specific light that He has allocated for the creatures.

And according to that desire, the light extended and filled it completely. This is regarded as the upper light filling the whole of reality, which is why it is called *Ein Sof*, since the will to receive did not put a stop and conclusion on the light, but rather expanded into the vessel of reception. That is, had that discernment been drawn back, there would have been no room where Godliness were felt in the world. Even when Adam was immersed in the lust for reception of pleasures only for himself, he still felt Godliness. Only once the *Tzimtzum* [restriction] on receiving with the intention for oneself alone took place, it came about that one who is immersed in lust does not feel Godliness and the beginning of one's work is to believe that there is Godliness in the world. This is so only because of the concealment that was done by the *Tzimtzum*.

We learned that in the world of *Ein Sof*, "it came up in His will ... and He restricted Himself." He interprets that by this he means that there was an ascent of the desire, since the will to receive is opposite from the desire to bestow, which is why he chose more *Dvekut* [adhesion]. *Dvekut* means equivalence of form, and he wanted to be similar to the giver, so he restricted himself. This means that in *Ein Sof* there seems to have been oppositeness between the *Kli* and the giver to the point that He had to correct it, and that for this correction he had set up the *Tzimtzum*.

He introduces *Pirkey de Rabbi Eliezer*, where it is written that before the world was created there was "He and His name are one." This means that there was no difference between the light, which is called "He," and "His name," which is the *Kli*, meaning the will to receive. He interprets that the *Kli* is called "His name" because *Shmo* [His name] in *Gematria* is *Ratzon* [desire]. But according to this, it is perplexing, for if there were no oppositeness between the *Kli* and the light, why was there a need to perform a correction that there will be equivalence, to the point that for this reason he performed the *Tzimtzum*? This is why he explains that this correction was not due to a lack, where he felt that there was oppositeness, but in order to decorate.

Letter No. 73

We can understand the difference between decoration and a lack through an allegory. A town's rabbi made a convention and sent for all the wealthy and respectable people in town to gather in the synagogue, for he wanted to tell them something. The rabbi came on stage and gave a heartfelt sermon about the greatness and importance of charity. Afterwards he told them that since a good man, a wise disciple, has just arrived from overseas, and he had children and a family of eight, and they did not have food for even one meal, no place to stay, and the family is now in the women's section of the synagogue, so he would like each one to donate even more than he can because it is really a matter of life and death, as they have no place to stay. And the rabbi wept bitterly.

Naturally, the people of Israel are all merciful and each one gave more than he could, and he collected thousands of pounds for that family, since everyone felt the lack, and therefore everyone took part in mending the lack that they felt.

The following year, the rabbi assembled the town's powerful and respectable and gave them another heartfelt sermon, and cried and sighed so bitterly that it could break one's heart. He let them know the merit of the *Mitzva* [good deed/commandment] of mercy—that through mercy we will come out of exile and be rewarded with complete redemption.

Afterwards he told them that his wife was at a wedding of a rich man who came from the United States, and she saw there that the rich man's wife wore a costly fur that costs 3,000 pounds, and a diamond ring that costs another 3,000 pounds, so now she is asking him to buy her these Jewels for 6,000 pounds. The rabbi wept bitterly and asked for them to have mercy on him and give him that amount. He would not have asked them for it had he not seen that last year they gave him 6,000 pounds for the poor man so he could get by with his family, and it must be because they have merciful hearts, so he is asking them for that amount for Jewels for his wife, so he was crying and yelling, "Jews, O merciful Jews!"

Naturally, the more the rabbi cried, the more they laughed at him and said, "Should we feel sorry for your wife because she wants to decorate herself? What mercy is there here? With the poor man there was necessity, and this is called a 'lack.' We all felt the lack, so each of us felt compelled to mend it."

From this allegory we can understand the difference between lack and decoration: a lack is when he is bare and destitute; then you can speak of mercy. But when you have a bountiful home but no jewelry, which is accessories that only a few in a generation have, you cannot speak of a lack, since they can live without it, too.

It is likewise here. The light filled the whole of the will to receive until there was no place empty, without abundance, as it is written that the upper light filled the whole of reality and there was no vacancy. This is called "He and His name are one," when there is no discerned difference between the light and the *Kli*, since without a *Kli*, the light would not be able to expand, since the desire to do good to His creations would not be able to work without the existence of a desire to receive. Therefore, there was no distinction between the light and the *Kli*, as both are equally important with respect to the goal.

This brings up the question, "Why was there a *Tzimtzum*?" The answer to this is that the *Tzimtzum* was in order to decorate. This means that decorations are needed in order to improve the gift. Although now he has abundance because the light fills the whole *Kli*, it is still possible to make it better, meaning that the reception of the abundance will not be regarded as reception, but as bestowal, by making it reception in order to bestow, which is regarded as actual bestowal.

This is why the *Tzimtzum* is regarded as free choice, meaning that he had the choice to not perform a *Tzimtzum*, for who forced him? After all he was given and he received, and if he wanted, he could stay in that state and have abundance. However, he chose that it is better to perform a *Tzimtzum* and receive only in order to bestow, for by that he will be equal to the Emanator.

Only afterwards, after the *Tzimtzum*, it become a lack, for it is a rule that a desire in the upper one becomes a mandatory law in the lower one. Hence, the lower one no longer has a choice, meaning that even when he wants, he is not given. It follows that now, after the *Tzimtzum*, the will to receive is regarded as a lack because you can no longer receive anything in it, and it is discerned as darkness. Only when beginning to do things in order to bestow do we begin to equalize in form and begin to come out of the rule of the *Tzimtzum*. Then we begin to feel Godliness, to the extent that we can work in order to bestow.

If you have any more questions on that topic write me the places you find confusing and I will try to explain to the best of my ability. But mainly, we should hope that the Creator will give and bestow upon us the reason of the upper one so we can understand and learn to hear, to learn and to teach ourselves, to keep, do, and observe.

Letter No. 74

February 13, 1966

Hello and all the best to my friend, whom I love as my own soul,

I long to hear how things are going for you—your health, your sustenance, and how your children are doing at school. I have no special news, and I will conclude my letter with words of Torah.

It is written in the weekly portion: "Six days you are to do your work, but on the seventh day you shall cease." This means that Shabbat was established for resting, and the weekdays were established for work. That is, we must work, and one who does not work during the weekdays does not keep, "Six days you are to do your work." What should wise disciples, whose Torah is their work, do?

We should interpret this by way of ethics, as well as explain the meaning of ethics. That is, what is required of us? What is the meaning of keeping Torah and *Mitzvot* [commandments]? According to what Baal HaSulam interpreted, they were given to us as a remedy by which to achieve the goal we must achieve.

Therefore, first we must understand the purpose of creation, the reason for which we came into this world. It is known from the holy books that the purpose of creation is to do good to His creations (and according to rule that the cow wants to nurse more than the calf wants to suckle). So who detains us from receiving the delight and pleasure that the Creator wants to give us?

They explained that it is in order to avoid the bread of shame. That is, one who receives a gift from one's friend is ashamed of him. Therefore, in order for one to not be ashamed upon the reception of the pleasure, we were given the work in Torah and *Mitzvot*, so that through labor and Torah and *Mitzvot* we will be rewarded with receiving the reward. This means that once we have the fit *Kelim* [vessels] to receive the pleasure and abundance from the Creator in a way that there is no shame in the reception of the pleasure, we will be given abundance and delight from above.

Now we will understand what we asked above. We were given six days to work on qualifying the *Kelim* for reception of the pleasure, which is called labor, and Shabbat is the time of reception of the pleasure, and not of the correction of the *Kelim*. This is why Shabbat is called *Shvita* [ceasing/resting] from the work, and all the *Kelim* that have been prepared on the eve of Shabbat are filled on Shabbat, for Shabbat is a "similitude of the next world."

According to the above we will understand the ethics in which we need to engage, meaning understand that we need the labor for ourselves, in order to receive the delight and pleasure, and the Creator will help us.

From your friend who wishes you and your family abundant blessings and success, joy and contentment,

Baruch Shalom HaLevi Ashlag

Letter No. 75

May 24, 1966, Eve of Shavuot

Hello and all the best to my friend,

I long to know how things are going with your work, and especially your health.

"If you walk in My statutes and keep My commandments." RASHI interprets, "Is this the keeping of the *Mitzvot* [commandments]? When he says, 'and keep My commandments,' then we are referring to keeping the *Mitzvot*. Thus, what am I keeping by 'If you walk in My statutes'—that you labor in the Torah. 'And keep My commandments'—labor in the Torah in order to keep and to observe."

We should understand why he had to say that the verse, "If you ... in My statutes," comes to point to laboring in the Torah. Could we not keep, "and keep My commandments," if we do not observe the study of Torah in order to know what we must do? After all, how can we observe *Mitzvot* if we do not keep "walk by My statutes"?

However, we can say that if the verse tells us to keep the *Mitzvot*, we must certainly learn the Torah first. It is not written that this is necessary because it is impossible to keep the *Mitzvot* if we do not know them.

Letter No. 75

However, there is a different issue here than the study of Torah in order to know how to observe the *Mitzvot*. That is, even when we know the *Mitzvot*, the body does not want to observe them. For example, everyone knows that there is a *Mitzva* [commandment] to love the Creator, but only a chosen few can observe the *Mitzva* of loving the Creator, while the whole world is under the governance of self-love.

In order to be able to observe the *Mitzvot* for the sake of the Creator we were given the remedy of Torah, as our sages said, "The light in it reforms him." This is done specifically through labor in the Torah. To the extent that one engages in the Torah, to that extent he draws the light of the Torah, and by that he will have the strength to observe the *Mitzvot*.

This is RASHI's precision: "'If you walk in My statutes,' meaning labor in the Torah." It is so because we know about learning the Torah in order to know the *Mitzvot* that we should keep from the verse, "And keep My commandments." Therefore, we say that the verse, "If you walk in My statutes," comes to show that we should labor in the Torah.

RASHI interprets about that: "and keep My commandments"—labor in the Torah in order to keep and to observe." Although there seems to be no connection, we should toil in the Torah in order to be able to keep and to observe because through labor we acquire the light in the Torah, and the light in it reforms him, hence the keeping and observing.

From all the above we see the power of labor—it can turn all the evil in man to good. We should also make two discernments in the study of Torah: 1) to learn the laws in order to know what we should do, 2) learn Torah by labor, in order to have the strength to keep and to observe. In the latter part, it does not matter if we are learning laws or learning Torah, which does not speak of laws at all, but only that in the Torah there is room for labor, and then the Torah grants one with the light in it.

May the Creator help us be rewarded with the light of Torah.

I conclude my letter with the blessing of Torah, and may the merit of the Torah protect us and we will be saved in every way, in corporeality and spirituality. May we be rewarded with complete redemption soon in our days, Amen.

Baruch Shalom HaLevi Ashlag
Son of Baal HaSulam

Letter No. 76

May, 1967

To my friend,

I long to hear from you and from your family, in general and in particular.

"If you walk in My statutes and keep My commandments so as to do them." The holy *Zohar* asks, "Since he already said, 'walk' and 'keep,' why also 'do'?" It replies, "One who does the *Mitzvot* [commandments] of the Torah and walks in His ways, it is as though he has made Him above. The Creator said, 'as though he had made Me.' This is the meaning of 'to do them,' as though you have made Me" (*Behukotai*, item 18).

We should understand what it means that one who walks in the way of the Creator makes the Creator. How can one think such a thing?

It is known that "The whole earth is full of His glory." This is what every person should believe, as it is written, "I fill the heaven and the earth." However, the Creator has made a concealment so that we cannot see Him so as to have room for choice, and then there is room for faith—to believe that the Creator "fills all the worlds and encompasses all the worlds." And after a person engages in Torah and *Mitzvot* and keeps the commandment of choice, the

Creator reveals Himself to him, and then he sees that the Creator is the ruler of the world.

Thus, at that time a person makes the king who will rule over him. That is, a person feels that the Creator is the ruler of the world, and this is regarded as a person making the Creator king over him. As long as one has not come to such a feeling, the Creator's kingship is concealed. This is why we say, "On that day, the Lord will be one and His name, 'One.'" That is, the glory of His kingship will appear over us.

This is the whole correction we must do in this world, and by that we extend abundance in the world, for all the bestowals from above are drawn by engaging in Torah and *Mitzvot* with the aim to extend His kingship on us.

This is the meaning of Moses sentencing the people, as it is written in the portion, *Yitro* [Jethro]: "And the people stood about Moses from the morning until the evening. ...and I judge between a man and his neighbor." In ethics, "between a man and his neighbor" means between the good inclination and the evil inclination, to show them the statutes of the Creator, so they will know the thoughts and desires of the good inclination and the thoughts and desires of the evil inclination, and will know what to sort, as it is difficult for one to scrutinize alone if the good inclination is speaking to him or that they are the words of the evil inclination.

By this we will understand what our sages said about the verse, "'Who is the wise man that may understand this? ...Why is the land ruined?' Rav Yehuda said, 'Rav said that they did not bless in the Torah first.' The RAN introduces there in the name of our rav Jonah, and these are his words: 'This verse is accurate—the land was lost because they did not bless in the Torah first. If it says, 'because they left My law,' literally, that they had left the Torah and did not engage in it, when we ask the sages and the prophets why they did not interpret it, for it is revealed and easy to interpret, they certainly always engaged in Torah. This is why the sages and the prophets were perplexed by why was the land ruined?

Letter No. 76

Finally, the Creator Himself explained it. He knows the depths of the heart—that they did not bless in the Torah first. That is, the Torah was not important enough to them that it would be worth blessing, meaning they did not engage in it *Lishma* [for Her sake], and therefore slighted its blessing." Thus far his words.

This means that the study of Torah and observing the *Mitzvot* is primarily in order to draw the disclosure of the light of His face downward. This is regarded as "the light in it reforms him," which appears through the choice, and when engaging *Lishma*. At that time what Rabbi Meir said comes true—"The secrets of Torah are revealed to he who learns Torah *Lishma*." This is regarded as His kingship appearing below, and this the meaning of "do them," as though you are making Me.

May the Creator help us merit drawing, and may the glory of the Creator appear over all the earth soon in our days, Amen.

From your friend who wishes you and your family all the best,

Baruch Shalom HaLevi Ashlag

Son of Baal HaSulam

Letter No. 77

February 18, 1973, Bnei Brak

To my friend,

I received your letter together with 18, etc., and concerning the group, it is known that "As water face to the face," etc., meaning that when a person feels his lowliness, it is because he feels His greatness. That is, normally, when we give to another, if he is of inferior degree, his giving is also very small.

Therefore, usually, when we collect donations, we search for influential and respectable people because according to the importance of the receiver, so is the measure of the donations. Therefore, when one wants to bestow upon the Creator, the evil inclination comes and depicts the *Shechina* [Divinity] in the dust. That is, whatever we give is enough and we need not give more.

But for one who wishes to receive reward for his work it is to the contrary. He appreciates the giver and says to himself that He must be benevolent and merciful. He mentions all the virtues of the giver because he wants Him to give him abundance.

Therefore, all those whose work is based on reward for the work, regardless of whether the reward is corporeal or spiritual—what one imagines to be spiritual, as long as it is a reward for one's work—then through a little bit of thought and effort he can appreciate and cherish the giver.

Letter No. 77

But in the way of Baal HaSulam, where the whole foundation is that one should ask that all of one's thoughts and desires will be only to benefit the Creator, a depiction of lowliness, called *Shechina* in the dust, immediately appears. Hence, we must not be impressed by the descent, since many pennies join into a great amount.

This is as we learned, "there is no absence in spirituality," rather that it has temporarily departed in order to have room for work to advance. This is so because every moment that we scrutinize into holiness enters the domain of holiness, and a person descends only in order to sort out more sparks of holiness.

However, there is an advice that one should not wait until his degree is lowered for him, and when he feels his lowliness he goes up again, and that ascent is regarded as sorting a part into holiness. Instead, he himself descends and elevates other sparks, and raises them into the domain of holiness.

It is as our sages said, "Before I lose, I search" (*Shabbat*, 152), meaning before I lose the situation I am in, I start searching. It is as Baal HaSulam said about King David, who said, "I awaken the dawn." Our sages said, "I awaken the dawn and the dawn does not awaken me."

Therefore, the keeping is primarily during the ascent, and not during the descent. During the ascent we need to extend fear, lest we are pushed out, God forbid. But after all these, all we need is to cry out to the King and ask for His mercy on us once and for all.

I will conclude my letter for I am not accustomed to letters.

Baruch Shalom HaLevi
Son of Baal HaSulam

Letter No. 78

Rav Baruch Shalom HaLevi Ashlag,
Son of Baal HaSulam,
4 Mintz St., Bnei Brak.
With God's help,

Thus far we did not engage in building buildings and matters that concern wide publicity. This is not our way. Rather, our sole intention is to spread the teaching of fear of heaven and serving the Creator among our willing friends, and especially the wisdom of Kabbalah and the wisdom of the hidden to those who walk humbly and are worthy of it, as I had received it from Baal HaSulam.

In this generation, when the wisdom of the poor is despised, and each city is built firm, while the city of God is lowered to the bottom, this is the time of the footsteps of the Messiah, as it is known to those who know the hidden wisdom.

Therefore, I have agreed this time to the request of our friends who wish to expand our ranks and build a synagogue for Torah and prayer to be named after the great man, Baal HaSulam, a place from which his fountain shall flow outwards and the wisdom shall sing in the street, and all who wish to take the Lord may come and take with great sanctification and proper preparation.

Letter No. 78

With this I appeal to all our brothers from the house of Israel that the spirit of the Lord is beating within them, and who regret the exile of the *Shechina* [Divinity], to assist the builders who are engaging in this great matter. By this merit we will be rewarded with complete redemption, as it is said in the holy *Zohar*, "By this the children of Israel will come out of exile."

Anticipating the general salvation and the raising of the value of Torah,

Your friend in heart and soul

THIS BOOK WAS PRINTED

IN LIVING MEMORY OF

DAVID AND MIRIAM MERON